VISUAL QUICKSTART

MACROMEDIA FIREWORKS 4

FOR WINDOWS AND MACINTOSH

Sandee Cohen

 Peachpit Press

Visual QuickStart Guide
Fireworks 4 for Windows and Macintosh
Copyright © 2001 by Sandee Cohen

Peachpit Press
1249 Eighth Street
Berkeley, CA 94710
800 283-9444 • 510 524-2178
fax 510 524-2221
Find us on the Web at http://www.peachpit.com

Published by Peachpit Press in association with Macromedia, Inc.
Peachpit Press is a division of Addison Wesley Longman.

Cover Design: The Visual Group
Production and additional design elements: Sandee Cohen
Illustrations: Sandee Cohen

ISBN 0-201-73133-9

0 9 8 7 6 5 4 3 2 1

Printed and bound in the United States of America

DEDICATED TO

Jeffry
With all my love and best wishes

THANKS TO

Nancy Ruenzel publisher of Peachpit Press.

Marjorie Baer executive editor at Peachpit Press.

Karen Dominey who has become an integral part of the team.

Pattie Belle Hastings who did the screen shots of the new interface. Her illustrations and icons are terrific. I look forward to reading her new book.

Myrna Vladic the production coordinator from Peachpit Press.

The staff of Peachpit Press all of whom make me proud to be a Peachpit author.

Steve Rath who does the best index in the business.

Diana Smedley of Macromedia. Congratulations on a great new interface.

David Morris of Macromedia who gave me a wonderful preview of all the new features.

Doug Benson of Macromedia who answered my continuing questions after the beta program ended.

Mark Haynes, Karen Duban, and Julie Hallstrom, the technical reviewers from Macromedia.

Joe Lowery author of *The Fireworks 4 Bible.* Joe has been a great resource, and I'm honored to call him a friend.

Linda Rathgeber author of *Playing with Fire.* Thanks for putting my technique in your new book.

Fireworks beta list participants, too numerous to name, who all gave me great insight into features and techniques.

Michael Randasso and the staff of the New School for Social Research Computer Instruction Center.

David Lerner of Tekserve who helped me do something I swore I would never do— change computers in the middle of an important project. Without his great shop, I would have never been able to get the book finished.

Susan Gladding of Xsense. She helped get my XRouter Pro back up in service to keep my cable modem connection to the Web.

Pixel my cat who thinks chapter 13 is all about her. And won't let me change the title to "Working with Bitmaps."

Colophon

This book was created using Macromedia Fireworks 4, Adobe Illustrator, Macromedia FreeHand, and Adobe Photoshop 6 for illustrations; QuarkXPress 4 for layout; and Ambrosia SW Snapz Pro for screen shots. The computers used were a 450 MHz Power Macintosh G4, a PowerBook G3.

Fireworks 4 for Windows ran on Virtual PC 3 from Connectix. (No Intel inside.) The fonts used were Minion and Futura from Adobe and two specialty fonts created using Macromedia Fontographer. A single cable modem Web connection was shared between computers using the miraculous Xsense XRouter Pro.

TABLE OF CONTENTS

Table of Contents

Table of Contents

INTRODUCTION

Welcome to learning Macromedia Fireworks 4. In a very short period of time Fireworks has become an important tool for creating all sorts of Web graphics.

What makes Fireworks so useful? Perhaps the most important reason is that it allows designers to work visually to create not just the images for Web sites but also the special code needed to assemble graphics and create interactive elements.

Another reason is that, instead of using three or more separate programs, Fireworks combines features found in image editing, Web optimizing, and vector drawing programs. So instead of requiring you to jump from one program to another, Fireworks lets you use one program from start to finish.

It has been very exciting to revise this book—my fourth time! Some features that used to be covered in a page or two have now been expanded into their own complete chapters. And yet, other features have been so simplified they can be covered in just a few pages.

Using This Book

If you have used any of the Visual QuickStart Guides, you will find this book very similar. Each chapter consists of numbered steps that explain how to perform a specific technique or work with a feature of the program. As you work through the steps, you gain an understanding of the technique or feature, helped along by insightful tips. The illustrations let you judge if you are following the steps correctly.

Instructions

Using a book such as this will be easier once you understand the terms I use. This is especially important because some other computer books use terms differently. So, here are the terms I use throughout the book and explanations of what they mean.

Click refers to pressing down and releasing the mouse button in the Macintosh, or the left mouse button in Windows. You must release the mouse button or else it's not a click.

Press means to hold down the mouse button or a keyboard key.

Press and drag means to hold the mouse button down and then move the mouse. In later chapters, I use the shorthand term *drag;* just remember that you have to press and hold as you drag the mouse.

Move the mouse or cursor means to move the mouse without pressing the mouse button.

Menu Commands

Like any application, Fireworks has menu commands that you choose to open dialog boxes, change artwork, and initiate certain actions. These menu commands are shown in bold type. The direction to choose a menu command is written like this: **Modify > Arrange > Bring to Front.** This means that you should first choose the Modify menu, then choose the Arrange submenu, and then the Bring to Front command.

Keyboard Shortcuts

Most of the menu commands for Fireworks have keyboard shortcuts that help you work faster. For instance, instead of choosing New from the File menu, it is faster and easier to use the keyboard shortcut.

Different software companies and authors differ as to the order in which they list the modifier keys used in keyboard shortcuts. I always list the Macintosh Command and the Windows Ctrl keys first, then the Option or Alt key, and then the Shift key. In actual practice, the order that you press those modifier keys is not important. However, it *is* very important that you always add the last key (the letter or number key) after you are holding the other keys.

Rather than cluttering up the exercises with long keyboard commands, I've listed the shortcuts in Appendix A, separated by platform.

Learning Keyboard Shortcuts

While keyboard shortcuts help you work faster, you don't have to start using them right away. In fact, most likely you'll learn more about the program by using menus. As you look for one command you may see a related feature you would like to explore.

Once you feel comfortable working with Fireworks, you can start adding keyboard shortcuts to your repertoire. My suggestion is that you look at the menu commands you use a lot. Then choose one of those shortcuts each day. For instance, if you import a lot of art from other programs, you might decide to learn the shortcut for the Import command. For the rest of that day, every time you import art use the Import shortcut. (It happens to be Cmd/Ctrl-R.) Even if you have to look at the menu to refresh your memory, use the keyboard shortcut to actually open the Import dialog box anyway. By the end of the day you will have memorized the Import shortcut. The next day you can learn a new one.

Cross-Platform Issues

One of the great strengths of Fireworks is that it is almost identical in look and function on both the Macintosh and Windows platforms. In fact, at first glance it is hard to tell which platform you are working on. However, because there are some differences between the operating systems themselves, there are some things you should keep in mind.

Modifier Keys

I always list the modifier keys with the Macintosh key first and then the Windows key second. So a direction to hold the Command/Ctrl key as you drag means that Macintosh users should hold the Command key while Windows users should hold the Ctrl key on the Windows platform. When the key is the same on both computers, such as the Shift key, only one is listed.

In most cases, the Mac's Command key (sometimes called the Apple key) corresponds to the Ctrl key on Windows. The Option key on the Macintosh usually corresponds to the Alt key on Windows. The Control key on the Macintosh has no Windows equivalent. Notice that the Control key for the Macintosh is always spelled out while the Ctrl key for Windows is not.

Platform-Specific Features

A few times in the book I have written separate exercises for the Macintosh and Windows platforms. These exercises are indicated by (Mac) and (Win).

Most of the time this is because the procedures are so different that they need to be written separately. Some features exist only on one platform. Those features are labeled to reflect this.

Fireworks Workflow: How to Use this Book

I structured this book so that you could start with an empty document and build your skills and understanding step by step. The first two chapters deal with the basics of Fireworks's onscreen elements and the document window. The next eight chapters cover the illustration and drawing tools in Fireworks. The rest go through all of the features in an orderly fashion. So, if you tend to be a little obsessive/compulsive, you should start right with Chapter 1 and march straight through the book, one chapter after another.

However, if your client is demanding that you finish the Web site tonight you may need to skip some features and jump right into specific techniques such as optimizing and exporting existing scans.

How you use this book depends on what you need to learn, how quickly you need to learn it, and what your learning style is. This workflow guides you as to how to move around and choose the chapters that most interest you—like a buffet dinner.

Basics ❶

Everyone needs some basics to cover the workings of the program. So whatever your ultimate goal, you should begin with:

- Chapter 1: Fireworks Basics
- Chapter 2: Document Setup

Optimizing ❷

If you're in a hurry to get scanned images up on the Web you can then skip directly to these chapters—this means you don't want to edit or add artwork to your images.

- Chapter 14: Importing
- Chapter 15: Optimizing
- Chapter 20: Exporting

Basics

❶ *Chapters 1 and 2 cover the Fireworks basics— the interface and document setup.*

Optimizing

❷ *Chapters 14, 15, and 20 cover the steps needed to optimize graphics and put them on the Web.*

Fireworks Workflow

Bitmap Images

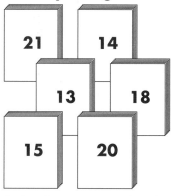

❸ *Photoshop users can explore these chapters to make the transition to Fireworks.*

Interactivity

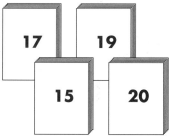

❹ *Chapters 17, 19, 15, and 20 show you how to add interactive elements to your graphics.*

Animations

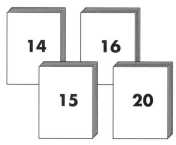

❺ *Chapters 14, 15, 16, and 20 explain how to make Web animations.*

Bitmap Images ❸

It's very possible that you are familiar with Adobe Photoshop and Adobe ImageReady, which many people use to produce Web graphics. If you're interested in learning how you can use Fireworks as you would use these programs, you should cover:

- Chapter 21: Compared to Photoshop
- Chapter 14: Importing
- Chapter 13: Working with Pixels
- Chapter 18: Slices
- Chapter 15: Optimizing
- Chapter 20: Exporting

Interactivity ❹

People expect to click buttons to move around Web pages. Here's a quick course for you if you want to know how to augment your pages with interactive elements such as buttons and links.

- Chapter 17: Hotspots and Links
- Chapter 19: Behaviors
- Chapter 15: Optimizing
- Chapter 20: Exporting

Animations ❺

Once you've succeeded with buttons, you'll be ready to try your hand at animations:

- Chapter 14: Importing
- Chapter 16: Animations
- Chapter 15: Optimizing
- Chapter 20: Exporting

Fireworks Workflow

Graphics Creation ❻

Fireworks is more than just optimizing and exporting graphics for the Web. Its graphics creation tools are among the best in the business. These are the chapters that show you how to create graphics:

- Chapter 3: Colors
- Chapter 4: Path Tools
- Chapter 5: Selecting Paths
- Chapter 6: Working with Objects
- Chapter 7: Fills
- Chapter 8: Strokes
- Chapter 9: Effects
- Chapter 10: Text
- Chapter 11: Masks and Interactions

Working Faster and Smarter ❼

It's not enough to know how to use Fireworks—you also want to finish your projects quickly. Here are the timesavers that let you automate your process, work more efficiently, and use Fireworks in conjunction with other Macromedia products:

- Chapter 12: Automation Features
- Chapter 20: Exporting
- Appendix A: Keyboard Shortcuts

Graphics

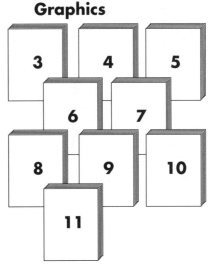

❻ *These chapters show you how to use Fireworks's extensive arsenal of drawing tools.*

Faster and Smarter

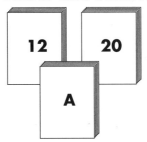

❼ *Once you understand the program, you can learn to work faster, which is covered in chapters 12, 20, and appendix A.*

Continuing Your Fireworks Education

One of the benefits of the Visual QuickStart series is that the books are straightforward and don't weigh you down with a lot of details you don't need. However, they were never designed to be a complete reference work. So, if you need the most complete reference book on Fireworks, I recommend that you look at *The Fireworks 4 Bible* by Joseph W. Lowery. Joe's book goes far beyond the scope of this QuickStart Guide, particularly in areas such as JavaScript actions and integration with Macromedia Dreamweaver. (Since many Fireworks features are designed to work with Dream-weaver, you may also want to get Joe's other book, *The Dreamweaver 4 Bible.*)

If you'd like to explore the creative aspects of Fireworks, you may also want to look at Linda Rathgeber's *Playing with Fire.* Outside of the fact that Linda's book features a technique I developed, she has a wealth of techniques for working with the program. Also, check out her Web site Playingwithfire.com.

But however you use Fireworks, don't forget to have fun!

Sandee Cohen

(Sandee@vectorbabe.com)
January, 2001

Easter Egg

Easter eggs are extra games or treats that the software engineers add to programs. They're called Easter eggs because you're supposed to search for them and find them yourself. However, if you want to see the Fireworks 4 development team, here's how to get to the Fireworks 4 Easter egg.

To see the Fireworks 4 Easter egg:

1. Choose About Fireworks from the Apple menu (Mac) or the Help menu (Win). The Fireworks splash screen appears ➌.

2. Option-click (Mac) or Ctrl-click (Win) the Macromedia logo in the splash screen.

3. Enjoy the show ➒!

TIP There is actually a more practical purpose for the splash screen. Click the splash screen to display your Fireworks 4 registration number. This can be useful if you need support from Macromedia.

➌ *Opt/Alt-click the Macromedia logo in the splash screen.*

➒ *A distorted view of the Fireworks 4 development team is available as an Easter egg.*

FIREWORKS BASICS

When I start learning a new application, I'm always in a rush to get started. I open it up and begin to explore. It's the same way when I pick up a book about the application—I never start with the first chapter. I don't want to read about buttons, fields, and controls—especially if I'm already familiar with other programs from the company such as Macromedia Dreamweaver, Macromedia Flash, and Macromedia FreeHand.

No, I rush right into the middle chapters of the book.

However, after a few hours of slogging helplessly through the book, I eventually realize there are many things I don't understand about the program. I recognize I'm a bit confused. So I come back to the first chapter to learn the foundation of the program.

Of course, since you're much more patient than I am, and probably wiser, you're already here—reading the first chapter.

System Requirements

There are certain minimum requirements of your computer and operating system needed for Macromedia Fireworks to perform correctly.

Minimum System Requirements (Mac)

- Macintosh Operating System 8.6 or higher

- Adobe Type Manager 4 or higher to use Type 1 fonts

- Power Macintosh processor G3 or greater

- 64 MB of application RAM with virtual memory on (32 MB or more recommended with virtual memory turned off)

- 100 MB or more of available hard disk space

- CD-ROM drive

- Mouse or digitizing tablet

- 640×480 resolution, 256-color monitor (1024×768 resolution, millions-of-colors monitor recommended)

To check memory (Mac):

- Choose About This Computer from the Apple menu to view the version of the operating system, the built-in memory, and the amount of virtual memory **❶**.

To check hard disk space (Mac):

- Open the hard disk and read the available disk space at the top of the window **❷**.

❶ *The Macintosh* **Memory** *display shows that this computer is operating under Mac OS 9.0.4 and has 640 megabytes of memory.*

❷ *The Macintosh* **Hard Disk space** *display shows that this computer has over 22 gigabytes of storage space available.*

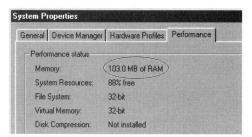

❸ *The Windows* **System Properties** *display shows that this computer has 103 megabytes of system memory.*

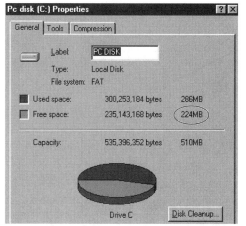

❹ *The Windows* **Hard Disk Properties** *display shows that this computer has 224 megabytes of free disk space.*

Minimum System Requirements (Win)

- Windows 95, 98, or Windows NT 4 (with Service Pack 3) or later
- Adobe Type Manager 4 or higher to use Type 1 fonts
- Intel Pentium processor (Pentium II recommended)
- 64 MB of system RAM
- 100 MB of available hard disk space
- CD-ROM drive
- Mouse or digitizing tablet
- 640×480 resolution, 256-color monitor (1024×768 resolution, millions-of-colors monitor recommended)

To check memory (Win):

Choose System Properties from the Control Panels directory to view the amount of memory, the available memory, the file system, amount of virtual memory, and if disk compression is active ❸.

To check hard disk space (Win):

1. Open the My Computer icon on the desktop.
2. Select the hard disk, usually named a letter such as C.
3. Click with the right mouse button to open the contextual menu.
4. Choose Properties from the contextual menu. This opens the Properties dialog box ❹.

System Requirements

Installing and Launching Fireworks

Once you have confirmed that your system meets the minimum requirements for running Fireworks, you can then install the application and begin to use it.

To install Fireworks (Mac):

TIP Disable any virus-protection software before installing the software.

1. Insert the Fireworks CD-ROM in the CD-ROM drive.
2. Double-click the Fireworks Installer ❺.
3. Follow the instructions that appear.
4. After installation, restart the Macintosh.

To install Fireworks (Win):

TIP Disable any virus-protection software and clear the TEMP directory before installing the software.

1. Insert the Fireworks CD-ROM in the CD-ROM drive.
2. Follow the instructions that appear ❻.
3. After installation, restart the computer.

Once you have installed Fireworks, you can then launch the application.

To launch Fireworks (Mac):

Open the folder that contains the Fireworks application and then double-click the Fireworks application icon ❼.

To launch Fireworks (Win):

Choose **Start** > **Programs** > **Macromedia Fireworks 4** ❽.

❺ *The* **Fireworks Installer** *for the Macintosh.*

❻ *The opening screen for the Fireworks Installer for Windows.*

❼ *The* **Fireworks application icon.**

❽ *The* **Fireworks application** *in the Start menu.*

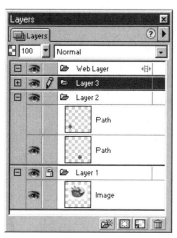

⑨ *The* Layers panel.

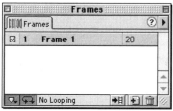

⑩ *The* Frames panel.

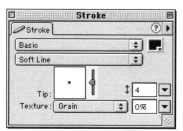

⑪ *The* Stroke panel.

Onscreen Panels

When you launch Fireworks, you see the various Fireworks onscreen panels. These panels control different aspects of the program. They can be closed, opened, resized, or rearranged to suit your own work habits.

TIP Fireworks remembers the layout of the onscreen panels when you quit the program. The next time you open the program, the panels are arranged in the same positions.

TIP You can use the JavaScript commands to rearrange the onscreen panels into different layouts *(see page 195).*

The Layers Panel

The Layers panel ⑨ allows you to control the order in which objects appear onscreen. *(For more information on the Layers panel, see Chapter 6, "Working with Objects.")*

The Frames Panel

The Frames panel ⑩ controls the elements used for creating rollovers and animations. *(For more information on the Frames panel, see Chapter 16, "Animations.")*

The Stroke Panel

The Stroke panel ⑪ contains controls for adjusting the look of the stroke that is applied to the edge of an object. *(For more information on strokes, see Chapter 8, "Strokes.")*

Onscreen Panels

The Fill Panel

The Fill panel ⑫ controls the colors, textures, gradients, patterns, and effects that are applied to the area inside an object. *(For more information on working with fills, see Chapter 7, "Fills.")*

The Effect Panel

The Effect panel ⑬ controls the effects such as lighting and dimensions that can be added to objects. *(For more information on effects, see Chapter 9, "Effects.")*

The Color Mixer Panel

The Color Mixer ⑭ allows you to define colors according to five different modes: RGB, Hexadecimal, HSB, CMY, or Grayscale. *(For more information on the color modes, see Chapter 3, "Colors.")*

The Swatches Panel

The Swatches panel ⑮ lets you work with preset palettes of color or store your own sets of colors. *(For more information on the color modes, see Chapter 3, "Colors.")*

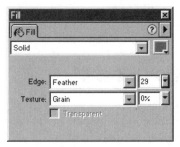

⑫ *The* Fill panel.

⑬ *The* Effect panel.

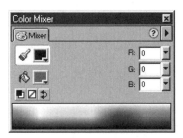

⑭ *The* Color Mixer panel.

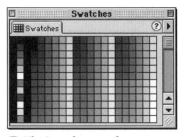

⑮ *The* Swatches panel.

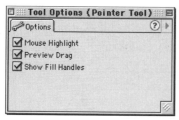

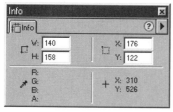

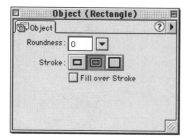

16 *The* Color Well Swatches panel.

17 *The* Options panel.

18 *The* Info panel.

19 *The* Object panel.

The Color Well Swatches Panel

Rather than repeatedly going to the Color Mixer or Swatches panel to apply colors, you can use the various Color Well Swatches panels **16** located in the Tools panel, panels and dialog boxes. Macromedia calls this a Color Box, but to avoid confusion in drawing boxes, I call it a Color Well. Besides, if you think of colors as inks, you definitely should find them in a well. *(For more information on using the Color Well Swatches panel, see pages 52–55.)*

The Tool Options Panel

The Tool Options panel **17** displays any options for working with the currently selected tool. These options change depending on the tool selected.

The Info Panel

The Info panel **18** provides feedback as to the color and position of selected objects. *(For more information on using the Info panel, see Chapter 6, "Working with Objects.")*

The Object Panel

The Object panel **19** controls various aspects of objects. For instance, the corner radius of a rectangle is controlled by the Object panel. The panel controls change depending on the object that is selected. *(For more information on using the Object panel, see Chapter 6, "Working with Objects.")*

Onscreen Panels

The URL Panel

The URL panel ❷⓿ allows you to add Web links to areas on the page. *(For more information on adding links to areas of your Web graphics, see Chapter 17, "Hotspots and Links" and Chapter 18, "Slices.")*

The Behaviors Panel

The Behaviors panel ❷❶ allows you to assign JavaScript actions to slices and image maps. *(For more information on working with Behaviors, see Chapter 19, "Behaviors.")*

The Find and Replace Panel

The Find and Replace panel ❷❷ allows you to make changes in text and vector objects elements within a specific document or throughout many different Fireworks documents. *(For more information on working with the Find and Replace panel, see Chapter 12, "Automation Features.")*

❷⓿ *The* URL panel.

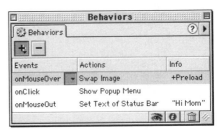

❷❶ *The* Behaviors panel.

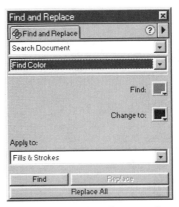

❷❷ *The* Find and Replace panel.

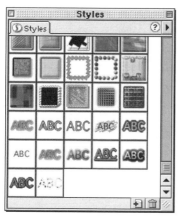

㉓ *The* Styles panel.

㉔ *The* Project panel.

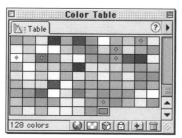

㉕ *The* Color Table panel.

The Styles Panel

The Styles panel **㉓** allows you to save the settings for an object's appearance and then apply them quickly to other objects. *(For more information on working with styles, see Chapter 12, "Automation Features.")*

The Project Panel

The Project panel **㉔** helps you keep track of the various files you are working with. You can then use the Project panel to perform various actions on those files. For example, you can apply find and replace commands to all the files in the Project list. *(For more information on working with the Project Panel, see Chapter 12, "Automation Features.")*

The Color Table Panel

The Color Table panel **㉕** lets you control the colors used in exporting 8-bit images. This is most commonly used when exporting GIF files. *(For more information on working with the Color Table, see Chapter 3, "Colors.")*

Onscreen Panels

The Optimize Panel

The Optimize panel ❷❻ allows you to control the colors and settings for exporting images. *(For more information on working with the Optimize panel, see Chapter 15, "Optimizing.")*

The History Panel

The History panel ❷❼ records the series of actions and commands you perform within Fireworks. You can then play those actions back as scripts in other documents that allow you to automate your work. *(For more information on working with the History panel, see Chapter 12, "Automation Features.")*

The Library Panel

The Library panel ❷❽ stores the items that you define as graphic, button, and animation symbols. You can drag items from the Library panel onto your pages. *(For more information on working with the Library panel, see Chapter 16, "Animations.")*

❷❻ *The* **Optimize** *panel.*

❷❼ *The* **History** panel *lets you record actions and save them as scripts that allow you to automate your work.*

❷❽ *The* **Library** *panel.*

Onscreen Panels

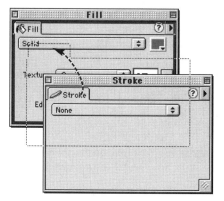

29 *Drag the tab of a panel to* **group a panel** *with another panel.*

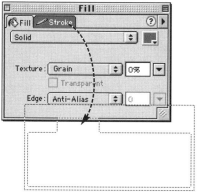

30 *Drag the tab of a panel to* **ungroup a panel.**

Working with Panels

The panels can all be customized to make it easier for you to work with Fireworks. You can change how panels are grouped, resize them, or quickly minimize or maximize their size. This is particularly helpful if you're working on a very small monitor.

TIP If you need more screen space to see what you're working on, tap the Tab key on your keyboard. This quickly hides or shows all the panels.

To group panels:

1. Drag a panel by its tab onto another panel.

2. When a black line appears around the second panel, release the mouse button **29**. The tabs of the panels appear stacked together.

To ungroup panels:

1. Drag a panel by its tab outside the area of the panel.

2. When an outline of the panel appears, release the mouse button **30**. The panel appears separated from the group.

Working with Panels

To resize panels (Mac):

◆ Drag the resize icon of a panel to change the size of the panel **③①**.

To resize panels (Win):

1. Move the cursor over the sides or corner of the panel. A double-headed arrow appears **③②**.

2. Drag with the double-headed arrow to change the size of the panel.

To minimize panels (Mac):

1. Click the minimize icon of a panel to display only the title bar of the panel **③③**.

2. Click the minimize icon to restore the panel to its full size.

③① (Mac) *Drag the* **resize icon** *of a panel (circled) to change the size of a panel.*

③② (Win) *Drag the* **sides or corners** *of a panel to change the size of a panel.*

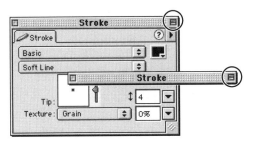

③③ (Mac) *Click the* **minimize icon** *(circled) to quickly show and hide the contents of a panel.*

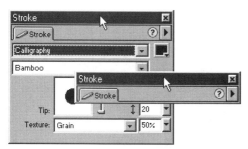

③④ (Win) *Double-click the* **title bar of a panel** *to quickly show and hide the contents of a panel.*

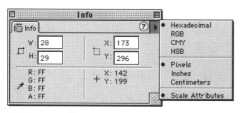

③⑤ *Each panel has an Options Panel menu that contains various settings for the panel.*

To minimize panels (Win):

1. Double-click the title bar of a panel to display only the title bar and selected panel tab **③④**.

2. Double-click the title bar to restore the panel to its full size.

Each of the panels has an Options panel menu that contains additional controls for the panel.

To use the Options menu for a panel:

1. Press the triangle to display the Option menu **③⑤**.

2. Choose the menu command.

Working with Panels

Window Elements

The Window elements allow you to display animations, see information about the file, change the magnification and open different panels.

The Animation Controls

The Animation controls **36** are at the bottom of the document window. Click the controls to see how an animation will play. *(For more information on playing animations see page 265.)*

The Document Controls

The Document controls **37** let you exit the bitmapped mode, see the document info, and change the magnification of your page. *(For more information on using the Document Controls, see page 33.)*

The Mini-Launcher

The Mini-Launcher **38** lets you quickly show or hide some of the onscreen panels. Each icon corresponds to the icon in the tab of the panel it controls. Click each icon to show or hide its panel.

TIP Each of the panels shown in the Mini-Launcher corresponds to one of the panel groups shown when Fireworks is first installed. So if you click the Stroke icon in the Mini-Launcher, you will see the Stroke, Fill, Effect, and Info panels.

36 *The* **Animation controls** *let you preview animations within the document.*

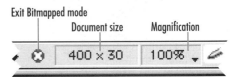

37 *The* **Document controls** *control the bitmapped mode and page view, and show the document size.*

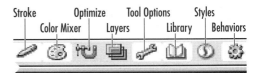

38 *The* **Mini-Launcher** *lets you show or hide some of the panels.*

39 *The* Text Editor.

40 *Click the icons in the* **Main toolbar** (**Win**) *to apply the commands.*

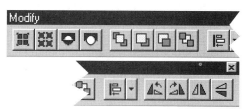

41 *Click the icons in the* **Modify toolbar** (**Win**) *to apply the commands.*

The Text Editor

The Text Editor **39** lets you enter and format text. *(For more information on working with text, see Chapter 10, "Text.")*

The Windows Toolbars

The Windows version of Fireworks provides two special toolbars that contain frequently used menu commands.

The Main Toolbar (Win)

The Main toolbar **40** can be fixed to the top of the screen or dragged into position as a floating panel. It contains commands for working with files and displaying panels.

The Modify Toolbar (Win)

The Modify toolbar **41** can be fixed to the top of the screen or dragged into position as a floating panel. It contains commands for working with objects. *(For more information on working with the commands in the Modify toolbar, see Chapter 6, "Working with Objects.")*

Using the Interface Elements

All the panels and dialog boxes use similar interface elements.

Tabs

◆ Click to choose a tab ❷. This changes the information displayed.

Fields

◆ Enter a value in a field ❸. This can be either numbers or text. (Macromedia calls these Boxes.)

Buttons

◆ Click to apply a button command ❹.

TIP A button surrounded by a border can be prompted by pressing the Return (Mac) or Enter (Win) keys.

Icons

◆ Click to select an icon ❺. The selected icon is indicated by a change in its appearance.

Checkbox

◆ Click to activate a checkbox ❻. A check appears to indicate the box is selected.

TIP Checkboxes allow you to select more than one item from a list.

Radio Button

◆ Click to activate a radio button ❼. A dot appears to indicate the button is selected.

TIP Radio buttons only allow you to select one item from a list.

Keyboard Prompts (Win)

◆ An underlined letter in an element or dialog box ❼ means you can press that letter to prompt the element.

❷ *Click to select a* **Tab**.

❸ *Enter a value in a* **Field**.

❹ *Click to apply a* **Button** command.

❺ *Click to select an* icon.

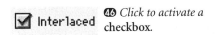

❻ *Click to activate a* checkbox.

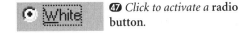

❼ *Click to activate a* **radio** button.

48 *Click the tab to open a pop-up menu.*

49 *Click the panel menu control (circled) to open a* **panel menu.**

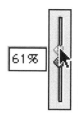

50 *Drag to adjust a* **wheel.**

51 *Click to choose a color in a* **color ramp.**

52 *Press the triangular arrow to open a* **slider** *and then drag up or down to change the setting.*

Icon cursors

Precision cursors

53 *The difference between* **icon cursors** *and* **precision cursors.**

Pop-up Menus

1. Click to reveal a pop-up menu **48**.
2. Choose from the menu items.

Panel Option Menus

1. Click the triangle in the right corner of a panel **49** to open the menu.
2. Choose from the menu items.

Wheels

◆ Drag the wheel handle **50** clockwise or counterclockwise to change the value.

Color Ramp

◆ Click anywhere in the color ramp **51** to select that color.

Pop-up Sliders

1. Press the triangle to reveal the slider control **52**.
2. Drag the small pointer to change the amount in the field.

Using the Precision Cursors

Each of the tools can be set for icon cursors or precision cursors **53**. The icon cursor shows the representation of the tool as it appears in the Tools panel. The icon cursor shows a crosshair and dot that indicates the center point or active point of the tool.

Choosing Icon or Precise Cursors

◆ Press the Caps Lock key. This switches between the two cursor modes.

or

1. Choose Edit > Preferences.
2. Choose the Editing controls.
3. Choose Precise Cursors.

Interface Elements; Precision Cursors

Tools panel and Keyboard Shortcuts

Fireworks has 37 different tools. You can choose a tool by clicking its icon in the Tools panel **54** or by pressing the group.

You can also access the tools by pressing the keyboard shortcut (shown in parentheses).

The tool shortcuts do not need modifiers such as Command or Ctrl.

TIP When tools share the same keyboard shortcut, press the key several times to rotate through the different tools.

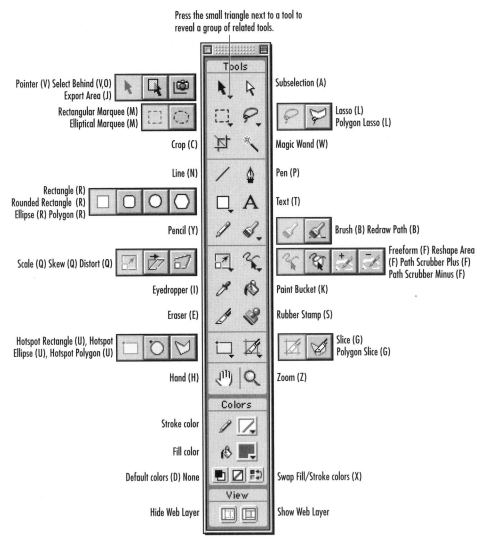

Press the small triangle next to a tool to reveal a group of related tools.

Pointer (V) Select Behind (V,O) Export Area (J)

Subselection (A)

Rectangular Marquee (M) Elliptical Marquee (M)

Lasso (L) Polygon Lasso (L)

Crop (C)

Magic Wand (W)

Line (N)

Pen (P)

Rectangle (R) Rounded Rectangle (R) Ellipse (R) Polygon (R)

Text (T)

Pencil (Y)

Brush (B) Redraw Path (B)

Scale (Q) Skew (Q) Distort (Q)

Freeform (F) Reshape Area (F) Path Scrubber Plus (F) Path Scrubber Minus (F)

Eyedropper (I)

Paint Bucket (K)

Eraser (E)

Rubber Stamp (S)

Hotspot Rectangle (U), Hotspot Ellipse (U), Hotspot Polygon (U)

Slice (G) Polygon Slice (G)

Hand (H)

Zoom (Z)

Colors

Stroke color

Fill color

Default colors (D) None

Swap Fill/Stroke colors (X)

View

Hide Web Layer

Show Web Layer

54 *The tools in the* **Tools panel** *and their keyboard shortcuts (in parentheses).*

Tools Panel and Keyboard Shortcuts

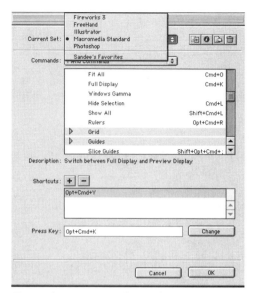

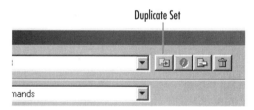

⑤⑤ *Use the* **Current Set list** *in the Keyboard Shortcuts dialog box to switch to a different set of keyboard shortcuts.*

Duplicate Set

⑤⑥ *Click the* **Duplicate Set icon** *to create a new shortcut set.*

⑤⑦ *The* **Duplicate Set** *dialog box lets you name a custom keyboard shortcut set.*

Customizing Keyboard Shortcuts

Keyboard shortcuts are the keys that you press to invoke commands and access tools. While most programs tend to use similar shortcuts for basic commands such as Copy and Paste, many programs have slightly different shortcuts for others such as Show Rulers. Fireworks lets you customize the keyboard shortcuts so that the command you use in one program is the same as the one you use in another.

Fireworks ships with different shortcut sets that let you easily switch to your favorite keyboard commands.

To change the keyboard sets:

1. Choose **Edit > Keyboard Shortcuts**. The Keyboard Shortcuts dialog box appears **⑤⑤**.

2. Choose a set from the Current Set list.

TIP The Macromedia Standard set contains the shortcut list that is most similar to other Macromedia products. This set makes it easy to learn the shortcuts for all Macromedia applications.

3. Click OK to apply the set.

You can't modify the shortcut sets that ship with Fireworks. However, you can duplicate a set and then make changes to design your own shortcuts.

To duplicate a keyboard set:

1. Click the Duplicate Set button in the Keyboard Shortcuts dialog box **⑤⑥**. This opens the Duplicate Set dialog box **⑤⑦**.

2. Name the new shortcut set and click OK. The new set appears in the Current Set list.

TIP The duplicate set uses the shortcuts of the current set. So if you want a set that is similar to Fireworks 3, make that set active before you make the duplicate.

Once you have created your own custom keyboard set, you can make changes to the keyboard commands.

To change the keyboard commands:

1. Use the Commands list **58** to choose shortcuts you want to change:
   - Menu Commands displays the shortcuts found in the menu bar. These shortcuts must use one of the modifier keys.
   - Tools displays the shortcuts that control the tools and commands in the Tools panel. These shortcuts must consist of letters or numbers without a modifier key.
   - Miscellaneous displays the shortcuts for actions that do not have a list in the menu bar. For example, nudging elements up and down using the arrow keys are under this heading. These shortcuts must use one of the modifier keys. The only exception is the up, down, left, or right arrow keys, which can be used alone.

2. Choose the command you want to change from the commands list.

3. Click the Plus Sign button to highlight the Press Key field.

4. On your keyboard, press the actual keys for the keystroke you want to assign **59**. The keystroke description is entered in the Press Key field.

5. Press the Change button to assign the keystroke.

TIP If the keystroke is used for another command, an alert sign appears under the Press Key field **60**. If you click the Change button, another dialog box asks you to confirm reassigning the shortcut **61**.

TIP Cmd/Ctrl-click on the Change button to avoid the Reassign dialog box.

58 *The* **Commands** *list lets you choose what type of shortcuts you want to change.*

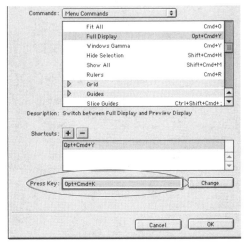

59 *Use the* **Press Key** *field (circled) to invoke the keystroke you want to use for the shortcut.*

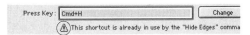

60 *The* **Alert sign** *(circled) indicates that the keystroke you have chosen is already in use by another command.*

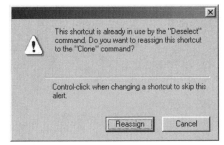

61 *The* **Reassign** *dialog box makes you confirm the choice to reassign one shortcut with another.*

Delete Set

Rename Set

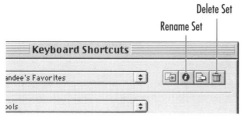

62 *The* **Current Set controls** *let you rename or delete a shortcut set.*

63 *The* Rename Set dialog box.

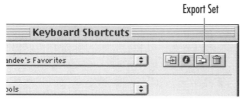

64 *The* Delete Set dialog box.

Export Set

65 *The* **Export Set button** *lets you export the current set as an HTML text file.*

To change the name of a keyboard set:

1. Select the keyboard set you want to rename from the Current Set list.

2. Click the Rename Set button from the Current Set controls **62**. The Rename Set dialog box appears **63**.

3. Enter the new name for the set and click OK.

To delete a keyboard set:

1. Select the keyboard set you want to delete from the Current Set list.

2. Click the Delete Set button from the Current Set controls. The Delete Set dialog box appears **64**.

3. Choose the set you want to delete and press the Delete button. The Delete Set dialog box automatically closes and the set is deleted.

TIP There is no way to cancel the command once you press the Delete key.

You can also export the list of keyboard shortcuts as an HTML text file that can be opened and printed.

To export a keyboard set as an HTML text file:

1. Select the keyboard set you want to export from the Current Set list.

2. Click the Export Set button from the Current Set controls **65**.

3. Use the operating system dialog box to name the file and save it to a specific location.

Customizing Keyboard Shortcuts

DOCUMENT SETUP 2

Remember back when you were in the fourth or fifth grade and you were going to the first day of school? Remember how the night before you would carefully lay out all of your new clothes for the next day? Remember how you'd spend extra time to set up your notebook, dividers, paper, pencils, and rulers?

Even then you knew the importance of document setup. You knew that setting things up properly right at the beginning of the term would help you later on in the school year.

That's how it is when you start each new Macromedia Fireworks document. The document setup helps you organize your work and will help you later on.

Opening Documents

When you start a new document, you must make certain decisions about the document that affect the final output. Fortunately, none of these decisions are final, and you can change your mind at any time as you work on your document.

To create a new document:

1. Choose **File** > **New**. This opens the New Document dialog box ❶.

2. Use the Height and Width fields to set the size of the document.

   TIP Use the pop-up lists to change the unit of measurement from pixels to inches or centimeters.

3. Use the Resolution field to set the number of points per inch for the graphics of the document.

   TIP Most Web graphics are saved at 72 pixels per inch. Print graphics usually need higher resolutions.

4. Set the Canvas Color of the document by choosing White, Transparent, or Custom.

   TIP The Canvas Color sets the color of the background of your document.

5. If you choose custom, click the Color Well to open the Swatches, where you can set your color.

6. Click OK to create the new document, which appears in an untitled document window ❷.

   TIP The Original, Preview, 2-Up, and 4-Up tabs at the top of the document window are used as part of the process in optimizing files *(see Chapter 15, "Optimizing").*

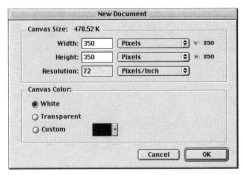

❶ *The* **New Document** *dialog box.*

❷ *The* document window.

❸ *The* **Page Preview** *shows the size, (in pixels) of the document.*

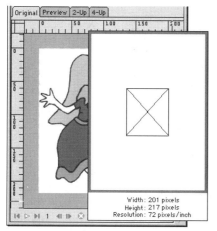

Width: 201 pixels
Height: 217 pixels
Resolution: 72 pixels/inch

❹ *Press the* **Page Preview** *to see more information about the file and how large it would print on the paper currently selected for the printer.*

Understanding Resolution

Resolution is the number of pixels or details of color per inch. The higher the resolution, the smaller the size of the pixels.

Resampling is the technique that increases or decreases the resolution of a document. You resample up when you increase the size of an image.

If you have scanned images in your Fireworks document, you should not increase the size of the document more than 50%.

However, if you only have native Fireworks objects, you can resample Fireworks documents up or down at any time.

To open a previously saved document:

1. Choose **File** > **Open**.
2. Navigate through your directories and folders to find the file you want to open.
3. Click OK.

When you open an existing document, Fireworks lets you protect the original file by opening it as an untitled document. This keeps you from inadvertently writing over a document that you want to keep.

To open a document as untitled:

1. Choose **File** > **Open** and navigate to find an existing Fireworks file.
2. Click Open as "Untitled" and then click Open. The document opens in an unsaved, untitled version.
3. Make any changes and save the document as you would any other file.

TIP (Mac) The native file format for a Fireworks file is an enhanced PNG file. If you are going to send your file to Windows users, add the PNG file extension to the file name.

To see the document information:

◆ Press the Document Info Display area ❸ to see a representation of the size of the document as well as a read out of the document's size and resolution ❹.

Altering Documents

Having created a document, you can still make changes to it. You can change the size of the image or the size of the canvas. You can also change the color of the background of a document.

To change the image size:

1. Choose **Modify** > **Document** > **Image Size** to open the Image Size dialog box ❺.

2. Use the Pixel Dimensions height and width fields to change the absolute number of pixels in the document.

TIP The Pixel Dimensions fields are not available if Resample Image is off.

3. Use the Print Size height and width fields to change the display size of the image.

TIP Press the pop-up menu for pixels or inches to change the size of the document by a percentage.

TIP Select Constrain Proportions to keep the image from being distorted.

4. Use the Resolution field to change the image size by increasing or reducing the number of pixels per inch.

TIP Scanned images may become blurred if the resolution or size of the image is increased by more than 50% ❻.

5. Use the resampling pop-up menu to choose how the scanned imaged will be changed ❼. The four choices are Bicubic, Bilinear, Soft, and Nearest Neighbor.

TIP Use Bicubic for scanned images such as photographs. Use Nearest Neighbor for images with straight lines and text such as screen shots. Use Bilinear or Soft only if you do not get acceptable results with the other two methods.

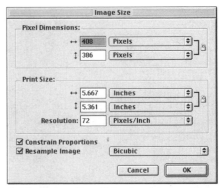

❺ *The* **Image Size** *dialog box lets you change the size and resolution of an image.*

Original image

Resampled image

❻ *The effects of* **resampling an image** *to increase its size while maintaining the resolution. Notice the blurry edges in the resampled image.*

❼ *The* **resampling choices** *control how scanned images are changed.*

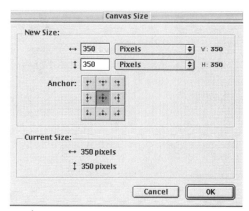

❽ *The* **Canvas Size** *dialog box lets you add space to, or delete space from, the canvas outside the image area.*

❾ *The* **Crop tool** *in the Tools panel.*

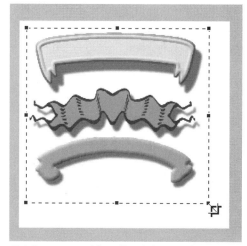

❿ *The* **Crop tool handles** *define the final canvas size after cropping.*

You can keep the image size constant while adding space to, or deleting space from, the canvas outside the image area. This changes the background relative to the image.

To change the canvas size numerically:

1. Choose **Modify** > **Document** > **Canvas Size** to open the Canvas Size dialog box **❽**.

2. Enter new amounts in the New Size height and width fields.

TIP Use the current size as a reference.

3. Choose one of the squares in the Anchor area to determine where the area is added to the canvas. For instance, if you click in the upper left corner, the added area will be added to the right and bottom of the canvas.

4. Click OK.

To change the canvas size visually:

1. Choose the Crop tool from the Tools panel **❾**.

2. Drag with the Crop tool to create the handles **❿** that define the area you want to remove from the document.

3. Double-click inside the crop area to apply the crop.

    or

    Double-click outside the crop area or choose a new tool to continue without applying the crop.

TIP To enlarge the canvas, extend the Crop handles beyond the area of the current canvas.

Altering Documents

Sometimes when you reduce the size of your document, some objects that were visible on the canvas end up positioned outside the canvas in the easel area. You have a choice as to whether or not Fireworks keeps those objects or deletes them.

To control objects off the canvas:

1. Choose **Edit** > **Preferences** to open the Preferences dialog box **⓫**.

2. Choose Editing from the menu.

3. Select Delete Objects when Cropping.

The canvas color is the color automatically applied behind all the images in a document. You can change the canvas color at any time while you work on a document.

To change the canvas color:

1. Choose **Modify** > **Document** > **Canvas Color** to open the Canvas Color dialog box **⓬**.

2. Click White, Transparent, or Custom.

TIP The transparent background is designated by a gray and white checkerboard **⓭**.

3. If you choose Custom, click the Color well to open the Swatches panel to choose a specific color.

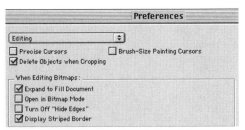

⓫ *Choose* **Delete Objects when Cropping** *from Editing Preferences to determine what happens to objects when the canvas is cropped.*

⓬ *The* Canvas Color *dialog box.*

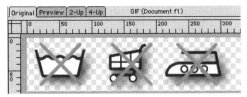

⓭ *The* **checkerboard grid** *indicates a transparent background.*

Vertical ruler   Horizontal ruler

⑭ *The* **rulers** *in the document window.*

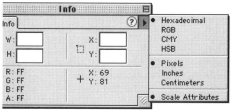

⑮ *Use the Info panel menu to* **change the unit of measurement.**

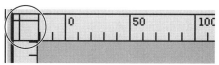

⑯ *Drag the* **zero point crosshairs** *(circled) onto the page to set the new zero point.*

Working with Rulers

In order to work precisely in your document, you need to work with the rulers.

To display the document rulers:

Choose **View > Rulers**. The rulers appear at the top and left sides of the document **⑭**.

TIP Two lines appear on the rulers— one on the vertical ruler and one on the horizontal ruler—to track your position as you move around the document.

Fireworks ships with pixels as the default unit of measurement for Info panel and dialog boxes. You can change that unit at any time.

To change the unit of measurement:

1. Make sure the Info panel is open. If not, choose **Window > Info ⑮**.

2. Use the Info panel menu to choose a new unit of measurement. The choices are:
   - Pixels
   - Inches
   - Centimeters

TIP Even if you change the unit of measurement, the rulers are still displayed in pixels.

Fireworks uses the upper left corner of a document as its *zero point*, or the point where the rulers start. You can change the zero point for a document. This can help you position items on the page.

To change the zero point:

1. Drag the zero point crosshairs onto the page **⑯**.

2. Double-click the zero point crosshairs in the corner of the document window to reset the zero point to the upper left corner.

Using Ruler Guides

The rulers also let you place additional guides that you can use to align objects.

To create guides:

1. Drag from the left ruler to create a vertical guide ❼. Release the mouse button to place the guide.

2. Drag from the top ruler to create a horizontal guide. Release the mouse button to place the guide.

3. Repeat to add as many horizontal or vertical guides as you need.

TIP Release the mouse button over the canvas area to create a guide. If you release over the easel area, you will not create the guide.

To position guides:

Drag an existing guide to move it to a new position.

or

Double-click the guide to open the Move Guide dialog box ❽ and enter the exact position of the guide.

TIP The Move Guide dialog box shows the position of the guide in pixels.

TIP Use **View** > **Guide Options** > **Snap To Guides** to have objects automatically snap, or align, to the guides.

❼ **Drag a guide** *from the ruler onto the active area.*

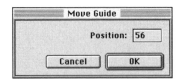

❽ *The* **Move Guide** *dialog box lets you enter the exact pixel position of the guide.*

⓲ *The* **Guides (Win)** *dialog box.*

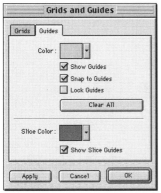

⓳ *The* **Grids and Guides (Mac)** *dialog box in the Guides mode.*

There are several ways you can edit or control the look of guides.

To edit guides:

1. Choose **View** > **Guide Options** > **Edit Guides** to open the Guides dialog box ⓲–⓳.

2. Click the Color Well to open the swatches and choose a new color. This can help make the guides look more or less obvious when positioned over the artwork in the document.

3. Click Show Guides to show or hide the guides.

4. Click Snap to Guides to turn this feature on or off.

5. Click Lock Guides to keep the guides from being moved.

TIP You can also lock the guides by choosing **View** > **Guide Options** > **Lock Guides**.

6. Click Clear All to delete all the guides from the document.

7. Click OK to apply the changes.

TIP (Mac) Click the Grids tab to switch from editing the guides to editing the grids (*see the steps on the next page*).

Working with Snap to Guides

The Snap to Guides feature means that as you move objects or anchor points, they will automatically jump, or snap, to a guide as you get near the guide.

Most people leave the feature turned on when they want to keep things aligned to guides.

However, you may want to turn off the features, especially if you are trying to move an object slightly away from a guide.

Using Ruler Guides

Using the Document Grid

Ruler guides are terrific for inserting at variable positions. If you need guides at repeated intervals, you should use Fireworks's document grid. The grid can also be used to align objects.

To view the document grid:

Choose **View**>**Grid** to display the document grid . You can use the grid to arrange your images into certain areas, or to make sure objects are aligned, or are the same size.

TIP You can use **View**>**Grid Options**>**Snap to Grid** to have objects automatically snap, or align, to the grid.

TIP When Snap to Grid is turned on, objects snap to the grid even if the grid is not visible.

You can also change the size of the grid. This makes it easy to create many different buttons or other objects that are all the same size or shape.

To edit the document grid:

1. Choose **View**>**Grid Options**>**Edit Grid** to open the Grids and Guides dialog box ㉒–㉓.

2. Click the Color Well to open the swatches and choose a new color for the grid.

3. Use the Horizontal slider or type in the field to increase or decrease the horizontal spacing.

4. Use the Vertical slider or type in the field to increase or decrease the vertical spacing.

5. Click Snap to Grid to turn this feature on or off.

6. Click Show Grid to show or hide the document grid.

㉑ *The **document grid** shown over the art.*

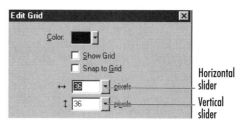

Horizontal slider
Vertical slider

㉒ *The **Edit Grid** (Win) dialog box.*

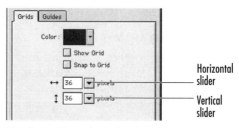

Horizontal slider
Vertical slider

㉓ *The **Grids and Guides** (Mac) dialog box in the Grids mode.*

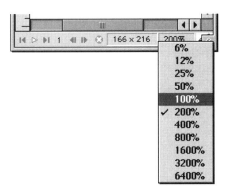

⓴ *The* **Magnification control menu** *at the bottom of the document window.*

Don't Sweat the Details...Yet!

Unlike print graphics, you don't have to worry too much about tiny details of your graphics as you lay out your Web graphics and pages.

That's because the process of optimizing your graphics, which is covered in Chapter 15, "Optimizing," can drastically change the look of colors and details.

Just relax and set up your graphics the way you want. There's plenty of time later to sweat out the details.

Magnification

You may need to zoom in or out to see specific areas of the big picture.

To use the magnification commands:

To zoom to a specific magnification, use the Magnification control **⓴**. Fireworks lets you view your artwork from 6% to 6400%.

TIP These are the same limits when using any of the other magnification or zoom controls.

or

Choose **View > Magnification** and then choose a specific magnification.

or

Choose **View > Zoom In** or **View > Zoom Out** to jump to a specific magnification.

or

Choose **View > Fit Selection** to display the object selected.

or

Choose **View > Fit All** to display the entire document.

Magnification

You can use the Zoom tool to jump to a specific magnification and position.

To use the Zoom tool:

1. Click the Zoom tool in the Tools panel **⑳**.

TIP The Zoom tool changes your view using the amounts listed in the Magnification control menu **㉔**.

2. Click the Zoom tool on the area you want to zoom in on. Click as many times as you need to get as close as necessary to the area you want to see.

or

Drag the Zoom tool diagonally across the area you want to see. Release the mouse button to zoom in **㉖–㉗**.

TIP Press the Option/Alt key while in the Zoom tool to zoom out from objects. The icon changes from a plus sign (+) to a minus sign (–).

Honestly, I haven't touched the Zoom tool in the Tools panel in years. Does that mean I don't zoom in and out? No, it means I zoom in and out by using the following keyboard shortcut. I've used this shortcut so often that I can do it in my sleep. In fact, the shortcut is so important, it has its own exercise.

To access the Zoom tool using the keyboard:

1. Press Command/Ctrl and the Spacebar. The currently selected tool is replaced by the Zoom tool.

2. Continue to hold the modifier keys as you drag or click with the Zoom as described in the previous exercise.

3. Release the modifier keys to return to the currently selected tool.

㉕ *The* **Zoom tool** *in the Tools panel.*

㉖ *Use the* **Zoom tool** *to zoom in on a specific area by dragging a marquee around that area.*

㉗ *After dragging, the* **selected area** *fills the window.*

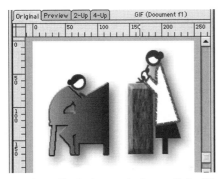

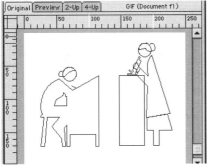

❽ *The* **Full Display** *mode shows all the fills, brushes, and effects for the objects.*

❾ *The* **Draft Display** *mode shows only the paths for the objects.*

Using the Display Options

Fireworks lets you work in two different display modes. The Full Display mode **❽** shows all the objects in the document with their fills, brushes, and effects. It gives you the best idea of what your final image will look like.

The Draft Display mode **❾** shows only the paths for objects. Switch to the Draft Display to improve the speed of your monitor's screen redraw. The Draft Display can also help you select objects located behind others.

To change the display options:

◆   Choose **View** > **Full Display** to switch between the two display modes.

TIP A check mark next to the Full Display listing indicates that you are viewing the document in the Full Display mode. No check mark indicates that you are in the Draft Display mode.

Using the Hand Tool

If you have used a computer for any type of program, you should be familiar with the scroll bars of a window that let you reposition the document so you can see horizontal and vertical areas that are outside the view of the window. Fireworks also has a Hand tool that lets you move around the window without using the scroll bars.

⑩ *The **Hand tool** in the Tools panel.*

To use the Hand tool:

1. Choose the Hand tool in the Tools panel **⑩**

2. Position the Hand tool inside the document window and drag in any direction **㉛**. This reveals the areas of the image that were previously hidden.

TIP Hold the spacebar to access the Hand tool without leaving the tool that is currently selected.

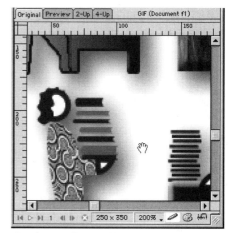

㉛ *The **Hand tool** allows you to move an image within the document window.*

Using the Hand Tool

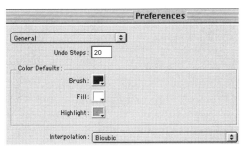

㉜ *The* **Undo Steps field** *allows you to set how many actions can be reversed.*

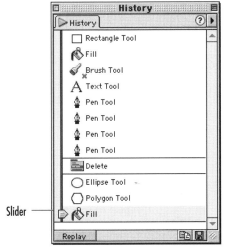

Slider

㉝ *The* **History panel** *shows a list of the undo steps.*

Controlling Actions

Like most applications, Fireworks lets you undo or reverse actions and commands. The number of steps is defined by the user.

To undo actions:

1. Choose **Edit > Undo**. This reverses the most recent action or command.

2. Choose **Edit > Undo** again to reverse the next most recent action.

TIP You'll work faster if you use the keyboard shortcut Command/Ctrl-Z.

Of course, you can also undo the undo—which is also called a redo.

To redo actions:

◆ Choose **Edit > Redo** to reverse the previously chosen Undo command.

To set the number of undo steps:

1. Choose **Edit > Preferences**.

2. Set the number of undo steps in the General Preferences options **㉜**.

TIP You must relaunch Fireworks for the change in the number of undo steps to take effect.

To jump to a previous action:

1. Choose **Window > History** to open the History panel. The panel shows the commands that can be reversed **㉝**.

2. Drag the slider up to the point where you want to reverse the actions. You add new steps to the History panel from that point on.

TIP The History panel can also be used to make scripts that automate a series of commands. *(See Chapter 12, "Automation Features" for more information on working with the History panel to create scripts.)*

Saving Your Work

Computers are nasty beasts. Just as you've worked several hours on an important project, they can suddenly quit or freeze on you. Any work that you haven't saved will be lost—totally lost. That's why it's an excellent idea to save your work often.

The first time you save a new file, there are several steps you have to perform.

To name and save a file:

1. Choose **File** > **Save** or **File** > **Save As**. There is no difference between the two commands when working on an untitled file. This opens the Save or Save As dialog box ❸❹.

2. Use the navigation controls to choose a destination disk and folder for the file.

3. Use the Name or File name field to name the file.

4. (Mac) Click Add File name Extension to automatically add the .png extension to the name of the file.

TIP The Windows operating system automatically adds the extension to the file name.

TIP Mac users should add the .png extension, especially if they will be sending files to their Windows friends.

5. Click Save to save the file and return to the Fireworks application.

Once you have named a file, it is very simple to save additional changes.

To save changes:

◆ Choose **File** > **Save**. The previous version of the file will be replaced by the current version.

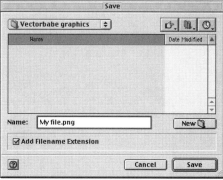

❸❹ *The* Save As dialog box (Win, top) *or* Save dialog box (Mac, bottom) *allows you to name a file and select its destination.*

A Special PNG

The Fireworks native file format has the extension .png. Although it has the same file extension, this is not the same as the PNG file type that can be created for the Web.

A Fireworks PNG is considered an enhanced PNG. This means that added information appears within the code for the file that is not found in a regular PNG.

You shouldn't publish a Fireworks PNG to a Web site. It will be far too big. You should export it as an optimized PNG. *(For more information on optimizing PNG files, see Chapter 15, "Optimizing.")*

COLORS 3

When I worked in advertising, the low-budget print jobs were limited to just black and white. As I worked my way up to the big-budget clients, I got to work on four-color jobs.

Designers working on Web graphics are luckier. Low-budget clients can afford color just like the big-budget companies. I think that's why so many designers enjoy creating Web graphics.

Of course, there are some limitations as to the number and types of colors you can use. But, unless it's your design decision, you should not have to limit your graphics to black and white.

Setting the Color Modes

Fireworks uses five different color modes to set color. You choose the different modes with the Color Mixer.

To use the Color Mixer:

1. If you do not see the Color Mixer, choose **Window** > **Color Mixer**.

   or

   Click the title bar of the Color Mixer panel to bring it in front of other onscreen elements.

2. Use the Color Mixer Options menu to choose one of the five color modes ❶.

One of the most common ways of defining colors for Web graphics is to use the *RGB* (red, green, blue) color system, also called *additive* color. *(See the color pages for a diagram that shows how additive colors can be mixed.)*

To define RGB colors:

1. Make sure the Color Mixer mode is set to RGB. If not, use the Options menu to change it.

2. To choose the R (red) component, drag the slider or enter a value in the R field. Do the same for the G (green) component and the B (blue) component ❷.

   or

   Click anywhere along the RGB color ramp at the bottom of the Color Mixer to choose colors by eye, rather than by numeric values.

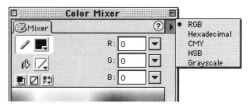

❶ *The* **five color mode choices** *of the Color Mixer Options menu.*

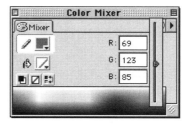

❷ **Drag the slider** *to set the value for one of the RGB color components or enter a number in each field. The RGB colors are set with numbers from 0 to 255.*

Understanding RGB Colors

RGB colors are called *additive* colors. They are formed from light such as the light from the sun, a movie projector, or a scanner, as opposed to pigments as in printer's inks. In the RGB additive color system, all three colors (red, green, and blue) combine to create white.

When all three colors are taken away, you get black. (Think about what happens when you turn off the lights in a room.)

Each of the RGB components is given a number between 0 and 255. So, for example, a yellow color could have the RGB values of R: 250, G: 243, and B: 117.

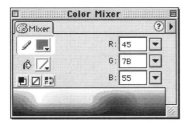

❸ Hexadecimal colors *use combinations of letters and numbers to define colors.*

Understanding Hexadecimal Color

Text, links, and background colors of Web graphics are defined in HTML documents using a color system called *hexadecimal.*

Hexadecimal colors are defined using the numbers from 0 to 9 and the letters A through F. So, the yellow mentioned in the sidebar on the previous page would be defined in hexidecimal code as R: FA, G:F3, B: 75.

Web-safe colors *(covered on pages 52 and 55)* are limited to those colors whose hexidecimal values include matched pairs of numbers or letters (00, 11, 22, 33, 44, 55, 66, 77, 88, 99, AA, BB, CC, DD, EE, FF). For example, the values R: FF, G: 00, B: 99 indicate a Web-safe color. The values R: 34, G: AA, B: F3 do not.

There is no difference in download speeds if you define colors using hexadecimal values. However, you may find it easier to match the colors in HTML documents if you use hexadecimal values.

Another way of defining colors is to use the *hexadecimal* color system. This is the same system used in HTML code.

TIP You may want to define your colors using hexidecimal values so you can match the colors in your Fireworks file with the colors on your HTML page layout.

To define hexadecimal colors:

1. Make sure the Color Mixer mode is set to Hexadecimal.

2. To choose the R (red) component, drag the slider or enter a value in the R (red) field. Do the same for the G (green) component and the B (blue) component ❸.

   or

   Click in the color ramp at the bottom of the Color Mixer to choose colors by eye rather than by numeric values. The hexidecimal values appear in the R, G, B fields.

TIP The color ramp in the hexadecimal mode limits you to working with the 216 Web-safe colors *(see page 52).*

TIP The hexadecimal system uses one or two combinations of the following numbers or letters: 0, 1, 2, 3, 4, 5, 6, 7, 8, 9, A, B, C, D, E, F. Other characters are ignored.

TIP You can also use the hexadecimal codes from your Fireworks graphics as part of the HTML code for your Web pages.

Setting the Color Modes

Fireworks also lets you define colors using *CMY* mode. This is a variation of the *subtractive* CMYK colors used in process-color printing. *(See the color pages for a diagram that shows how subtractive colors can be mixed.)* The special CMY mode in Fireworks mixes cyan, magenta, and yellow to create colors.

To define CMY colors:

1. Make sure the Color Mixer mode is set to CMY. If not, use the Color Mixer Options menu to switch to the CMY mode.

2. To choose the C (cyan) component, drag the slider or enter a value in the C (cyan) field. Do the same for the M (magenta) component and the Y (yellow) component ❹.

   or

   Click anywhere along the CMY color ramp at the bottom of the Color Mixer to choose colors by eye, rather than by numeric values.

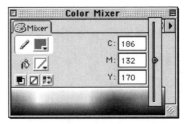

❹ **CMY colors** *use the numbers from 0 to 255 to set the amount of each color component.*

Understanding CMY Colors

The CMY colors in Fireworks are not the same as the CMYK colors used in printing.

Theoretically (and in Fireworks), combining the three pure CMY—cyan, magenta, and yellow—colors produces black. They are called *subtractive* colors because when you take away each of the colors you get white. (Take away the ink from a page and you're left with white.)

In actual printing, combining the three CMY inks produces a muddy brown-black so an extra black printing plate is added to create real black.

Fireworks provides the CMY mode as a convenience for those designers who (like your humble author) find it difficult to think in RGB. We can't remember that you add green to red to make orange. Our finger painting experiences make it easier for us to remember that magenta plus yellow make orange.

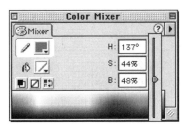

❺ **HSB colors** *use a combination of degrees around the Color Wheel for hue and percentages of saturation and brightness to define colors.*

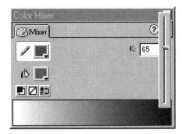

❻ **Grayscale colors** *use percentages of black to define colors.*

Understanding HSB Colors

The most classic form of defining colors is the HSB—hue, saturation, and brightness system.

Hue uses the principle of arranging colors in a wheel. Changing the colors from 0° to 360° moves through the entire color spectrum. Saturation uses percentage values, where 100% is a totally saturated color. Lower saturation values create pastel versions of a color. Brightness uses percentage values, where 100% is a color with no darkness or black. The lower the brightness percentage, the more darkness or black is added to the color.

You can also define colors using the classic *HSB* or hue, saturation, and brightness system.

To define HSB colors:

1. Make sure the Color Mixer mode is set to HSB. If not, use the Color Mixer Options menu to switch to the HSB mode.

2. To choose the H (hue) component, drag the slider or enter a degree value in the H (hue) field ❺.

3. To choose the S (saturation) component, drag the slider or enter a percentage value in the S (saturation) field. Do the same for the B (brightness) component.

   or

   Click anywhere along the HSB color ramp at the bottom of the Color Mixer to choose colors by eye, rather than by numeric values.

Although all Web graphics are exported in RGB or indexed colors, you may need to match colors used in grayscale images. So, the Color Mixer also lets you define colors using values of a single black (K) color plate.

To define Grayscale colors:

1. Make sure the Color Mixer mode is set to Grayscale. If not, use the Color Mixer Options menu to switch to the HSB mode.

2. To choose the K (black) component, drag the slider or enter a value in the K (black) field ❻.

   or

   Click anywhere along the Grayscale color ramp at the bottom of the Color Mixer to choose colors by eye, rather than by numeric values.

Setting the Color Modes

Using the Swatches Panel

It would be cumbersome to have to go to the Color Mixer every time you needed a color. The Swatches panel lets you store commonly used colors so they are always available.

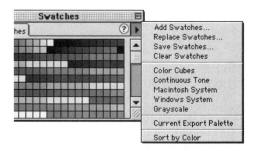

To use the Swatches panel:

1. If you do not see the Swatches panel, choose **Window** > **Swatches**.

   or

   If the Swatches panel is behind another panel, click the title bar of the Swatches panel to bring it in front of any other onscreen elements.

2. Click the Swatches panel Options menu to access the Swatches commands ❼.

One of the most important considerations in creating Web graphics is using *Web-safe colors*. You can access the 216 Web-safe colors via the Swatches panel. There are two arrangements of the Web-safe colors.

The Color Cubes palette displays the Web-safe colors in groups of related colors.

To choose the Color Cubes Swatches:

- Open the Swatches panel menu and choose Color Cubes. The color swatches appear in the panel ❽. *(See the color pages for a color display of the palette.)*

The Continuous Tone palette displays the Web-safe colors so that the colors flow from one color to another.

To choose the Continuous Tone swatches:

- Open the Swatches panel menu and choose Continuous Tone. The color swatches appear in the panel ❾. *(See the color pages for a color display of the palette.)*

❼ *The* Swatches panel Options menu.

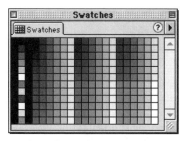

❽ *The* **Color Cubes** *arrangement of the Web-safe colors.*

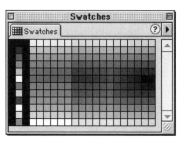

❾ *The* **Continuous Tone** *arrangement of the Web-safe colors.*

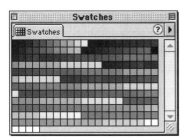

❿ *The* **Macintosh System colors** *in the Swatches panel.*

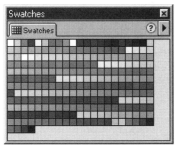

⓫ *The* **Windows System colors** *in the Swatches panel.*

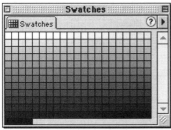

⓬ *The* **Grayscale colors** *in the Swatches panel.*

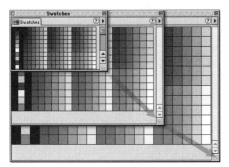

⓭ *As you* **increase the size of the Swatches panel** *you also increase the size of the color chips.*

You can also limit your colors to those found in the Macintosh operating system. This can be helpful if you are designing graphics for a intranet Web site to be viewed only on Macintosh computers that display only 256 colors.

To choose the Macintosh System Swatches:

◆ Open the Swatches panel menu and choose Macintosh System. The 256 color swatches appear in the panel **❿**. *(See the color pages for a color display of the palette.)*

You can also pick colors using the Windows System colors. This can be helpful if you are designing graphics for an intranet Web site to be viewed only on Windows computers that display only 256 colors.

To choose the Windows System Swatches:

◆ Open the Swatches panel menu and choose Windows System. The 256 color swatches appear in the panel **⓫**. *(See the color pages for a color display of the palette.)*

You can also limit your colors to grayscale colors. This is done by choosing the Grayscale swatches.

To choose the Grayscale Swatches:

◆ Open the Swatches panel menu and choose Grayscale. The 256 grayscale color swatches appear in the panel **⓬**.

If you find the color chips in the Swatches panel too small to use, you can make them bigger by enlarging the Swatches panel.

To change the size of the Swatches color chips:

◆ Use the resize control of the Swatches panel to increase the size of the Swatches panel. The color chips change their size accordingly **⓭**.

Using the Swatches Panel

You can use the Swatches panel to store colors that you create in the Color Mixer. This makes it easy to maintain a consistent look in all your graphics.

To add colors to the Swatches panel:

1. Use the Color Mixer to define a color that you want to store.

2. Move the mouse over to the gray area at the end of the Swatches panel where there are no swatches. A Paint Bucket cursor appears ⓮.

3. Click the mouse button. The new color appears in its own color swatch.

You can also delete colors from the Swatches panel.

To delete colors from the Swatches panel:

1. Move the cursor over the swatch for the color you want to delete.

2. Hold the Command/Ctrl key. A Scissors cursor appears ⓯.

3. Click to delete the color from the Swatches panel.

You can also delete all the colors from the Swatches panel at once.

To delete all the colors from the Swatches panel:

◆ Choose Clear Swatches from the Swatches panel Options menu.

If you keep adding many colors to the Swatches panel, you may want to arrange the swatches so that similar colors are grouped together.

To sort the swatches by color:

◆ Choose Sort by Color from the Swatches panel Options menu.

TIP The color swatches are sorted first by hue and then from light to dark ⓰.

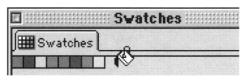

⓮ *The* **Paint Bucket** *cursor indicates you can store a color in the Swatches panel.*

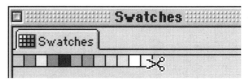

⓯ *The Command/Ctrl key displays the* **Scissors cursor**, *which allows you to delete a color from the Swatches panel.*

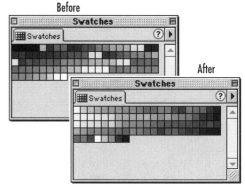

⓰ *The Swatches panel before and after* **sorting** *the colors.*

When to Use Web-safe Colors

At the risk of starting a controversy, let me try to explain when (or if) you should limit your colors to only the Web-safe palette.

Some people have monitors that can display only 256 colors. There are 256 colors for Windows monitors and 256 colors for Macintosh monitors, but only 216 colors that appear on both platforms. These are the 216 Web-safe colors.

If you limit your Fireworks graphics to only those 216 colors, you ensure that the colors of your document do not change when they are displayed on different monitors using different browsers.

These days, though, most people have monitors that can display more than 256 colors—most likely millions of colors. The question is: Should you limit yourself to designing Web sites for the oldest, most backward monitors or should you design for the majority?

My own opinion is that, unless you have a very good reason, you should design for the most advanced audience. The Web-safe palette is far too limiting to create sophisticated effects such as shadows, highlights, and bevels.

However, if you are designing a site with maps or financial charts, you might want to limit those images to the Web-safe colors. This guarantees that the images are displayed the same on all monitors.

Once you have created a custom Swatches panel with your own colors, you can save that Swatches panel to use at other times.

To save colors in the Swatches panel:

1. Choose Save Swatches from the Swatches panel Options menu.

2. Give the file a name and then save the file wherever you want. The saved file can be loaded into the Swatches panel at any time.

To load colors to the Swatches panel:

1. Open the Swatches panel menu and choose Replace Swatches.

2. Navigate to find a saved Swatches panel file.

3. Click Open. This replaces the current set of swatches with those from the saved file.

To add colors to the Swatches panel:

1. Open the Swatches panel menu and choose Add Swatches.

2. Navigate to find a saved Swatches panel file.

3. Choose Open. Unlike the Replace Swatches command, this adds the new swatches to those already in the Swatches panel.

Using the Swatches Panel

Using the Default Colors

Fireworks has a set of default colors for the Stroke and Fill colors. The default color for Stroke is black. The default color for Fill is white. These are simply the colors that the folks at Macromedia thought you would like to have when you first open Fireworks. However, the default colors can be accessed easily and changed to suit your needs.

To work with the default colors:

1. Click the default colors icon ⑰ in either the Tools panel or the Color Mixer to set the Stroke and Fill colors to their default settings.

   TIP Press the letter D to apply the default colors to an object.

2. Click the swap colors icon ⑱ in either the Tools panel or the Color Mixer to reverse the Stroke and Fill colors.

   TIP Press the letter X to swap the Stroke and Fill colors applied to an object.

To change the default colors:

1. Choose **Edit** > **Preferences** to open the Preferences dialog box ⑲.

2. Click the Color Well in the Color Defaults for the Brush or Fill colors.

3. Use the swatches to choose a new default color.

4. Click OK to apply the changes.

   TIP Macromedia used to call the Stroke color the Brush color. They forgot to change the label in the Preferences for Color Defaults. So, instead of Stroke, the color is labeled Brush. Let's hope they fix it in the next version of the program.

   TIP The Color Defaults also lets you change the highlight color, which is the color used to indicate that an object is about to be chosen.

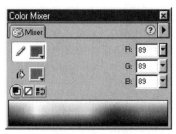

⑰ *Click the* **Default Colors icon** *(circled) in the Color Mixer to reset the Stroke and Fill colors to their default setting.*

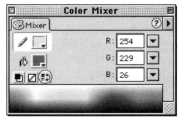

⑱ *Click the* **Swap Colors icon** *(circled) in the Color Mixer to reverse the Stroke and Fill colors.*

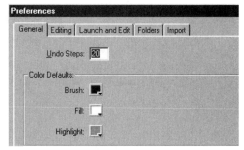

⑲ *The* **Color Defaults of the General Preferences** *lets you control the defaults for the Stroke, Fill, and Highlight colors.*

㉑ *The* **Eyedropper** *in the Tools panel.*

㉑ *The Eyedropper sampling for a* **Fill color.**

㉒ *The Eyedropper sampling for a* **Stroke color.**

㉓ *The* **Paint Bucket** *in the Tools panel.*

Sampling Colors

The Eyedropper tool lets you pick colors from objects or images so you can apply an exact match elsewhere.

To sample colors with the Eyedropper:

1. Choose the Eyedropper in the Tools panel **㉑**.
2. Position the Eyedropper over the color you want to sample.
3. Click. The color appears as either the Fill or Stroke color.

TIP When the Fill color is chosen, the Eyedropper shows a black square next to it **㉑**.

TIP When the Stroke color is chosen in the Tools panel, the Eyedropper shows a curved line next to it **㉒**.

The Paint Bucket lets you drop Fill colors onto objects whether or not they are selected. *(See page 218 for information on settings the options for the Paint Bucket.)*

To fill objects with the Paint Bucket:

1. Choose the Paint Bucket in the Tools panel **㉓**.
2. Click inside an object. The object fills with the currently selected Fill color. *(For more information on working with fills, see Chapter 7, "Fills.")*

Using the Info Panel

Fireworks lets you see the details of an image in the Info panel.

To change the Info panel settings:

1. Make sure the Info panel is open. If not, choose **Windows > Info.**

2. Click the triangle to open the Info panel Options menu ❷❹.

3. Choose a color mode to change how the Info panel displays color values.

4. Choose a unit of measurement to change how the Info panel displays the size and position of objects.

As you are working, you may want to know the exact composition of the color of an object or image.

To determine the color of an object:

◆ Pass the pointer over the object. The color area shows the values for the color the pointer is over ❷❺.

TIP Changing the way the Info panel displays colors does not actually change the colors. Colors in Fireworks are not set until they are exported as a finished file *(see Chapter 20, "Exporting").*

You can also find the alpha, or transparency, value of an object or image. *(See Chapter 11 "Masks and Interactions" for information on applying transparency values to artwork.)*

To determine the transparency of an object:

◆ Pass the pointer over the object. The alpha value is listed next to the letter A ❷❻.

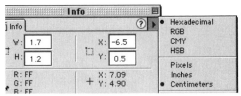

❷❹ *The* Info *panel menu.*

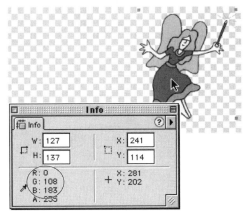

❷❺ *The* **color values** *(circled) of the Info panel show the RGB values for the area under the pointer.*

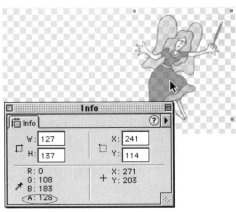

❷❻ *The* **alpha value** *(circled) of the Info panel shows the transparency values for the area under the pointer.*

PATH TOOLS 4

Many of my students ask me which is better for them to know in order to learn Macromedia Fireworks: a bitmapped editing program such as Adobe Photoshop, or a vector illustration program such as Adobe Illustrator or Macromedia FreeHand. Without a doubt the answer is a vector program.

While Fireworks does offer image editing features in bitmap mode *(see Chapter 13, "Working with Pixels")*, there is added power from the fact that it uses vector containers to hold bitmap information. So, unlike pixel images that are difficult to change, the paths in Fireworks remain "always editable, all the time."

If you are familiar with a vector program, you will quickly pick up the principles here. If you have never used a vector program, pay attention to this chapter, because creating paths is the primary source of images in Fireworks.

Creating Basic Shapes

There are four tools that allow you to quickly make a variety of basic shapes: rectangles, ellipses, polygons, stars, and straight lines.

Both the Rectangle tool and the Rounded Rectangle tool create rectangles, squares, and rounded-corner rectangles. One of the most common uses for these tools is to create the shapes for buttons and banners for your Web graphics.

To create a rectangle:

1. Click the Rectangle tool in the Tools panel ❶. If the Rectangle tool is not visible, press the triangle for the pop-up group in the Tools panel to choose the Rectangle tool.

2. Move the pointer to the Canvas area. The cursor changes to a plus sign (+) indicating that you can draw the rectangle.

3. Press and drag diagonally from one corner to the other of the rectangle you want to draw.

   TIP Hold the Shift key as you press and drag to constrain the Rectangle tool into creating a square ❷.

   TIP Hold the Option/Alt key as you press and drag to draw from the center point outward.

4. Release the mouse button to create the rectangle.

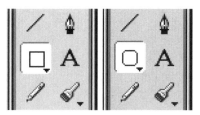

❶ *The* **Rectangle tool and Rounded Rectangle tool** *in the Tools panel.*

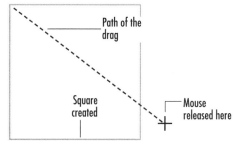

❷ **Holding the Shift key** *constrains the Rectangle tool to create a square. As long as you hold the Shift key down, the sides will remain equal.*

Rectangle or Rounded Rectangle?

All rectangles created by either the Rectangle tool or the Rounded Rectangle tool can have a roundness setting applied to them from the Object panel.

The Rounded Rectangle tool remembers the last setting of roundness. If you create a rectangle and change its roundness to 80, the next time you draw a Rounded Rectangle, its roundness will be 80. The Rectangle tool does not remember the roundness. If you set the roundness to 0, the next rectangle drawn by the Rounded Rectangle tool will be 30%—its default setting.

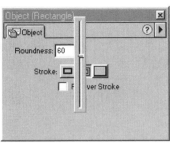

❸ *The* **Roundness slider** *lets you round the corners of a rectangle. You can also enter a precise number in the Roundness field.*

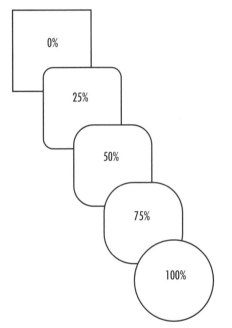

❹ *Squares drawn with different percentages for the corner radius.*

❺ *The* **Ellipse tool** *in the Tools panel.*

A rectangle with rounded corners is a very popular look for buttons and other interactive Web elements.

To create a rounded-corner rectangle:

1. Use either the Rounded Rectangle or the Rectangle tool to create a rectangle as described in the previous exercise.

2. Choose **Window > Object** to display the Object panel **❸**.

3. Use the Roundness slider to change the corners of the rectangle. The corners are rounded according to the percentage set for the corner radius **❹**.

TIP You can change the roundness interactively as you drag by pressing the up or down arrow keys on the keyboard.

TIP You can select the rectangle and use the Object panel to change the roundness of the rectangle at any time as long as you don't ungroup the rectangle.

You can create ellipses, ovals, and circles using the Ellipse tool.

To create an ellipse:

1. Click the Ellipse tool in the Tools panel **❺**. If the Ellipse tool is not visible, click the pop-up group to choose the Ellipse tool.

2. Move the pointer to the Canvas area.

3. Press and drag a line that defines the diameter of the ellipse.

TIP Hold the Shift key as you drag to constrain the ellipse into a circle.

TIP Hold the Option/Alt key as you drag to draw from the center point outward.

4. Release the mouse button to complete the ellipse.

Creating Basic Shapes

You can use the Line tool to quickly create straight line segments.

To create a line:

1. Click the Line tool in the Tools panel ❻.
2. Move the pointer to the Canvas area. The cursor changes to the plus sign.
3. Drag to set the length and direction of the line.

TIP Hold the Shift key to constrain the angle of the line to 45° increments ❼.

4. Release the mouse button to complete the line.

❻ *The* **Line tool** *in the Tools panel.*

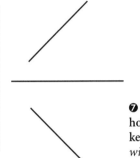

❼ *The results of* **holding the Shift key** *while drawing with the Line tool.*

Polygons give your Web graphics a special look. The Polygon tool can create both polygons and stars.

To create a polygon:

1. Click the Polygon tool in the Tools panel ❽. If the Polygon tool is not visible, press the pop-up group to choose the Polygon tool.
2. Double-click the Polygon tool to display the Polygon Options panel ❾.
3. Choose Polygon from the pop-up list.
4. Use the slider or enter a number from 1 to 360 in the field to set the number of sides for the polygon.

TIP The more sides to the polygon, the closer it gets to a circle.

5. Move the pointer to the Canvas area and press and drag. The point where you start the drag is the center of the polygon.
6. Release the mouse button to create the polygon.

❽ *The* **Polygon tool** *in the Tools panel.*

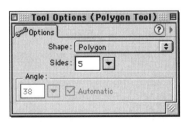

❾ *The* **Polygon tool** *Options panel.*

⑩ *The Polygon tool set for the* **Star** *options.*

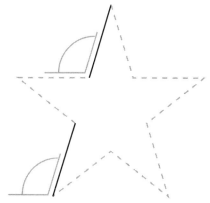

⑪ *The two black segments are parallel as a result of setting the star to* **Automatic.**

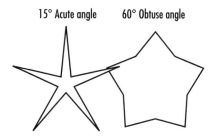

⑫ *Choose low angle values to create* **acute-angled stars** *with sharp points. Choose high angle values to create* **obtuse-angled stars** *with broad points.*

The same tool that you use to create polygons can be used to create stars. Stars with many points are sometimes called *bursts* and are useful for calling attention to special information.

To create a star:

1. Click the Polygon tool in the Tools panel. If the Polygon tool is not visible, open the pop-up group to choose the Polygon tool.

2. Double-click the Polygon tool in the Tools panel to display the Polygon tool Options panel.

3. Choose Star from the pop-up list in the Polygon Options. This adds the Angle controls to the panel **⑩**.

4. Use the slider or enter a number from 1 to 360 in the sides field to set the number of external points for the star.

5. Check Automatic to create stars with parallel line segments **⑪**.

    or

    Use the slider to set the angle of the points. Low settings create acute angles. High settings create obtuse angles **⑫**.

Working with the Pen Tool

One of the most important tools in any vector program is its Pen tool. The Pen tool allows you to precisely create a wide variety of shapes. The Fireworks Pen tool is similar to those found in Macromedia FreeHand and Adobe Illustrator. Before you learn to use the Pen, you should understand the elements of paths.

⑬ *The* **Pen tool** *in the Tools panel.*

 ⑭ *The* **start icon** *for the Pen tool.*

Anchor points define places in a path where the path changes direction or curvature. *Segments* are the paths that connect anchor points. *Control handles* extend out from anchor points; their length and direction control the shape of curved segments.

The best way to learn to use the Pen is to start by creating straight segments.

To create a straight path segment:

1. Click the Pen tool in the Tools panel ⑬.

2. Move the pointer to the Canvas area. The Pen cursor displays an *X* next to it. This indicates the start of the path ⑭.

3. Click to create an anchor point which defines the beginning of the segment of the path.

4. Move the cursor to where you want the next anchor point of the path. The Pen cursor changes so there is nothing next to it. This indicates that you can create a second point, connected to the first.

TIP If you use Precise Cursors *(see page 25)*, you do not see the Pen cursor. Rather you see a crosshair cursor.

5. Click. This connects the two anchor points with a straight line segment ⑮.

6. Continue to create straight segments by repeating steps 4 and 5.

7. To finish the path, hold the Command/Ctrl key, and click.

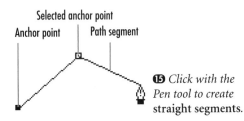

Selected anchor point

Anchor point | Path segment

⑮ *Click with the Pen tool to create* **straight segments**.

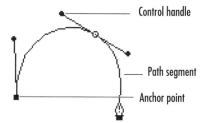

⓰ *Dragging with the Pen tool creates* **curved segments.**

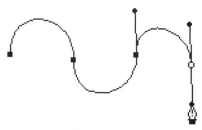

⓱ *A path with a series of curved segments.*

⓲ *Hold the Option/Alt key to pivot the handles and create a* **corner curve.**

You can also the Pen tool to create curved segments. Think of a curved segment as the shape that a roller coaster follows along a track.

To create a curved path segment:

1. Click the Pen tool in the Tools panel.

2. Move the Pen cursor to the Canvas area. The Pen cursor displays an *X* next to it.

3. Press and drag to create an anchor point with control handles.

4. Release the mouse button. The length and direction of the handle control the height and direction of the curve **⓰**.

5. Move the cursor to where you want the next anchor point of the path.

6. Press and drag to create the curved segment between the two anchor points.

7. Continue to create curved segments by repeating steps 3 and 4 **⓱**.

8. To finish the path, hold the Command/Ctrl key, and click.

Curves do not have to be smooth. A corner curve has an abrupt change in direction. Think of a bouncing ball. Where the ball hits the ground, its path is a corner curve.

To create a corner curve:

1. Press and drag to create an anchor point with control handles. Do not release the mouse button.

2. Hold the Option/Alt key and then drag to pivot the second handle **⓲**.

TIP The longer the handle, the steeper the curve.

3. Release the mouse button when the second handle is the correct length and direction.

Working with the Pen Tool

Once you have created a curved segment with two handles, you can retract the second handle back into the anchor point. This allows you to make the next path segment a straight path.

To retract the handle into a point:

1. Press and drag with the Pen tool to create an anchor point with two control handles.

2. Move the cursor back over the anchor point. A small caret appears next to the Pen cursor.

3. Click. The handle retracts back into the anchor point **⑲**.

4. Continue the path with either a straight segment or a curved segment.

TIP Click to make the next path segment straight. Drag to make the next path segment curved.

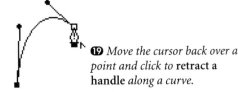

⑲ *Move the cursor back over a point and click to* **retract a handle** *along a curve.*

⑳ *Hold the Command + Option keys (Mac) or Ctrl + Alt keys (Win) to* **extend a handle** *out from an anchor point.*

Once you click to create an anchor point with no control handles, you can extend a single handle out from that anchor point. This allows you to make the next path segment a curved path.

To extend a handle out from a point:

1. Click to create an anchor point with no control handles.

2. Move the pointer back over the anchor point you just created. A small caret appears next to the Pen cursor.

3. Hold the Command + Option keys (Mac) or Ctrl + Alt keys (Win). The Pen cursor changes to a white arrow head.

4. Press and drag out from the anchor point **⑳**. A single control handle extends out from the anchor point.

5. Continue the path with a curved segment.

㉑ *An* Open path.

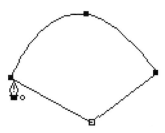

㉒ *The* **Closed path** *icon next to the Pen tool indicates that you are about to create a closed path.*

There are two ways to finish a path in Fireworks. The first way is to leave the end points of the path open. An open path is like a piece of string.

The second way to finish a path is to join the last point of the path to the first. This creates a closed path. A closed path is like a rubber band.

To create an open path:

1. Move the Pen tool away from the last point of the path.

2. Hold the Command/Ctrl key, and click. This leaves the path open ㉑ and allows you to continue using the Pen tool.

   or

   Switch to another tool in the Tools panel. This leaves the path open.

To create a closed path:

1. Move the cursor to the first anchor point of the path. A small circle appears next to the Pen cursor. This indicates you are about to close the path ㉒.

2. Click to close the path.

Working with the Pen Tool

Setting the Pen and Points Display

The Pen tool options control how the path is displayed as you draw with the Pen tool. The Pen preview helps to see what the next segment of the path will look like as you position the Pen cursor.

To set the Pen preview:

1. Double-click the Pen tool in the Tools panel to open the Options panel for the Pen tool 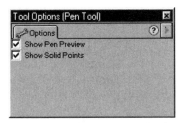.

2. Select Show Pen Preview to see a continuation of the path as you move the Pen tool to the next point ㉔.

   or

   Deselect Show Pen Preview to leave a gap between the Pen tool and the previous point on the path ㉔.

The Pen tool options also control the display of selected points on a path.

To set the points preview:

1. Double-click the Pen tool in the Tools panel to open the Options panel for the Pen tool.

2. Select Show Solid Points to display unselected points as filled squares and selected points as hollow squares ㉕.

   or

   Deselect Show Solid Points to display unselected points as hollow squares and selected points as filled squares ㉕.

TIP When Show Solid Points is deselected, Fireworks displays points similarly to the way Adobe Illustrator and other Adobe products display points. It is also the way previous versions of Fireworks displayed points.

TIP The Show Solid Points option changes the display of all points, regardless of the tool that was used to create them.

㉓ *The* **Pen options** *control the display of the path and the points on the path.*

㉔ *Turn the* **Pen Preview** *on to show the path between the last point and the next click of the Pen.*

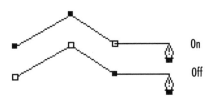

㉕ **Show Solid Points** *changes how selected points are displayed.*

㉖ *The* **Brush tool** *in the Tools panel.*

㉗ *The* **Brush** *allows you to draw freeform paths without placing anchor points.*

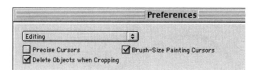

㉘ *Check* **Brush-Size Painting Cursors** *to see the size of the brush stroke.*

㉙ *The* **Brush icon** *is shown when Brush-Size Painting Cursors is deselected.*

Using the Brush Tool

Fireworks also has a Brush tool that lets you draw more freely, without worrying about how and where you place points. The Brush tool can also be used in the bitmap mode to paint images. *(For more information on working in the bitmap mode see Chapter 13, "Working with Pixels.")*

To draw with the Brush tool:

1. Click the Brush tool in the Tools panel **㉖**.

2. Move the pointer to the Canvas area.

3. Drag to create a path that follows the movements of the mouse **㉗**.

4. Release the mouse button to end the path.

TIP To make a closed path with the Brush tool, move the mouse close to the starting point of the path.

TIP Hold the Shift key to create straight lines with the Paintbrush.

The Paintbrush cursor shows the current size of the stroke width *(see page 121)*. However, you can change the preferences to show the Paintbrush cursor as you draw.

To change the Paintbrush cursor:

1. Choose **Edit** > **Preferences**.

2. Choose Edit from the pop-up menu. This shows the Editing preferences **㉘**.

3. Deselect Brush-Size Painting Cursors. This displays the Paintbrush cursor **㉙** instead of the size and shape of the stroke width.

Using the Pencil Tool

Like the Brush tool, the Pencil tool lets you draw without worrying about placing anchor points or creating handles. The Pencil tool can also be used in the bitmap mode to color pixels. *(See Chapter 13, "Working with Pixels.")*

30 *The* **Pencil tool** *in the Tools panel.*

To draw with the Pencil:

1. Click the Pencil tool in the Tools panel **30**.

2. Move the pointer to the Canvas area.

3. Drag to create a line that follows the movements of the mouse.

4. Release the mouse button to finish drawing the line.

TIP Release the mouse button where you started to close the path.

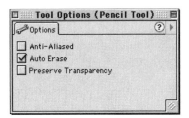

31 *The* **Pencil Tool Options** *panel.*

You can soften the look of Pencil lines by turning on the Anti-Aliased option. This adds lighter colors that blend to the background color or background objects. This softens the edge of the line.

TIP You can also apply anti-aliasing to the edges of objects *(see page 117)* or to text *(see page 159)*.

To add anti-aliased edges to Pencil tool lines:

1. Double-click the Pencil tool in the Tools panel to display the Pencil Options **31**.

2. Click the Anti-Aliased option to soften the lines created by the pencil **32**.

TIP The anti-aliased option creates additional colors in artwork. This can add to the size of the final Web graphic.

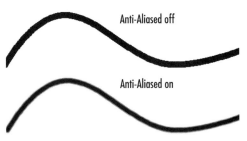

Anti-Aliased off

Anti-Aliased on

32 *The difference between drawing with the* **Anti-Aliased option** *on and off.*

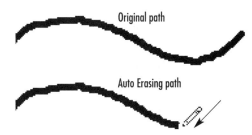

Original path

Auto Erasing path

33 *Dragging with the Pencil tool along a path with the **Auto Erase** option lets you erase the path by coloring it with the Fill color.*

Vectors vs. Pixels

I admit it, I love working with vector drawing tools. They're so precise, so mathematical. That's why I love working with the tools in Fireworks.

But many people, especially those used to image-editing programs such as Photoshop, find it difficult to get used to working with vectors.

If you absolutely cannot work with the vector tools, you can switch to the bitmap mode. But you'll miss out on some of the power of Fireworks.

The Auto Erase option lets you erase Pencil lines by drawing over them with the Fill color. *(For more information on Fill and Stroke colors, see Chapter 7, "Fills" and Chapter 8, "Strokes.")*

To use the Auto Erase:

1. Double-click the Pencil tool in the Tools panel. This opens the Options panel for the Pencil tool.

2. Click Auto Erase in the Options panel.

3. Place the Pencil over a path colored with the current Brush color.

4. Drag the Pencil. The path changes from the Brush to the Fill color **33**.

TIP When working in the path mode, the Auto Erase option of the Pencil does not actually change the colors of the previously drawn path. Rather, it creates a new path on top of the first one.

TIP The Auto Erase option works best when the path is not Anti-Aliased. This makes it easier to position the Pencil over a pixel colored exactly with the Brush color and not a shade created by the anti-aliasing.

TIP The auto-erase option works best in the bitmap mode. *(For more information on using the bitmap mode, see Chapter 13, "Working with Pixels.")*

Modifying Paths

Once you have created a path—with any of the drawing tools—you can modify its shape. Fireworks has several different ways you can modify paths. The Redraw Path tool is like the Brush tool except that, instead of just drawing paths, it modifies paths that it comes near to.

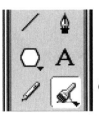

34 *The* **Redraw Path tool** *in the Tools panel.*

TIP The Redraw Path tool displays the Brush-Size Painting cursors or the the tool cursor depending on the Editing Preferences *(see page 25)*.

TIP Rectangles, ellipses, and polygons must be ungrouped *(see pages 82–83)* before they can be modified.

To use the Redraw Path tool to modify a path:

1. Select a path.

TIP Paths are automatically selected after you finish drawing them. You can also select paths using any of the selection tools. *(See Chapter 5, "Selecting Paths.")*

2. Press the triangle pop-up group in the Tools panel to choose the Redraw Path tool **34**.

TIP Although similar to the Brush tool icon, the Redraw Path tool shows a Paintbrush pulling at a line.

3. Move the tool to the part of the path that you want to redraw.

TIP If you have the tool cursor visible, a small triangle sign appears next to the Redraw Path cursor **35**. This indicates that the path will be redrawn.

4. Drag to create the new shape of the path. A red line appears that indicates the part of the path that is modified **36**.

5. Release the mouse to redraw the path.

TIP You can also modify the shape of a path by manipulating the anchor points and control handles of the path.

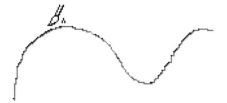

35 *The* **Redraw path cursor** *(with Brush-Size Painting Cursors deselected).*

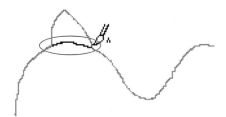

36 *A* **red line** *(circled) shows the original path as the Redraw Path tool creates the new path.*

㊲ *The* **Subselection tool** *in the Tools panel.*

㊳ *Click with the Pen tool to* **add a point** *to a path.*

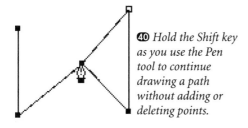

㊴ *A selected* **point on a path can be deleted** *by pressing the delete/backspace key.*

㊵ *Hold the Shift key as you use the Pen tool to continue drawing a path without adding or deleting points.*

Modifying Paths and Points

As you draw paths, you may find that you need to add or delete points. You may discover that you need to change a straight line into a curve or vice versa. Fortunately, the Pen tool not only creates points, it can also modify them—even as you are still drawing the path.

TIP You cannot use these techniques on rectangles unless you first ungroup them.

To add points to a path:

1. If you are not currently working on the path, use the Subselection tool **㊲** to select the path. *(See Chapter 5, "Selecting Paths" for more information on working with the Subselection tool.)*

2. If not already active, choose the Pen tool and position the cursor on the segment where you want to add the point. A plus sign (+) appears next to the cursor **㊳**.

3. Click. A new point appears.

To delete points from a path:

1. If you are not currently working on the path, use the Subselection tool to select the path.

2. If not already active, choose the Pen tool and position the cursor over the point that you want to delete. A minus sign (-) appears next to the cursor **㊴**.

3. Click. The point is deleted.

TIP If the anchor point has control handles, you must first click to delete the handles, then click again to delete the point.

TIP Hold the Shift key before you click with the Pen to override the add points or delete points features of the Pen tool **㊵**. Hold the Shift key after you click with the Pen to constrain the movements of the Pen tool.

Modifying Paths and Points

You can also use the Pen tool to change between the two types of anchor points: corner and curved. For instance, you can change a curve point into a corner point.

To convert a curve point:

1. Position the Pen tool over the point you want to convert. A small caret (^) indicates that the point will be converted 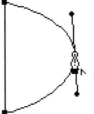.

2. Click. The Bézier handles of the point retract.

It's a little trickier to convert a corner point into a curve point. This is because you have to ignore the delete point icon.

To convert a corner point:

1. Position the Pen tool over the point you want to convert. Although the minus sign appears, ignore it. You are not going to delete that point.

2. Press and drag (do not click) with the Pen tool. Bézier handles will appear as the point is converted into a curve point ❹❷.

TIP You can also hold the Shift key to avoid the minus sign.

❹❶ *Click with the Pen tool to* **convert a curve point to a corner point.**

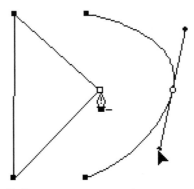

❹❷ *To* **convert a corner point to a curve point** *press and drag with the Pen tool to extend the Bézier handles. (Ignore the minus sign.)*

Modifying Paths and Points

SELECTING PATHS 5

When I was young, we didn't have personal computers. (Hey, that doesn't make me *that* old!) However, instead of computer graphics, we had other types of arts and graphics. Yes, there were arts and graphics before computers. One of my favorites was nail-and-string art.

You started with a plywood rectangle and spent the entire morning hammering thin nails into the wood in a grid pattern. This was the noisy part. After lunch, you took colored strings and wrapped them around the nails to create shapes—a much quieter activity.

That's why I enjoy working with the vector paths in Macromedia Fireworks. The anchor points are like the nails and the paths are the string.

Unlike the nails of my old art projects, Fireworks anchor point are much more flexible. This chapter shows that instead of pulling at each nail, you use Fireworks's selection tools to select and move anchor points and objects.

Selecting Entire Objects

The main selection aid is the Pointer tool. The Pointer tool selects objects as complete paths, not individual points.

❶ *The* **Pointer tool** *in the Toolbox.*

To use the Pointer tool:

1. Click the Pointer tool in the Toolbox ❶.

   TIP Hold the Command/Ctrl key to temporarily access the Pointer tool while working in any other tool. Release the key to return to the original tool.

2. Position the Pointer arrow over an object and click. A highlight color appears along the path indicating that the object is selected ❷.

   TIP If the object has no fill color, you must click the path or stroke color to select the object.

   TIP If you are working in the Draft Display mode *(see page 43),* you must click the path directly to select the object.

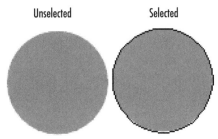

Unselected   Selected

❷ *A highlight color appears on the path of a* **selected** *object.*

You can also select many objects at once by dragging a marquee with the Pointer tool.

To select objects with a marquee:

1. Place the Pointer tool outside the area of the objects you want to select.

2. Drag diagonally with the Pointer tool to create a rectangle that encloses your selection.

3. Release the mouse button. All objects inside the rectangle are selected ❸.

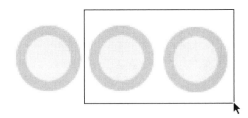

❸ *Drag with the Pointer tool to select objects within the* **rectangular marquee.**

Selecting Methods

With all the different ways to select objects, you might ask: Which one is the best way?

The best way depends on where your hands are, what tool is currently chosen, and how many objects you want to select. And there's an element of personal preference.

For instance, if you want to select all the objects on a page except one, it might be easier to use the Select All command and then Shift-click to deselect one.

If you want to select all the objects on the left side of the page, it may be quicker to drag to select the objects within a rectangular marquee.

There are many times I see my students laboriously clicking, one-by-one, to select objects. Before you start clicking, think about what would be the most efficient way to select the objects.

Once you have a selection of objects, you can add objects to, or subtract from, the selection.

To add objects from a selection:

♦ Hold the Shift key and click to select any additional objects.

To subtract objects from a selection:

♦ Hold the Shift key and click to deselect any objects.

TIP Sometimes it is easier to select a group of objects within a marquee and then use the Shift key to deselect the one or two you do not want as part of the selection.

In addition to the selection tools available from the Tools panel, you can use the commands from the Select menu to select and deselect objects.

To select objects using the menu commands:

♦ Choose **Select** > **Select All** to select all the objects in a file.

TIP The Select All command will not select objects on locked or hidden layers or if the Layer is set to Single Layer Editing . *(See pages 104–106 for information on working with layers.)*

or

Choose **Select** > **Deselect** to deselect any selected objects.

TIP These commands can also be used when working in the bitmap mode *(see Chapter 13, "Working with Pixels")*.

TIP You can also deselect any objects in a file by clicking the empty space in a document with the Pointer tool.

Selecting Entire Objects

Selecting Points

Instead of selecting an entire object, you can also select individual points. You can then manipulate or delete them to change the shape of the path. The Subselection tool is used to select individual anchor points.

To use the Subselection tool:

1. Click the Subselection tool in the Toolbox **❹**.

2. Click the object to select it. The anchor points will be displayed but not selected **❺**.

TIP The Pen tool options determine the appearance of selected and unselected points *(see page 68).*

3. Click a specific point or marquee—drag to select multiple points. The anchor points of the object are selected.

4. Hold the Shift key and click to select additional points **❺**.

5. Use the Subselection tool to move the selected points **❻**.

TIP If you switch from the Pointer tool to the Subselection tool while an object is already selected, you see the unselected anchor points for that object.

❹ *The* **Subselection tool** *in the Toolbox.*

Object selected but points unselected   Object and points selected

❺ *The* **Subselection tool** *allows you to see the anchor points and handles of a selected object. Click to select the specific points.*

❻ Drag with the Subselection tool *to change the position of anchor points.*

Pointer or Subselection Tool?

If you select an object with the Pointer tool and then drag, you will always move the entire object.

If you use the Subselection tool you can select individual points and move them. However, you can also select and move all the points in the path with the Subselection tool.

That's why I use the Subselection tool almost all the time, and rarely use the Pointer tool.

Selecting Points

❼ *The* **Select Behind tool** *in the Toolbox.*

❽ *The Select Behind tool was used to select the star behind the other two objects. The first click selected the square. The second click selected the circle. The third click selected the star.*

Selecting Objects Behind Objects

Because transparency often figures into creating Fireworks graphics, you may find that your artwork consists of many objects stacked on top of each other. This can sometimes make it difficult to select an object behind the rest. The Select Behind tool makes it easy to select through other objects to one at the back.

To use the Select Behind tool:

1. Press the pop-up group for the Pointer tool to choose the Select Behind tool ❼.

2. Click with the Select Behind tool over the objects you want to select. The first click selects the object on top of the others.

3. Click as many times as necessary to select the object you want ❽.

TIP Hold the Shift key as you click to add each object to the selection. (In case you were wondering, no—you can't use the Select Behind tool to deselect behind.)

Controlling Selections

Fireworks gives you several options for the Pointer tool that make it easier to select and move objects. The Mouse Highlight feature allows you to know which object is about to be selected with the next click. The Preview Drag option controls what the object looks like as you move it.

TIP These options are also available for the Select Behind tool and the Subselection tool.

TIP The final option for the Pointer tool, Show Fill Handles, is used when working with gradients *(see Chapter 7 "Fills")*.

To set the Mouse Highlight:

1. Double-click the Pointer, Subselection, or Select Behind tool to open the Options panel.

2. Select Mouse Highlight in the panel ❾.

3. Move the tool over an object. A red line appears around the object indicating that the object can be selected with the next mouse click.

To set the Preview Drag:

1. Double-click the Pointer, Subselection, or Select Behind tool to open the Options panel.

2. Select Preview Drag in the Options panel.

3. Move an object. With Preview Drag turned on you see the fill, stroke, and effects of an object as you move it. With Preview Drag turned off, you see only the path shape of the object ❿.

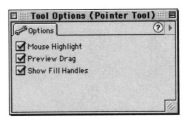

❾ *The* **Pointer tool options** *for the selection tools.*

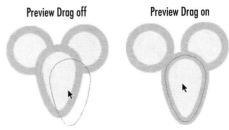

❿ *The* **Preview Drag** *controls what you see when an object is moved.*

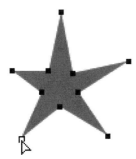

⓫ *The* **Hide Edges** *command hides the highlight along a path but keeps the anchor points and control handles visible when you use the Subselection tool.*

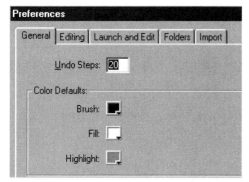

⓬ *Use the* **Highlight color well** *in the Preferences dialog box to change the color of the path highlight.*

If you find that the highlight effect interferes with your work, you can hide the highlight while keeping the object selected.

To control the highlight of selected objects:

◆ Choose **View** > **Hide Edges**. This hides the highlight along the path of an object.

or

To reveal the highlight, choose **View** > **Hide Edges** when there is a checkmark in front of the command.

TIP Anchor points and control handles are still visible when the Hide Edges command is applied **⓫**.

You may not be able to see the path highlight color if it is too similar to the color of the brush stroke around an object. You can use the Preferences to change the path highlight color.

To change the highlight color:

1. Choose **Edit** > **Preferences** to open the Preferences dialog box **⓬**.

2. Click the Highlight Color Well. The swatches appear.

3. Choose the color for the highlight and then click OK.

TIP The highlight color is an application preference. Changing it changes the highlight color for all Fireworks documents.

Controlling Selections

Working with Groups

If you have a graphic that consists of several objects and text, you may find it easier to select them all together as a unit, or group.

To group selected objects:

1. Select two or more objects.

2. Choose **Modify**>**Group**. Small anchor points appear around the objects indicating that they are a group ⓭.

TIP Fireworks lets you group a single object. This lets you select the object without highlighting its path.

3. You can add objects to the group by selecting the group and additional objects and then choosing the Group command again.

To ungroup objects:

1. Select the grouped objects.

2. Choose **Modify**>**Ungroup** to release the objects from the group.

TIP (Win) You can also use the Group/Ungroup icons on the Modify toolbar.

Grouped objects are considered a single object. However, you do not have to ungroup to select a specific object within the group.

To select objects within groups:

1. Choose either the Pointer, Subselection, or Select Behind tool.

2. Hold the Opt/Alt key and click the individual object of the group.

TIP Hold the Shift and Opt/Alt keys to add other items to the selection.

TIP If you want to move the object, be sure to release the Opt/Alt key before you start to drag or you will make a copy of the object (see page 87).

⓭ *Selected ungrouped objects (left) display their individual anchor points. Selected* **grouped objects** *display four points around the items in the group.*

Automatic Groups

The rectangles created by the Rectangle and Rounded Rectangle tools are automatically grouped. This is so you can change the roundness of the corners at any time.

If you ungroup them, you will not be able to change the roundness of the corners. The round corners will be converted into anchor points with handles.

Working with Groups

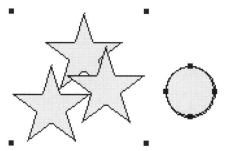

⓮ *The group of stars on the left is selected along with the circle on the right.*

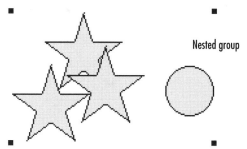

Nested group

⓯ *When the group of stars and circle are grouped, a* **nested group** *is created.*

Groups can be nested within other groups so that one group contains subgroups. The Subselect and Superselect commands then make it easy to work with nested groups.

To create a nested group:

1. Select two or more groups or one group and some other objects **⓮**.

2. Choose **Modify** > **Group**. The original selections are now subgroups of the nested group **⓯**.

3. Continue to select additional objects and choose the Group command to create more nested groups.

Once you group objects, you don't have to ungroup them to select the members of a group. The Subselect command lets you select a group and then easily select the individual members of the group.

To use the Subselect command:

1. Select a nested group.

2. Choose **Edit** > **Subselect**. This lets you see and work with the original objects of the nested group.

The Superselect command lets you select an individual object in a group and then easily select the entire group. This makes it easy to select different objects within a nested group.

To use the Superselect command:

1. Select a single item in a nested group.

2. Choose **Edit** > **Superselect**. This selects the group that contains the selection.

TIP You can reapply both the Subselect and Superselect commands to further select groups within nested groups.

Working with Groups

WORKING WITH OBJECTS 6

When I was a kid, I had an art toy called Colorforms®. It consisted of shiny black pages onto which I could place cutout vinyl shapes. The vinyl pieces stuck to the black pages without any glue or tape, which I found quite remarkable. I could put them down and pick them up and move them around however I wanted, creating all sorts of patterns and pictures.

Forty plus years later, as I play with Macromedia Fireworks, I see how similar it is to Colorforms. Unlike the plastic Colorforms pieces, objects on my Fireworks pages can be stretched, distorted, and otherwise transformed into unlimited variations.

Hundreds of pieces came in my Colorforms set, but with Fireworks I can duplicate them over and over. There is no limit to how many objects I can have on the page. Not only that, Fireworks objects don't ever get lost under the cushions of the couch!

Moving Objects

It's not critical where you originally create an object. You can always select it and move it to a new position. Or you can change its numeric coordinates in the Info panel.

To move an object by eye:

1. Select the object.

2. Using any of the selection tools, drag the object to the new position.

TIP Place your cursor anywhere on the object, except on a point to avoid reshaping the object.

TIP You can also move an object by pressing the arrow keys on the keyboard.

To move an object numerically:

1. Select the object.

2. Choose **Window**>**Info**. The Info panel appears ❶.

3. Change the number in the X field to set the position of the left edge.

4. Change the number in the Y field to set the position of the top edge.

TIP The Info panel also gives you read outs of the color and alpha settings under the current cursor positions. *(For more information see page 58.)*

Duplicating Objects

Because you work with objects, you can easily duplicate them in a variety of ways.

To copy and paste an object:

1. Select the object.

2. Choose **Edit**>**Copy**.

3. Choose **Edit**>**Paste** to paste the object into the same position as the original.

4. Move the object to a new position.

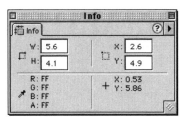

❶ *The* **Info panel** *lets you change the position of an object using the X and Y coordinates.*

The Computer Clipboard

The Copy and Cut commands place objects into an area of the computer memory called the Clipboard. The contents of the Clipboard stay within the memory until a new object is copied or the computer is turned off.

The Clipboard can only hold one set of information at a time. So, if you copy one item, and then later copy another, the first object is flushed from the Clipboard and replaced by the second.

Using the Clone; Duplicate; Drag and Drop; and Opt/Alt-Drag techniques allows you to make copies of objects without losing the current contents of the Clipboard.

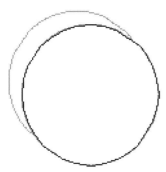

❷ *The* **Duplicate** *command copies the selected object. Cloning places a copy right on top of the original.*

❸ *Hold the Opt/Alt keys as you move an object to create a copy of that object while leaving the original in place.*

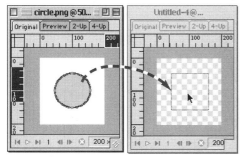

❹ *You can* **drag and drop** *an object from one document to another. (The dashed line with the arrow indicates the direction of the drag and drop.)*

To clone an object:

1. Select the object.

2. Choose **Edit** > **Clone**. A duplicate of the object appears in the same position as the original.

To duplicate an object:

1. Select the object.

2. Choose **Edit** > **Duplicate**. A duplicate of the object appears slightly offset from the original ❷.

To copy an object as you move it:

1. Choose any of the selection tools.

2. Hold the Opt/Alt key as you move the object. A small plus sign (+) appears next to the arrow as you move the object ❸.

3. Release the mouse button. A copy of the object appears.

You can also drag and drop objects from one document to another.

To drag and drop an object:

1. Position two document windows so that both are visible.

2. Use any of the selection tools to drag an object from one document to the other. (No need to hold the Opt/Alt key.)

3. Release the mouse button. A copy of the object appears in the new document ❹.

TIP Clone; Duplicate; Drag and Drop; and Opt/Alt-Drag leave the contents of the Clipboard unchanged. *(See the sidebar on the opposite page for a discussion of working with the Clipboard.)*

Duplicating Objects

Transforming Objects

Transformations change the size, shape, or orientation of an object. Fireworks provides many different ways to transform objects.

The Scale tool changes an object's size.

To Scale an object:

1. Choose the Scale tool in the Tools panel ❺.

    or

    Choose **Modify** > **Transform** > **Scale**. The transformation handles appear on a bounding box around the object.

2. Place the cursor directly over any of the handles. A small double-headed arrow appears ❻.

3. Drag a handle toward the object to reduce it or away to enlarge it.

TIP Drag one of the corner handles to scale both the horizontal and vertical dimensions of the object.

TIP Drag an edge handle to change just the horizontal or vertical dimension.

4. Double-click within the bounding box to apply the transformation.

    or

    Press Return/Enter.

TIP As you use the Scale tool, the Info panel shows the percentage amount of the scaling ❼.

TIP You can use the W and H fields in the Info panel to change the width and height of an object.

TIP You can also use the bounding box handles to rotate an object (*see page 91*).

❺ *The* Scale tool *in the Tools panel.*

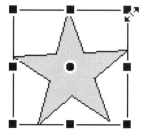

❻ *Drag a corner handle with the* Scale tool *to change the horizontal and vertical dimensions of the object proportionally.*

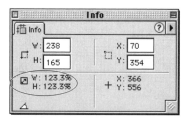

❼ *The Info Panel displays the* scaling percentages *(circled) as you drag with the Scale tool.*

Cancelling a Transformation

If you change your mind in the middle of using the bounding box handles, you can exit the transformation mode by pressing the Esc key on the keyboard. You can also press Command/Ctrl-period. Finally, you can switch to another tool in the Tools panel.

Transforming Objects

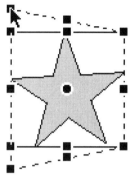

❽ *The* **Skew tool** *in the Tools panel.*

❾ *Drag a corner handle with the* **Skew tool** *to change the dimension of that side of the object.*

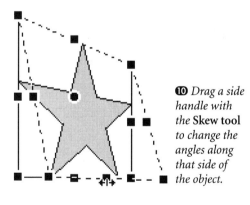

❿ *Drag a side handle with the* **Skew tool** *to change the angles along that side of the object.*

The Skew tool distorts an object by moving two sides of the bounding box together or two control handles in opposite directions. Skewing creates a perspective effect for objects or for text *(see page 161).*

To skew an object:

1. Choose the Skew tool in the Tools panel ❽.

   or

   Choose **Modify** > **Transform** > **Skew**. The transformation handles appear around the object.

2. Place the cursor directly over any of the handles.

3. Drag one of the corner handles in or out to move that handle and the one opposite it. This changes the dimension of that side of the object ❾.

4. Drag one of the side handles to change the angle of that side of the object ❿.

5. Double-click within the box created by the transformation handles to apply the transformation.

   or

   Press Return/Enter.

Transforming Objects

Transforming Objects

The Distort tool allows you to modify the proportions of an object by changing the shape of the box that defines it. Unlike Skew, the Distort tool lets you manipulate each corner handle individually.

To distort an object:

1. Choose the Distort tool in the Tools panel ⓫.

   or

   Choose **Modify > Transform > Distort**. The transformation handles appear around the object.

2. Place the cursor directly over a handle.

3. Drag to change the shape of the object ⓬.

4. Double-click within the bounding box to apply the transformation.

   or

   Press Return/Enter.

TIP As you use the Distort tool, the Info panel shows the new coordinates of the points ⓭.

⓫ *The* **Distort tool** *in the Tools panel.*

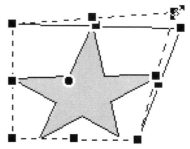

⓬ *Drag a handle with the* **Distort tool** *to change the shape of an object.*

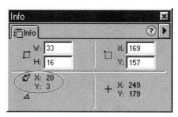

⓭ *The Info Panel displays the* x *and* y *coordinates of the distorted points (circled) as you drag with the Distort tool.*

Switching Transformation Tools

You don't have to apply a transformation to move between the transformation tools.

This means you can scale an object, skew it, distort it, and then apply the transformation.

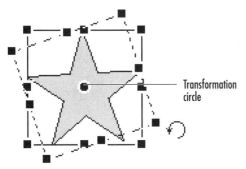

Transformation circle

⓮ *Drag with the* **Rotation cursor** *to change the orientation of an object.*

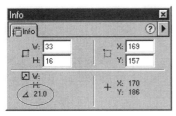

⓯ *The Info Panel displays the* **rotation angle** *(circled) as you use the Rotation mode of the Scale tool.*

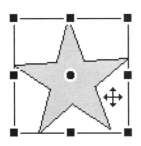

⓰ *The* **four-headed arrow** *appears when you move an object in a transformation mode.*

When you use any of the transformation tools, you have an additional transformation option available: rotation.

To rotate an object:

1. Choose any of the Transformation tools.

2. Position the cursor outside the handles. A rounded arrow appears.

3. Drag either clockwise or counter-clockwise to rotate the object ⓮.

TIP Move the small circle inside the bounding box to change the point around which the object rotates.

4. Double-click within the box created by the transformation handles to apply the transformation.

TIP As you use the Distort tool, the Info panel shows the new coordinates of the points ⓯.

You can also move an object while in the transformation mode.

To move an object in the transformation mode:

1. Position the cursor inside the box created by the transformation handles. A four-headed arrow appears ⓰.

2. Drag to move the object.

3. Continue working with the transformation tools or apply the transformation by double-clicking within the box created by the transformation handles.

Transforming Objects

Fireworks also gives you a set of Transformation menu commands that make it easy to rotate or flip objects 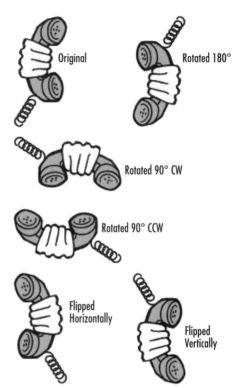 **⓱**.

To use the Transform menu commands:

1. Select an object.

2. Choose one of the following commands to rotate the object:
   - **Modify > Transform > Rotate 180°** turns the object upside down.
   - **Modify > Transform > Rotate 90° CW** rotates the object 90 degrees clockwise.
   - **Modify > Transform > Rotate 90° CCW** rotates the object 90 degrees counter-clockwise.

3. Choose one of the following commands to flip the object:
   - **Modify > Transform > Flip Horizontal** flips the object along its horizontal axis.
   - **Modify > Transform > Flip Vertical** flips the object along its vertical axis.

(Win) To use the Transform menu commands:

◆ Use the rotate buttons on the Modify toolbar **⓲** to apply rotations.

⓱ *The effects of* **Transform** *menu commands on the original object (upper left).*

⓲ *The* **Modify toolbar (Win)** *contains icons that rotate and flip objects.*

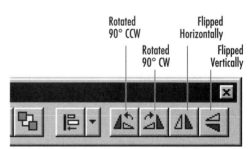

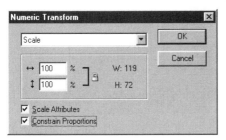

⓳ *The* **Numeric Transform** *dialog box set to the* **Scale** *controls.*

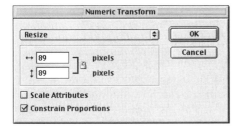

⓴ *The* **Resize controls** *of the Numeric Transform dialog box.*

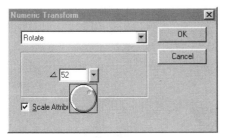

㉑ *The* **Rotate controls** *of the Numeric Transform dialog box.*

The Numeric Transform dialog box makes it easy to scale, resize, or rotate an object using precise values, rather than by judging by eye.

To use the Numeric Transform dialog box:

1. Select an object.

2. Choose a command from the **Modify >** **Transform >Numeric Transform**. The Numeric Transform dialog box appears.

3. Use the pop-up list to choose Scale, Resize, or Rotate.

4. In Scale mode, enter the percentage of change in the width or height fields **⓳**.

   or

   In Resize mode, enter the pixel amount in the width or height fields **⓴**.

   or

   In Rotate mode, use the wheel or enter the angle in the field **㉑**.

5. Click OK to apply the transformation.

TIP Both Scale and Resize change the size of the object. Scale does so using percentages; Resize by changing the pixel dimensions.

TIP In Scale or Resize modes, select Constrain Proportions to keep the horizontal and vertical dimensions in proportion to the original object.

TIP *See page the next page for a description of the Scale Attributes command.*

Transforming Objects

Controlling Transformations

When you choose any of the Transform tools, you can set two options to control how the transformation occurs.

Scale Attributes controls how the Scale tool affects the attributes such as the fill or stroke of an object.

To use the Scale Attributes option:

1. Double-click any of the Transformation tools in the Tools panel. The Options panel appears ㉒.

2. Choose Scale Attributes to extend any scaling to the size of the stroke, pattern fill, gradient fill, or effect applied to the object ㉓.

   or

   Deselect Scale Attributes to restrict the scaling only to the size of the object, not to any attributes applied to the object.

   TIP You can also set Scale Attributes in the Numeric Transform dialog box.

The *Auto-crop Images* option controls how the bounding box of a pixel-based image changes to fit a transformed image. *(For information on pixel-based images, see Chapter 13, "Working with Pixels.")*

To set the Auto-crop Images option:

1. Double-click any of the Transformation tools in the Tools panel. The Options panel appears.

2. Choose Auto-crop Images to automatically shrink the bounding box of an image to fit the new area of any transformed image ㉔.

   or

   Deselect Auto-crop Images to leave control of the size of the bounding box to Fireworks.

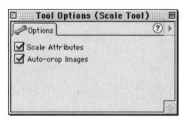

㉒ *The* **Tool Options** *for the Scale, Shear, and Distort tools.*

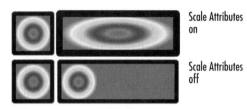

Scale Attributes on

Scale Attributes off

㉓ *The* **Scale Attributes** *options controls whether attributes such as this gradient fill scale when an object is resized.*

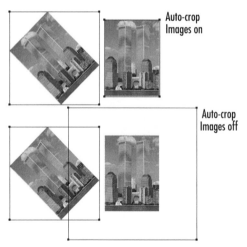

Auto-crop Images on

Auto-crop Images off

㉔ *The* **Auto-crop Images** *option controls if extra area is added to the bounding box around scanned images when the image is rotated.*

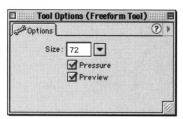

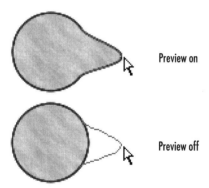

㉕ *The* **Freeform tool** *in the Tools panel.*

㉖ *The* **Freeform tool** *options.*

Preview on

Preview off

㉗ *The* **Freeform Preview** *displays the artwork as you change its shape. Turning off the Preview helps if you have a slower computer.*

Reshaping Objects

Once you have created an object, you may find it difficult to work with the control handles to reshape the path. Fireworks gives you several other ways to easily change the object's shape.

The Freeform tool allows you to change the shape of an object without worrying about adding or modifying points.

To set the Freeform tool options:

1. Double-click the Freeform tool in the Tools panel **㉕** to open the Freeform Options panel **㉖**.

2. Use the slider or enter a numeric value in the Size field to set the size of the tool. This controls how large an area (in pixels) is pushed by the tool.

3. If you have a pressure-sensitive pen and tablet, click Pressure to allow your pressure on the tablet to affect the size of the effect.

4. Choose Preview to see the artwork change as you use the Freeform tool **㉗**.

    or

    Deselect Preview to see only the outline of the path change **㉗**.

    TIP If you do not have a pressure-sensitive tablet, press the left arrow, left bracket ([), or 1 key as you drag to *decrease* the size of the Freeform tool effect.

    TIP If you do not have a pressure-sensitive tablet, press the right arrow, right bracket (]), or 2 key as you drag to *increase* the size of the Freeform tool effect.

Reshaping Objects

The Freeform tool has two modes: Push and Pull. In the Push mode the Freeform tool acts like a rolling pin to modify the shape of the path.

To use the Freeform tool in Push mode:

1. Set the Freeform tool options, as described on *the previous page.*

2. Move the cursor near, but not on, the edge of a selected object. The cursor displays the Push Freeform tool icon, an arrow with a circle next to it ❷❽.

3. Drag around the edge of the object. The shape of the object changes accordingly ❷❾.

TIP As you drag, the Push Freeform tool icon changes to a circle that indicates the size of the effect of the tool.

TIP The Push Freeform tool can work from either the inside or the outside of an object.

In Pull mode the Freeform tool acts like a magnet that pulls out new segments from the path.

To use the Freeform tool in the Pull mode:

1. Set the Freeform tool options, as described on *the previous page.*

2. Move the cursor to the edge of a selected object. The cursor displays the Pull Freeform tool arrow icon ❸⓿.

3. Drag in or out from the edge of the object. The shape of the object changes accordingly ❸❶.

❷❽ *The* **Push Freeform tool** *cursor.*

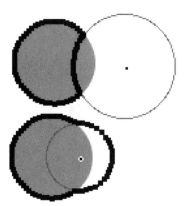

❷❾ *The* **Push Freeform tool** *allows you to push on the edges of an object to reshape it.*

❸⓿ *The* **Pull Freeform tool** *cursor.*

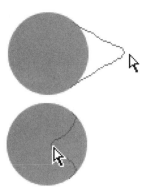

❸❶ *The* **Pull Freeform tool** *allows you to pull segments on an object.*

32 *The* **Reshape Area tool** *in the Tools panel.*

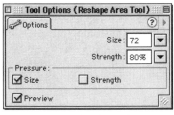

33 *The options for the* **Reshape Area tool.**

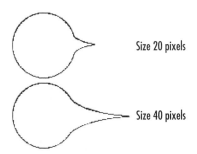

Size 20 pixels

Size 40 pixels

34 *The effect of changing the* size *of the* Reshape Area tool.

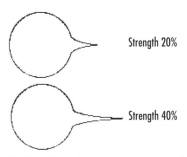

Strength 20%

Strength 40%

35 *The effect of changing the* strength *of the* Reshape Area tool.

The Reshape Area tool also lets you distort paths without manually adding or modifying anchor points or handles.

To set the Reshape Area tool options:

1. Choose the Reshape Area tool in the Tools panel **32**.

2. Double-click the Reshape Area tool in the Tools panel to open the Reshape Area Options panel **33**.

3. Use the slider or enter a numeric value in the Size field to set the size of the Reshape Area tool. The higher the number, the larger the area that the tool distorts **34**.

4. Use the slider or type in the Strength field to set how long the tool will work during a drag—the higher the setting, the longer the tool distorts the path **35**.

5. If you have a pressure-sensitive tablet, check the Size or Strength boxes to set how the pressure on the tablet affects the tool.

6. Choose Preview to see the artwork change as you use the Reshape Area tool.

    or

    Deselect Preview to see only the outline of the path change.

    TIP If you do not have a pressure-sensitive tablet, press the 1, left bracket ([), or left arrow key as you drag to *decrease* the size of the Reshape Area tool effect.

    TIP If you do not have a pressure-sensitive tablet, press the 2, right bracket (]), or right arrow key as you drag to *increase* the size of the Reshape Area tool effect.

Reshaping Objects

The Reshape Area tool modifies paths as if they were taffy. The size of the tool controls the amount that is pulled. The strength of the tool controls the length of the pull.

To use the Reshape Area tool:

1. Choose the Reshape Area tool.
2. Position the tool either inside or outside the path.
3. Drag to reshape the path **36**.

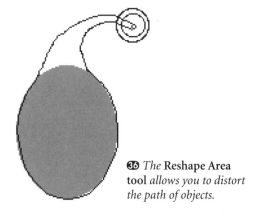

36 *The* **Reshape Area tool** *allows you to distort the path of objects.*

You can also reshape paths by cutting them with the Knife tool.

To use the Knife tool:

1. Choose the Knife tool in the Tools panel **37**.
2. Drag the Knife tool across a path. This cuts the path **38**.

TIP Segments created by the Knife tool can be moved away from the other objects with any of the selection tools.

TIP The Knife tool changes to an Eraser tool and erases pixels in the Bitmap mode *(see page 217).*

TIP The Knife tool cursor resembles an X-acto knife when used to cut paths. It resembles a rubber eraser when erasing pixels.

37 *The* **Knife tool** *in the Tools panel.*

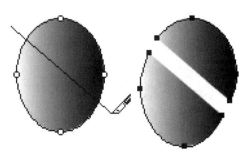

38 *Cutting an object with the Knife tool. (The objects were separated after cutting to show the effect of the Knife tool.)*

Original objects   Objects after Union command

❸❾ The Union command *forms one object from two or more overlapping objects.*

Original objects   Objects after Intersect command

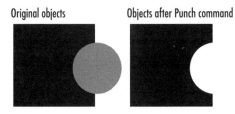

❹⓿ The Intersect command *creates an object just where two or more objects overlap.*

Original objects   Objects after Punch command

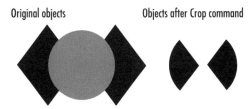

❹❶ The Punch command *uses one object to punch a hole in the objects below it.*

Original objects   Objects after Crop command

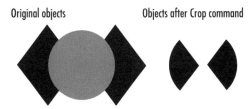

❹❷ The Crop command *trims away all the area outside the top object.*

Combining Vector Objects

One of the secrets to working with vector objects is to combine simple paths into more complex shapes. Some programs call these Path operations. In Fireworks they are the Combine commands. Each of the Combine commands creates a new object from two or more overlapping objects.

To unite objects:

1. Select two or more overlapping objects.

2. Choose **Modify** > **Combine** > **Union**. The path of the new object follows the path of the overlapping objects **❸❾**.

To form the intersection of objects:

1. Select two or more overlapping objects.

2. Choose **Modify** > **Combine** > **Intersect**. The path of the new object follows the shape where the paths overlap **❹⓿**.

To create a hole:

1. Select two or more overlapping objects.

2. Choose **Modify** > **Combine** > **Punch**. The top object punches holes in all the objects below it **❹❶**.

To crop objects:

1. Select three or more overlapping objects.

2. Choose **Modify** > **Combine** > **Crop**. This trims away parts of the paths that were outside the original top object **❹❷**.

   TIP The object created by the Combine commands take its appearance from the bottommost object.

Combining Vector Objects

Using the Alter Path Commands

You can also change the shape of paths using the Alter Path commands. The Simplify command lets you reduce the number of points on a path. Fewer points makes it easier to reshape objects.

TIP Artwork from clipart collections or converted from bitmap images often contains too many anchor points.

To simplify the shape of a path:

1. Select a path.

2. Choose **Modify** > **Alter Path** > **Simplify**. The Simplify dialog box appears **43**.

3. Enter an amount of simplification in the dialog box and click OK. Fireworks removes as many points as possible to simplify the path **44**.

TIP The higher the number, the greater the distortion that may occur.

You can also expand the stroke of an open path into a closed path. This lets you apply a fill such as pattern or a gradient *(see Chapter 7, "Fills")*.

To expand a path:

1. Select a path.

2. Choose **Modify** > **Alter Path** > **Expand Stroke**. The Expand Stroke dialog box appears **45**.

3. Enter the desired width or thickness of the path (in pixels).

4. Set shape of the corners.

5. Enter an amount for the Miter Limit to control the length of the points of any corners.

6. Set the shape of the ends of the path.

7. Click OK. The path is converted into a filled shape **46**.

TIP Use the Expand Stroke command on a closed path to quickly punch a hole the object.

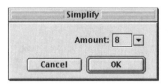

43 *The* **Simplify** *dialog box.*

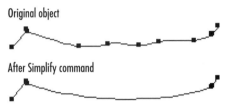

44 *The* **Simplify command** *reduces the number of points on a path.*

45 *The* **Expand Stroke** *dialog box.*

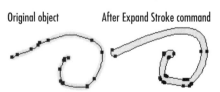

46 *The* **Expand Stroke command** *converts an open path into a filled shape.*

47 *The* **Inset Path** *dialog box.*

Outside inset

Original

Inside inset

48 *The* **Inset Path command** *changes the shape of the object so that it lies inside or outside the original.*

Fireworks also lets you increase or decrease the size of a path using the Inset Path command.

To inset a path:

1. Select a path you want to inset.
2. Choose **Modify >Alter Path >Inset Path**. The Inset Path dialog box appears **47**.
3. Choose the direction of the inset. Inside moves the contours of the path inside the original. Outside moves the contours of the path outside the original **48**.
4. Enter the width or amount that the path should be changed.
5. Set the shape of the corners.
6. Enter an amount for the Miter Limit to control the spikes of any corners.
7. Click OK. The path is converted into a filled shape.

TIP Use the Clone command before applying the Inset Path. This keeps the original image and moves the object created by the Inset Path command inside or outside the original.

TIP While it might seem like Inset Path is the same as the Scale command *(see pages 88 or 93)*, it actually allows you to create a smaller or larger path that follows the contours of the original. For example, the Scale command could not have created a path that fit inside the original object shown in **48**.

Using the Alter Path Commands

Aligning Objects

You can use the Align menu commands to align the objects or distribute them along the horizontal or vertical axis **❹❾**–**❺❷**.

To use the Align menu commands:

1. Select two or more objects to align.

   or

   Select three or more objects to distribute.

2. Align or distribute the objects by choosing a command from the **Modify** > **Align** menu—for example, **Modify** > **Align** > **Left**.

TIP Fireworks uses the left-most object as the point to align to on the left. It uses the right-most object to align to the right.

TIP Fireworks uses the topmost object to align to the top. It uses the bottommost object to align to the bottom.

The Modify toolbar (Win) gives you buttons to apply many object commands. All the Align commands are available in a pop-up list on the Modify toolbar.

To use the Align pop-up list (Win):

1. Select two or more objects to align.

   or

   Select three or more objects to distribute.

2. Press the Align button on the Modify toolbar **❺❸** *(on the following page)* and choose an alignment or distribute command.

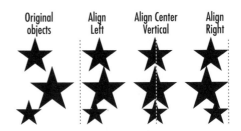

❹❾ *The results of using the **Align** commands for the vertical axis.*

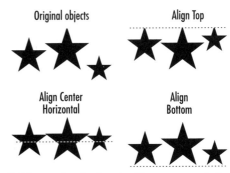

❺❿ *The results of using the **Align** commands for the horizontal axis.*

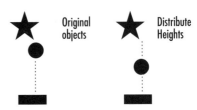

❺❶ *The effect of applying the **Distribute Heights** command.*

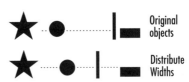

❺❷ *The effect of applying the **Distribute Widths** command.*

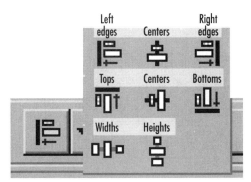

⑤ *The* **Align pop-up list** *on the Modify toolbar (Win).*

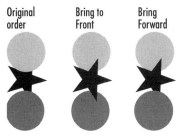

㉨ *The results of applying the* **Arrange menu** *commands to the star.*

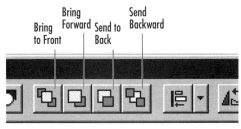

⑤ *The* **Arrange commands** *on the Modify toolbar (Win).*

Arranging Objects

The order in which overlapping objects appear depends on the order in which they were created. Objects created first are at the back of their layer. Objects created later are in front. You can change the order of objects using the Arrange menu commands **㉨**.

To send objects to the front or back of a layer:

1. Select the object.

2. Choose **Modify > Arrange > Bring to Front** to move the object in front of all the other objects on that layer.

   or

   Choose **Modify > Arrange > Send to Back** to move the object behind all the other objects on that layer.

TIP (Win) You can also use the Front/Back icons on the Modify toolbar **⑤** to easily move objects within a layer.

Objects can also be moved forward or backward one place at a time in their layer.

To move objects forward or backward in a layer:

1. Select the object.

2. Choose **Modify > Arrange > Bring Forward** to move the object in front of the next object in the layer.

   or

   Choose **Modify > Arrange > Send Backward** to move the object behind the next object in the layer.

3. Repeat as necessary to put the object where you want it.

TIP (Win) You can also use the Forward/Backward icons on the Modify toolbar to easily move objects in front or behind each other.

Arranging Objects

Working with Layers

As you add more objects to your documents, you may want to take advantage of the Fireworks Layers panel. This panel lets you show and hide objects on each of the layers, lock the layers from changes, and change the order in which objects appear.

To work with the Layers panel:

1. Open the Layers panel by choosing **Window**>**Layers** ⑤⑥. The two default layers, Layer 1 and Web Layer, appear in the panel.

   TIP The Web Layer holds objects used to add Web addresses to images and to slice them for exporting. *(For more information on working with Web addresses and HTML information in Fireworks, see Chapter 17, "Hotspots and Links" and Chapter 18, "Slices.")*

2. To make all the objects on a layer invisible, click the Show/Hide icon for that layer.

   TIP To make all the layers invisible, hold the Opt/Alt key as you click the Show/Hide icon for any layer.

3. To prevent any objects on a layer from being selected, click the space in the lock area. A Padlock icon appears indicating the layer is locked.

   TIP Click the layer's padlock icon to unlock the layer.

4. Click the name of a layer to make that layer the active layer. New objects are automatically created on that layer.

5. Drag the name of a layer up or down to a new position in the panel to move that layer to a new position ⑤⑦.

Show/hide icon
Active layer   New Layer

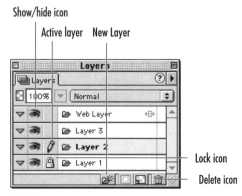

Lock icon
Delete icon

⑤⑥ *The* Layers *panel.*

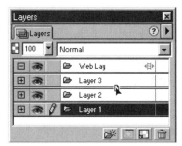

⑤⑦ **Drag a layer** *from one position to another to change the order of the layers.*

Working with Layers

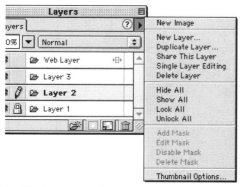

⑱ *The* **Layers** *panel menu.*

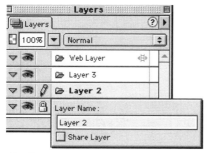

⑲ *The* **Layers Options** *field lets you change the name of a layer.*

The Layers panel menu controls additional features of the Layers panel.

To use the Layers panel menu:

1. Press the triangle at the top of the Layers panel to view the panel menu **⑱**.

2. Choose New Layer or click the New Layer icon to add a new layer.

3. Choose Duplicate Layer to duplicate the layer currently selected along with its contents.

4. Choose Share This Layer to display the objects on a layer on all the frames of a document. *(For more information on working with frames, see Chapter 16, "Animations.")*

5. Choose Delete Layer or click the icon to delete a layer.

6. Choose Hide All or Show All to change the display status of all the layers in the document.

7. Choose Lock All or Unlock All to change the protection applied to all the layers in the document.

To change the name of a layer:

1. Double-click the name of the layer. This opens the Layers Options **⑲**.

2. Type the new name for the layer.

3. Click OK to apply the name change.

The Single Layer Editing mode makes it easy to work only with the objects on one layer.

To use Single Layer Editing:

◆ Choose Single Layer Editing from the Layers panel menu. The currently selected layer becomes the only layer you can work on. Objects on other layers cannot be selected.

You can use the Layers panel to move objects from one layer to another.

To move an object between layers:

1. Select the object. A small square appears next to the name of the layer that the object is on.

2. Drag the small square to the layer where you want to place the object ⑥⓪.

3. Release the mouse. The object appears on the new layer.

TIP Hold the Opt/Alt key as you drag the square to copy the object from one layer to another.

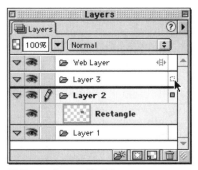

⑥⓪ **Drag the small object square** *to move an object from one layer to another.*

The Layers panel can also display the individual objects on each layer.

To change the display of objects on layers:

1. Click the plus sign (Win) or right-pointing triangle (Mac) to see the a thumbnail displays of any objects on the layer ⑥①.

2. Click the minus sign (Win) or the down-pointing triangle (Mac) to close the thumbnail display of any objects on the layer.

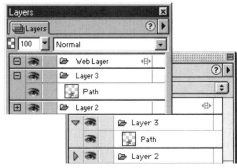

⑥① *Click the* **plus sign** (**Win**) *or the* **triangle** (**Mac**) *to display the objects on a layer.*

You can also change the size of the thumbnail displayed in the Layers panel.

To change the thumbnail options:

1. Choose Thumbnail Options from the Layers panel menu. The Thumbnail Options dialog box appears ⑥②.

2. Choose None to display the objects with no thumbnail.

3. Click each of the thumbnail sizes to change the display in the Layers panel.

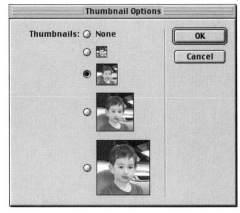

⑥② *The Thumbnail Options dialog box lets you change the size of the thumbnail displayed in the Layers panel.*

FILLS 7

I was amazed to find recently that the Colorforms I played with as a child are still popular—even in this age of computer and video games. In fact, a box of Colorforms is great preparation for any budding artist. I found them at www.areyougame.com.

Great as the objects in Colorforms are, though, you can't change their colors with just a click of a mouse.

Fireworks objects can be filled with colors, textures, patterns, gradients, and even other Fireworks objects. Even better, once an object has one type of fill, you can still go back later and change it. Also, Fireworks objects don't have to be hard-edged objects. They can have a slight softening or fade applied to their edges.

Creating Basic Fills

Fills are the colors, patterns, and gradients that are applied inside paths.

To apply a solid color fill:

1. Choose **Window**>Fill to open the Fill panel.

2. Choose Solid from the Fill category pop-up list. This displays the options for solid fills ❶.

3. Click the Fill Color Well to open the Swatches to pick a color.

   or

   Use the Color Mixer to select a color. *(For more information on working with the Color Mixer, see Chapter 3, "Colors.")*

You can also set an object to have no fill. This makes the inside of the object completely transparent ❷.

To set a Fill to None:

◆ Choose None from the Fill category pop-up list.

   or

   Click the None button in the Tools panel ❸.

   or

   Click the None button in the Color Well Swatches ❹.

TIP Click the edge to select an object with a None fill, or use a selection marquee.

Fill list   Texture list

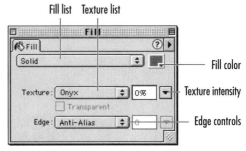

Fill color
Texture intensity
Edge controls

❶ *The* Fill panel.

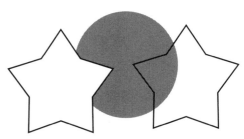

❷ *The difference between a white fill and a fill of* None *becomes obvious when the objects appear over another image.*

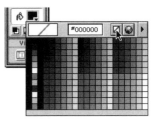

❸ *Click the* None button *in the Tools panel.*

❹ *The* None button *in the Color Well Swatches.*

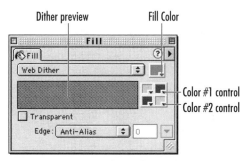

Dither preview   Fill Color

Color #1 control
Color #2 control

❺ *The* **Web Dither Fill** *controls.*

The Benefits of a Web Dither Fill

One of the benefits of the Web Dither fill is that you can limit the number of colors in your document, which keeps the file size down, but still have areas that simulate the look of other colors.

For instance, if you use only four colors—black, white, red, and blue—the Web Dither fill lets you combine them into others. For instance, black and white create gray; white and red create pink; black and red create dark red; black and blue create dark blue; and red and blue create purple.

So, although the final GIF image uses only four colors, your viewers see nine.

Creating a Web Dither Fill

In addition to a solid color fill, Fireworks offers a Web Dither Fill. This allows you to choose two colors that are combined together in a pattern (also called a *dither*) to simulate a third color. This gives you more control over the number of colors in your document. *(For a color print-out of a Web Dither Fill, see the color pages.)*

To apply the Web Dither Fill setting:

1. Choose Web Dither from the Fill category pop-up list. This displays the options for Web Dither fills ❺.

2. Use the Color #1 control to set the first of the two dithered colors.

3. Use the Color #2 control to set the second of the two dithered colors. The Dither preview shows how the combination of the two colors will look.

4. Select Transparent to set one of the colors as transparent. This lets any objects behind the color show through the fill.

TIP Use the Fill Color control to convert the dithered color into a solid color.

Creating a Web Dither Fill

Creating Gradient Fills

In addition to solid colors, Fireworks lets you fill objects with gradients, which gradually blend one color into another.

To apply a gradient fill:

1. Select an object.

2. Choose one of the types of gradient fills from the Fill category pop-up list **⑥**.

   TIP Each type of gradient changes how the colors of the gradients are manipulated. For instance, Linear creates a gradient that changes the colors along a line.

3. If necessary, change the colors by choosing a new set from the Gradient Colors list **⑦**.

To edit the colors in a gradient fill:

1. Click the Edit button next to the Gradient Colors list **⑧**. This opens the editing area for the gradients.

   TIP You can also choose Edit Gradient from the Gradient panel menu.

2. To change the position of a color, drag the Gradient Color control along the top ramp **⑨**. The bottom ramp displays a preview of the final gradient.

3. To delete a Gradient Color control, drag it off the Fill palette.

4. Choose a new set of colors from the Gradient preset colors list.

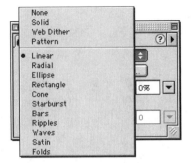

⑥ *The* **gradient category** *list.*

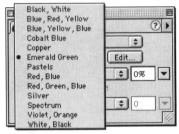

⑦ *The* **gradient preset colors** *list.*

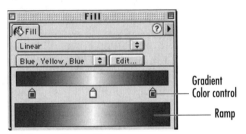

Gradient Color control

Ramp

⑧ *The* **gradient editing area.**

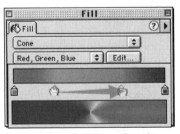

⑨ **Drag the color control** *to change the position of the color in the gradient.*

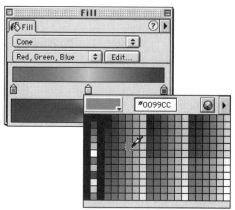

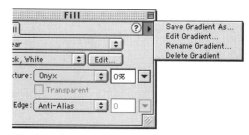

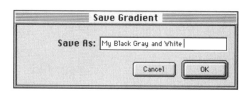

To change the colors in a gradient fill:

1. Double-click a Gradient Color control. This opens the Swatches **⑩**.

2. Click to choose one of the color swatches.

   or

   Move the cursor outside the panel and click anywhere on the screen to sample a color.

6. Click OK to apply the changes to the gradient.

To add colors to a gradient:

1. Move the cursor to an empty area under the top color ramp. A plus sign appears next to the cursor **⑪**.

2. Click. A new Gradient Color control appears.

3. Double-click the Gradient Color control to change its color as described above.

You can also save a gradient so that it appears in the Gradient preset list.

To save a gradient:

1. Choose Save Gradient As from the Fill panel Options menu **⑫**. This opens the Save Gradient dialog box **⑬**.

2. Give the gradient a name and click OK.

TIP If you give the gradient a new name, you add a new preset to the list.

TIP Gradient colors are saved in the document where they were created. To have a gradient available for all documents, use a style. *(For more information on working with styles, see Chapter 12, "Automation Features.")*

⑩ *The* **Swatches panel** *lets you choose a color for a Gradient Color control.*

⑪ *Click to* **add a Gradient Color control** *to the gradient.*

⑫ *The* **Fill panel menu** *lets you save, edit, rename, or delete gradients.*

⑬ *The* **Save Gradient** *dialog box.*

Creating Gradient Fills

You can also delete or rename gradients from the Fill panel menu.

To delete a gradient fill:

1. Select the gradient preset you want to delete.

2. Choose Delete Gradient from the Fill panel Options menu. A dialog box appears asking you to confirm the deletion of the gradient.

3. Click OK to delete the gradient from the list.

To rename a gradient fill:

1. Select the Gradient preset you want to rename.

2. Choose Rename Gradient from the Fill panel menu. This opens the Rename Gradient dialog box .

3. Type a new name for the gradient.

4. Click OK. The new name appears in the gradient preset list for that document.

TIP You can't change the names of the presets that ship with Fireworks. To rename those gradients you need to use the Save Gradient As command described on page 111.

⓮ *Use the* **Rename Gradient** *dialog box to change the name of your own custom gradients.*

Gradients Use Tons of Colors

Watch out when you apply gradients to your Fireworks documents. Even though you use only two or three colors in the Gradient Color controls, the gradient itself requires many colors to display properly.

A gradient that blends black into white may require as many as 256 colors to look smooth. Add another Gradient Color control and you may find it difficult to optimize the file using the 256 colors in a GIF images.

Creating Gradient Fills

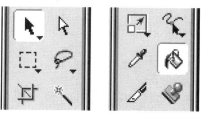

⓯ *Select the* **Pointer tool or the Paint Bucket** *to work with the Gradient Vector controls.*

⓰ *The* **Gradient Vector controls.**

⓱ *The* **Circle Vector control** *defines the start point of a gradient.*

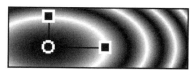

⓲ *A* **Square Vector control** *defines the end point of the gradient. A short gradient repeats to fill the object.*

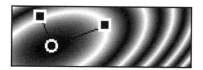

⓳ *The* **angle of the Vector controls** *defines the rotation of the gradient.*

In addition to controlling the colors in a gradient, you can also change the appearance of a gradient by changing its direction, length, and center.

To change the appearance of a gradient:

1. Select an object filled with a gradient.

2. Click the Pointer tool or the Paint Bucket tool in the Tools panel **⓯**. The Vector controls appear in the object **⓰**.

TIP If you don't see the Gradient Vector controls when you choose the Pointer tool, check Show Fill Handles in the Pointer tool Options panel.

3. Move the circle control to change the start point of the gradient **⓱**.

4. Drag the square control to change the end point of the gradient **⓲**.

TIP Some gradients provide two control handles to control two separate axes of the gradient.

5. Drag the line of the control to change the rotation of the gradient **⓳**.

TIP Double-click with the Paint Bucket tool to reset the Vector controls to the default setting.

Creating Gradient Fills

Working with Patterns

Another way to fill objects is to apply a pattern. Fireworks ships with a preset number of patterns which you can modify and augment.

To apply a pattern fill:

1. Choose Pattern from the Fill category pop-up list. The pattern list appears.

2. Choose one of the preset pattern fills from the pattern list **20**.

TIP A small preview appears next to each name as you move through the list.

TIP The Vector controls can also be used to modify the appearance of patterns as well as gradients *(see previous page)*.

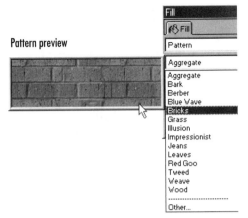

Pattern preview

20 *The* **Patterns** *pop-up list.*

In addition to the patterns that ship with Fireworks, you can add artwork to use as patterns. There are three ways to add patterns: individually, to the pattern folder, or by creating a second pattern folder.

To add individual patterns:

1. Choose Other from the pattern list.

2. Navigate and select the file you want to use as a pattern.

3. The name of the file appears at the end of the pattern list and can be applied to any object **21**.

TIP Individual patterns are contained in that document only.

TIP You can transfer an individual pattern from one document to another by copying an object containing the pattern to another file.

TIP Use the same technique to add individual textures to files. *(See page 116 for information about working with textures.)*

21 *An* **individual pattern** *inside an object.*

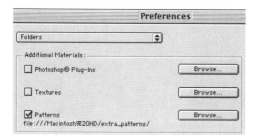

㉒ *Use the* **Folders Preferences** *to specify a second folder to hold patterns.*

Adding Patterns and Textures

Fireworks supports any file format that it exports as a file format for patterns and textures. So, if you use Fireworks to create your patterns or textures, you can save the file as a PNG or any of the other bitmap formats Fireworks uses for exporting.

If you use another program, such as Adobe Photoshop, you can save the file as a PNG, TIFF, or other bitmapped formats.

Fireworks ships with default patterns that appear in the Fill panel. You can add to the patterns that ship with Fireworks or create your own pattern folder.

To add to the pattern folder:

1. Scan or create artwork that can be tiled as a pattern.

2. Give the file a name and save it as any file format Fireworks can read. *(See the "Adding Patterns and Textures" sidebar on this page for a list of those file formats.)*

3. Put the file in the Patterns folder (Fireworks: Configurations: Patterns). The name of the file appears as the name of the pattern in the pop-up list.

TIP Use the same technique to add files to the Textures folder (Fireworks: Configurations: Textures). *(See the next page for information on working with textures.)*

To add a second pattern folder:

1. Place the files that you want to be patterns in a folder (directory).

2. Choose **File > Preferences**.

3. Choose Folders from the pop-up menu **㉒**.

4. Choose Patterns and then use the Browse button to navigate to the folder that holds the files.

TIP The patterns will not be available until the next time you launch Fireworks.

TIP Use the same technique with the Textures control to add a second folder for textures. *(See the next page for information on working with textures.)*

Working with Patterns

Using Textures

Textures change the intensity of fills. You can apply textures to any of the fills—solids, patterns, or gradients. Once a texture is applied to a fill, you can then change the intensity of the texture.

To apply a texture to a fill:

1. Choose one of the textures from the Texture pop-up list 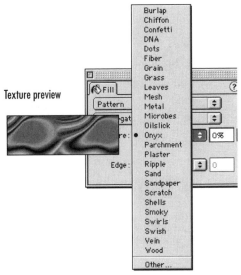.

TIP There is always a texture applied to every fill. However, with an intensity of 0% the effect of the texture is not visible.

2. Use the slider or enter a number in the Intensity field to see the effects of the texture on the fill **24**.

3. Check Transparent to allow background objects to appear in the light-colored areas of the texture **25**.

23 *The* **Texture** *pop-up list.*

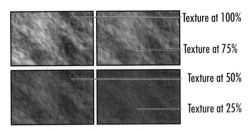

24 *Different settings of the Parchment texture on a solid fill.*

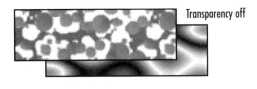

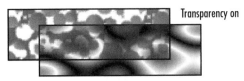

25 *The effect of the* **Transparent** *settings for a texture.*

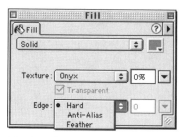

㉖ *The* **Fill Edge** *list controls the appearance of the edges of filled objects.*

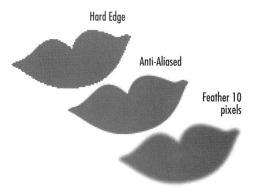

Hard Edge

Anti-Aliased

Feather 10 pixels

㉗ *The three different* **edge** *choices.*

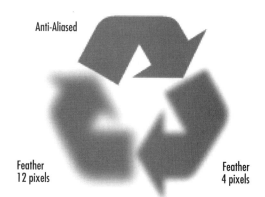

Anti-Aliased

Feather 12 pixels

Feather 4 pixels

㉘ *Feathering allows you to create softer, more blurred edges than anti-aliasing.*

Modifying Fill Edges

Once you have filled an object, you can control how the edges of the object display that fill.

To change the edges of a fill:

1. Select and fill an object.

2. Use the Fill Edge list **㉖** to change the edge treatment of the fill **㉗**.

   - **Hard** leaves the edge of the object as single-colored pixels.
   - **Anti-Alias** softens the edge of the object by changing the color of the pixels so they blend into the background or other objects.
   - **Feather** blurs the edge of the object. Use the slider to set the amount. The higher the feather, the greater the amount of blurring **㉘**.

   TIP The feather amount is in pixels and is applied equally to both sides of the edge of the path.

Anti-Aliasing Adds Colors

Anti-aliasing smooths out the harsh edges of objects. Remember, though, that when you apply anti-aliasing you also add colors to the object.

Those extra colors can add to the size of your file. You can reduce the number of colors by selectively changing the anti-alias setting to a hard edge when objects have similar colors.

For instance, a yellow object with a hard edge is very noticeable over a blue background—and needs anti-aliasing to avoid looking jagged. But a light yellow object over a gold background may not need anti-aliasing.

STROKES $\boxed{8}$

In addition to fills, Macromedia Fireworks also lets you change the appearance of objects by applying a stroke to the edge of the path. In an ordinary vector program, strokes are limited to just colors or dashes. In Fireworks, however, strokes are much more versatile.

Fireworks lets you set strokes to resemble all sorts of natural media such as paint brushes, crayons, chalk, pencils, oils—even toothpaste and confetti! You can also apply textures to strokes for even more varied appearances.

Finally, you can set strokes in Fireworks so that they work with pressure-sensitive tablets. You can also simulate the look of a tablet, even if you work with a mouse.

Setting Stroke Attributes

A stroke in Fireworks can be a simple colored line resembling a pencil stroke, or it can be a multicolored paint splatter. You control the look of strokes with the Stroke panel. The best way to understand strokes is to start with a basic stroke and then work your way up to the more sophisticated effects.

To view the Stroke panel:

◆ Choose **Window**>**Stroke** to open the Stroke panel ❶.

To apply a basic stroke:

1. Select the Brush tool in the Tools panel ❷.

   TIP Although strokes can be applied to closed paths, such as rectangles, it is easier to understand strokes by creating open paths with the Pen, Pencil, or Brush tools.

2. Choose **Window**>**Stroke** to open the Stroke panel and select Basic from the stroke category pop-up list.

3. Drag the Brush tool in the document area. A brush stroke appears along the path you just created.

4. Use the Stroke Color Well to choose a Stroke color.

   TIP You can also use the Color Well in the Color Mixer or the Tools panel to set the stroke color. *(For more information on working with the Color Mixer, see Chapter 3, "Colors.")*

   TIP When you create a path with the Brush or Pencil tools, the fill automatically changes to None. This gives the look of a simple brush stroke, rather than a vector object.

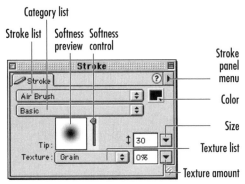

Category list
Stroke list   Softness   Softness
              preview   control
Stroke panel menu
Color
Size
Texture list
Texture amount

❶ *The* Stroke *panel.*

❷ *The* Brush tool *in the Tools panel.*

Difference Between Paths and Strokes

Paths are the objects that you create in Fireworks. A stroke is an effect applied to the edge of paths. You might have a path that doesn't contain a stroke but you'll never have a stroke that isn't applied to a path.

Setting Stroke Attributes

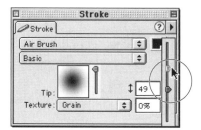

❸ *The* Stroke size *slider.*

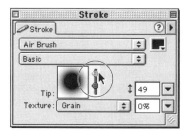

❹ *The* Stroke softness *slider.*

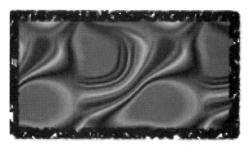

❺ *Two different textures applied to the stroke and fill of an object.*

The easiest way to understand the nature of strokes is by experimenting with the attributes of a selected path.

To change the stroke attributes:

1. Start with the basic stroke created in the previous exercise.

2. In the Stroke panel, drag the size slider or enter an amount in the field to change the size of the stroke **❸**.

3. Drag the softness slider to blur the edge of the stroke **❹**.

TIP You may need to increase the size of the stroke to see the difference in the edge softness.

4. Choose one of the preset strokes from the stroke name pop-up list to change the shape of the stroke.

TIP Each of the 11 stroke categories has its own preset strokes making a total of 48 different strokes to choose from.

You can apply a texture to a stroke, just as you can with fills.

To apply a texture to a stroke:

1. Select a Stroke.

2. Open the Stroke panel and choose one of the textures from the Texture list.

TIP The list of textures for strokes is the same as the list of textures used for fills. However, a stroke can have a different texture than the fill for the object **❺**.

3. Use the slider or enter a number in the Intensity field to see the effects of the texture on the fill.

TIP As with patterns, you can create your own textures to use within Fireworks *(see page 115).*

Saving Stroke Settings

Any changes you make to the Stroke panel, such as the size, edge softness, or texture, are modifications of the original stroke preset. You can save those changes as your own stroke preset.

To save Stroke panel settings:

1. Make whatever changes you want to the Stroke panel settings.

2. Choose Save Stroke As from the Stroke panel menu ❻. The Save Stroke dialog box appears.

3. Type the name of the new stroke and click OK. The new stroke appears as one of the stroke presets.

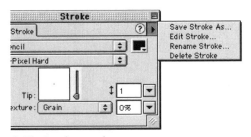

❻ *The* Stroke panel *menu.*

❼ *The* Pencil tool *in the Tools panel.*

Using the Pencil

Like the Brush tool, the Pencil tool creates paths. However, the default setting for the size and shape of the Pencil tool creates thin lines that resemble a pencil.

To use the Pencil tool:

1. Click the Pencil tool in the Tools panel ❼.

2. Drag a path on the page. The Stroke panel settings automatically change to the Pencil tool settings.

3. Choose one of the preset settings for the Pencil tool ❽.

4. Drag to create a Pencil path. The path that is created is stroked with the Pencil stroke settings.

TIP When you select the Brush or the Pencil tools, any fill that was set in the Fill panel resets automatically to None.

TIP Paths created by the Pencil tool can be changed by applying any of the stroke categories.

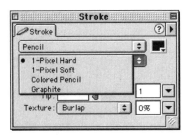

❽ *The* Pencil tool *presets.*

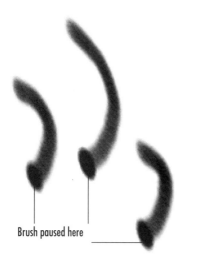

Brush paused here

❾ *The effect of pausing while creating three brush strokes.*

Creating Pressure Effects

Pressure means more than just meeting tight deadlines. It can be a good thing, too. If you work with a pressure-sensitive tablet, you can see how Fireworks strokes respond to changes in how you press with the stylus. Even if you draw with a mouse, you can still make a more natural stroke based on how you drag with the mouse.

To create a natural brush stroke:

1. Select the Brush tool.

2. Choose a brush such as Airbrush set to Basic or Calligraphy set to Quill.

TIP These strokes respond very well to variations in mouse movements.

3. Drag along a path pausing without releasing the mouse button. The width of the stroke increases where you pause in the drag ❾.

Creating Pressure Effects

Even after you've applied a stroke to a path, you can still alter it by by using the Path Scrubber tool. This tool allows you to increase or decrease the effect of pressure on a path. The Path Scrubber has two modes: Path Scrubber Plus and Path Scrubber Minus.

TIP If you have a pressure-sensitive tablet, you can use the Path Scrubber to further refine the look of the path. If you do not have a pressure-sensitive pen and tablet, you can use the Path Scrubber to simulate those effects.

To use the Path Scrubber tool:

1. Select a path with a stroke.

2. Choose the Path Scrubber Plus tool in the Tools panel ❿. (If you do not see the Path Scrubber Plus tool, press the pop-up group to select the tool.)

3. Drag along the path. The width of the stroke increases as you drag ⓫.

4. Choose the Path Scrubber Minus tool in the Tools panel ⓬.

5. Drag across to intersect the path. The width of the stroke decreases as you drag ⓭.

TIP Hold the Opt/Alt key to switch between the Path Scrubber Plus and Minus modes.

❿ *The* **Path Scrubber Plus tool** *in the Tools panel.*

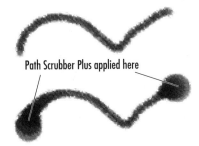

Path Scrubber Plus applied here

⓫ *The effect of the Path Scrubber Plus tool on a brush stroke.*

⓬ *The* **Path Scrubber Minus tool** *in the Tools panel.*

Path Scrubber Minus applied here

⓭ *The effect of the Path Scrubber Minus tool.*

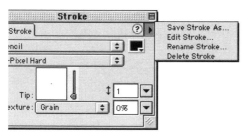

⓮ *Choose* **Edit Stroke** *from the Stroke panel Options menu to change the settings for a stroke.*

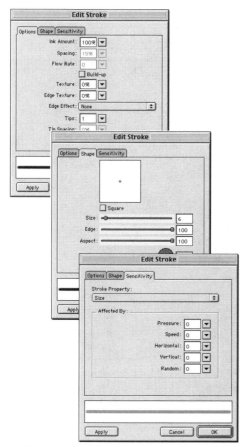

⓯ *The three panel settings for the* **Edit Stroke** *dialog box.*

Editing Strokes

In addition to the settings in the Stroke panel, other controls can affect the appearance of strokes. You do not have to open these settings to use Fireworks. However, as you become more comfortable with the program, you may want to experiment with these controls. For instance, these controls let you create strokes that are dashed or dotted lines.

TIP Draw a sample path and keep it selected to see how the settings affect the path.

To create your own strokes:

1. Choose Edit Stroke from the Stroke panel menu **⓮**. The Edit Stroke dialog box appears.

2. Click the tab for Options to control the appearance of the stroke **⓯**. *(See the exercise on the following page for details on working with the Edit Stroke Options controls.)*

3. Click the tab for Shape to control the size, edge softness, shape, roundness, and angle of the stroke **⓯**. *(See the exercise on page 127 for details on working with the Edit Stroke Shape controls.)*

TIP You can override the settings for size by changing the size and edge in the main Stroke panel.

4. Click the tab for Sensitivity to control how the stroke reacts to changes in the mouse or stylus movements **⓯**. *(See the exercise on page 128 for details on working with the Edit Stroke Sensitivity controls.)*

5. Click Apply to see how the settings appear on the selected path.

6. Click OK to apply the settings to the stroke and close the Edit Stroke dialog box.

Editing Strokes

To use the Edit Stroke Options settings:

1. Click the tab for Options to control the appearance of the stroke ⑯.

2. Set each of the Options controls as follows:

   • **Ink Amount** changes the opacity of the stroke color.
   • **Spacing** breaks the solid lines into dots and dashes.
   • **Flow Rate** adds to the size of the stroke if the cursor remains pressed over time. This is similar to the setting of an airbrush.
   • **Build-up** allows separate stroke tips interact with each other.
   • **Texture** makes the stroke more responsive to the texture set in the Stroke panel.
   • **Edge Effect** applies one of the special edge effects to the stroke ⑰.
   • **Edge Texture** makes the Edge Effect more apparent.
   • **Tips** lets you apply more than one stroke to each path.
   • **Tip Spacing** increases the distance between multiple tips.
   • **Variation** controls the colors of multiple tips ⑱.

   TIP The area at the bottom of the Edit Stroke dialog box shows a preview of the stroke as you change each of the settings.

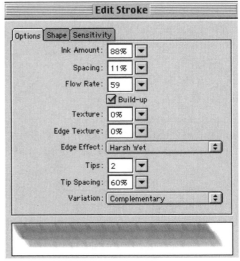

⑯ *The **Options panel** of the Edit Stroke dialog box.*

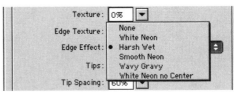

⑰ *The **Edge Effect list** lets you apply special effects to the edges of a stroke.*

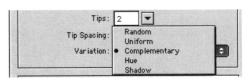

⑱ *The **Variation list** controls how multiple tips are colored.*

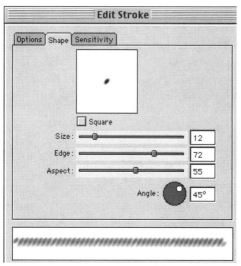

⓮ *The* **Shape panel** *of the Edit Stroke dialog box.*

To use the Edit Stroke Shape settings:

1. Click the tab for Shape to control the shape of the stroke **⓮**.

2. Set each of the Options controls as follows:

   - **Square** changes the stroke tip from an ellipse to a rectangle.
   - **Size** increases or decreases the size of the stroke.
   - **Edge** softens the edges of the stroke.
   - **Aspect** changes the appearance of the ellipse or rectangle used to create the stroke. The lower the Aspect the flatter the ellipse or rectangle appears.

   TIP Changing the Aspect creates strokes that resemble calligraphy pens.

   - **Angle** changes the orientation of the stroke tips.

Understanding the Edit Stroke panels

The three panels in the Edit Stroke dialog box can be confusing. My favorite way to understand what the panels do is to pick one of the preset strokes that ship with Fireworks and then analyze the settings in the Edit Stroke dialog box.

For instance, the 3D stroke under the Unnatural category is created by creating three tips set for a Shadow.

The Ribbon stroke under Calligraphy is created by setting the Aspect amount.

Don't be afraid to change the settings in the Edit Stroke dialog box. The three panels let you create an infinite variety of strokes.

Editing Strokes

To use the Edit Stroke Sensitivity settings:

1. Click the tab for Sensitivity to control how the mouse or pressure-sensitive tablet stylus affects the stroke ⓴.

2. Choose one of the attributes from the Stroke Property list ㉑:

3. Use the Affected By settings to control what type of action will vary the selected property:

   • **Pressure** makes the stroke responsive to a pressure-sensitive tablet.
   • **Speed** varies the attribute based on how fast or slow the mouse or tablet stylus is moved.
   • **Horizontal** changes the stroke along a horizontal axis.
   • **Vertical** changes the stroke along a vertical axis.
   • **Random** changes the stroke according to the whim of the computer gods.

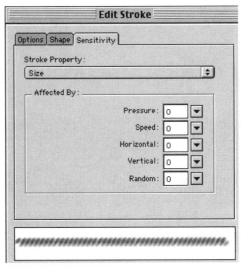

⓴ *The* **Sensitivity panel** *of the Edit Stroke dialog box.*

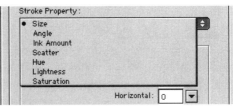

㉑ *Choose from the* **Stroke Property** *list of the Sensitivity panel to change the attributes of the stroke.*

Centered
Inside Outside

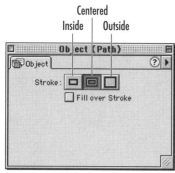

㉒ *The Stroke Position controls in the* Object *panel.*

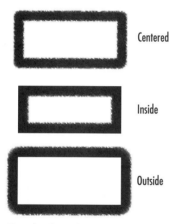

Centered

Inside

Outside

㉓ *The three choices for the* **position of a brush** on a path.

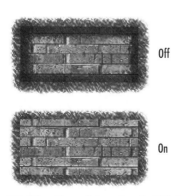

Off

On

㉔ *The effects of changing the* **Fill Over Stroke** *setting.*

Modifying Stroke Positions

Unlike other vector programs, Fireworks gives you a choice as to where a stroke is displayed on a path.

To change the position of a stroke on a path:

1. Select the path.

2. Choose **Window**>**Object** to open the Object panel **㉒**.

3. Click the Centered, Inside, or Outside buttons to change the position of the stroke along the path **㉓**.

When a path has both a stroke and a fill, you have a choice as to how the fill interacts with the stroke.

To change how the fill meets a stroke:

1. Select the path.

2. Choose **Window**>**Object** to open the Object panel.

3. Check Fill over Stroke to have the fill of the object extend over the path **㉔**.

Modifying Stroke Positions

129

EFFECTS 9

You could think of fills and strokes as the basic utilitarian features for styling objects. Effects, on the other hand, are the razzle-dazzle features that alter the look of objects. Unlike fills that are limited to just the inside of objects, and strokes that are limited to just the outside, effects in Macromedia Fireworks can change the look of either the inside or the outside of objects—or both.

For instance, you can add a bevel effect to the inside or the outside of an object to give the appearance of dimensionality. A shadow effect added to the outside of an object makes the object appear to float above its background. However, a shadow effect added inside an object will make it look as if it is punching a hole in the background.

Effects can also be used to enhance the appearance of scanned images. These effects may be just a subtle sharpening of the image's details or dramatic changes in color, brightness, and tones.

Effects allow you to give added flourishes to your Fireworks objects and scanned images.

Applying Effects

Effects are applied to objects and images using the Effect panel.

Effect panel list

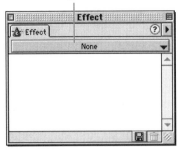

❶ *The* **Effect** panel *without an effect chosen.*

To open the Effect panel:

Choose **Window**>**Effect** to open the Effect panel ❶.

When you first open the Effect panel, it will be empty. As you add effects to an object, they appear in the Effect panel list.

To add effects to an object:

1. Select an object.

2. Use the Effect pop-up list ❷ to apply an effect to the object.

TIP When you choose an effect, another set of controls appears. These are the specific controls for the effect. *(Pages 133–149 explain how to set the controls for each of the effects.)*

TIP If you choose Use Defaults, you add a set of effects to the Effect panel without applying those effects. The effects can then be turned on using the Effect panel controls. ❸. *(See page 150 for information on working with the Effect panel.)*

❷ *The* **Effect** pop-up list *lets you apply effects to selected objects.*

❸ *The* **Effect** panel Defaults.

④ *Different looks that can be created using the* Outer (left) and Inner (right) Bevels.

Color Well   Size   Bevel Edge Shape list

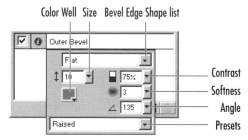

Contrast
Softness
Angle
Presets

⑤ *The* Outer Bevel *controls.*

Size   Bevel Edge Shape list

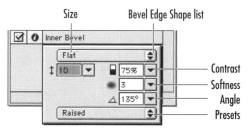

Contrast
Softness
Angle
Presets

⑥ *The* Inner Bevel *controls.*

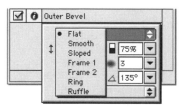

⑦ *The* bevel *shape choices.*

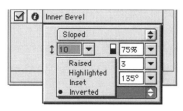

⑧ *The* bevel effects *button presets.*

Applying Bevel Effects

The bevel effects simulate the look of 3D objects such as chiseled letters or carved forms **④**. Fireworks lets you apply bevels to either the inside or outside of objects.

To apply a bevel effect:

1. Select an object.

2. Choose Outer Bevel from the Effect list. The Outer Bevel controls appear **⑤**.

   or

   Choose Inner Bevel from the Effect list. The Inner Bevel controls appear **⑥**.

3. Choose one of the bevel shapes from the Bevel shape list **⑦**.

4. Use the Size control to change the pixel size of the bevel.

5. If you have chosen Outer Bevel, use the Color Well to change the color of the bevel.

TIP The color of an inner bevel comes from the color of the original object.

6. Use the Contrast control to change the intensity of the light creating the bevel highlights and shadows.

7. Use the Softness control to change the hardness of the edges of the bevel.

TIP If the bevel around curved objects appears bumpy, increase the softness to smooth the bevel.

8. Use the Angle control to change the angle of the light on the beveled edge.

9. Use the Button presets **⑧** to apply special effects to the bevels. (*See the next page for a discussion on how to use the button presets.*)

Applying Bevel Effects

The Button menu for the bevel effects is used to easily apply variations to the bevels. The four states are Raised, Highlighted, Inset, and Inverted.

Using the bevel button choices menu:

The four states change bevels as follows **❾**:

- **Raised**, the default, leaves the object as originally styled.

- **Highlighted** lightens the object as if a 25% white tint were applied over it.

- **Inset** reverses the lighting of the bevel to invert the 3D effect.

- **Inverted** reverses the lighting and lightens the object with a tint.

TIP The four states of the Button menu are provided as a convenience for quickly changing the appearance of buttons. They do not actually create the code for making operational buttons. *(For more information on creating rollover buttons, see Chapter 19, "Behaviors.")*

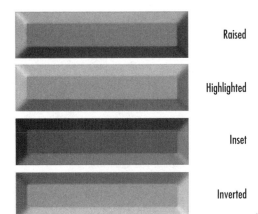

Raised

Highlighted

Inset

Inverted

❾ *The effects of applying each of the* **Bevel Preset choices.**

⑩ *Different looks that can be created using the* Inner Shadow and Drop Shadow *effects.*

Color Well Distance

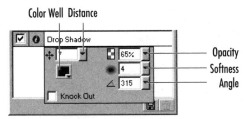

Opacity
Softness
Angle

⑪ *The* Drop Shadow *controls.*

Color Well   Distance

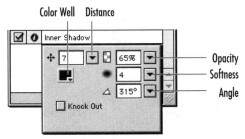

Opacity
Softness
Angle

⑫ *The* Inner Shadow *controls.*

Applying Shadow Effects

The shadow effects simulate the look of objects casting a shadow on a wall or cutting out a hole in a background **⑩**.

To apply a Drop Shadow or Inner Shadow effect:

1. Choose Drop Shadow from the Effect list. The Drop Shadow controls appear **⑪**.

   or

   Choose Inner Shadow from the Effect list. The Inner Shadow controls appear **⑫**.

2. Use the Opacity control to change the transparency of the shadow. The lower the number, the more transparent the object.

3. Use the Softness control to change the softness or feather applied to the edge of the shadow.

4. Use the Angle control to change the angle of the light casting the shadow.

5. Use the Distance control to change how far the shadow falls from the object.

6. Use the Color Well to choose a color for the shadow.

7. Select Knock Out to have only the shadow appear, not the object casting the shadow.

Applying Shadow Effects

Applying Emboss Effects

The emboss effect pushes the shape of one object into another object or out from the background .

To apply a Raised Emboss or Inset Emboss effect:

1. Choose Raised Emboss from the Effect list. The Raised Emboss controls appear ⓮.

   or

   Choose Inset Emboss from the Effect list. The Inset Emboss controls appear ⓯.

2. Use the Width control to change the width or size of the embossed edge.

3. Use the Contrast control to change the intensity of the light creating the embossing highlights and shadows.

4. Use the Softness control to change the sharpness of the edges of the embossing.

5. Use the Angle control to change the angle of the light on the embossing.

6. Choose Show Object to see any fill or strokes that are applied to the object ⓯ and ⓰.

   or

   Deselect Show Object to have the background color or any other objects seen within the emboss effects ⓯ and ⓰.

⓭ *Different looks that can be created using the* Inset Emboss (left) *and* Raised Emboss (right) *effects.*

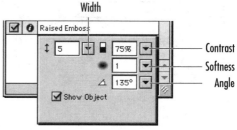

⓮ *The* Raised Emboss controls *which are also the same as the* Inset Emboss controls.

⓯ *A Raised Emboss effect with Show Object turned on (top). Show Object is turned off for the bottom text.*

⓰ *An Inset Emboss effect with Show Object turned on (top). Show Object is turned off for the bottom text.*

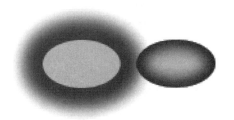

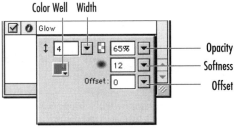

⑰ *Different looks that can be created using the* **Outer Glow** *(left) and* **Inner Glow** *(right).*

Color Well   Width

Opacity

Softness

Offset

⑱ *The* **Glow** *controls.*

Applying Glow Effects

The glow effect lets you add a color all around the edges of an object **⑰**.

To apply a Glow effect:

1. Choose Glow from the Effect category pop-up list. The Glow effect choices appear **⑱**.

2. Use the Opacity control to change the transparency of the glow. The lower the number, the greater the transparency.

3. Use the Softness control to change the softness, or feather, applied to the glow.

4. Use the Width control to change the size of the glow.

5. Use the Offset control to add a space between the object and the glow **⑲**.

6. Use the Color Well to choose a color for the glow.

⑲ *The* **Offset** *for the glow allows you to add space between the glow and the object.*

Applying Blur Effects

The blur effects soften the details in objects. They can be used to make one object appear to be behind others. The effects are most obvious when applied to pixel-based images, but they also affect patterns, textures, and gradients applied to objects.

TIP The blur effects work by changing some of the blacks and whites in an image to shades of gray. This means that some of the details of an image are lost.

To apply the Blur or Blur More effects:

◆ Choose Blur or Blur More from the Effect category pop-up list. The name of the effect appears in the Effect panel.

TIP The Blur ❷⓪ and Blur More ❷① effects each apply a fixed amount of blur and do not have a dialog box to let you control the amount of the blur.

You can also apply a Gaussian Blur which lets you control the amount of the blur.

To apply the Gaussian Blur effect:

1. Choose Gaussian Blur from the Effect category pop-up list. The Gaussian Blur dialog box appears ❷②.

2. Use the slider to increase or decrease the amount of the blur.

3. Check Preview to see the effects of the blur on the selected object.

4. Click OK. The name of the effect appears in the Effect panel as the effect is applied ❷③.

❷⓪ *The results of applying the* **Blur effect** *to an image.*

❷① *The results of applying the* **Blur More effect** *to an image.*

❷② *The* **Gaussian Blur** *dialog box.*

❷③ *The result of applying a 4 pixel setting of the* **Gaussian Blur** effect *to an image.*

Original   Sharpen effect

24 *The effect of applying the* **Sharpen effect** *to an image.*

Original   Sharpen More effect

25 *The effect of applying the* **Sharpen More** **effect** *to an image. Notice the added contrast created around the eye and below the mouth.*

Applying Sharpening Effects

Just as you can blur images, so can you sharpen them. This is especially useful when working with scanned images that tend to look a little soft, or out of focus.

TIP The sharpen effects work by changing some gray pixels in the image to black or white. Although it may seem that more detail is revealed, strictly speaking some of the detail is lost.

To apply the Sharpen or Sharpen More effects:

◆ Choose Sharpen or Sharpen More from the Effect category pop-up list. The name of the effect appears in the Effect panel.

TIP The Sharpen **24** and Sharpen More **25** effects each apply a fixed amount of sharpening and do not have a dialog box to let you control the amount of the blur.

Applying Sharpening Effects

The other type of sharpening effect goes under the unlikely name Unsharp Mask. This comes from a traditional photographic technique.

To apply the Unsharp Mask effect:

1. Choose Unsharp Mask from the Effect category pop-up list. The Unsharp Mask dialog box appears ㉖.

2. Drag the Sharpen Amount slider to change the amount of contrast that is applied—the greater the amount, the greater the sharpening.

3. Drag the Threshold slider to set how different the pixels must be before they are sharpened.

TIP A threshold of 0 means that all the pixels in the image are sharpened.

TIP A high threshold means that only those pixels that are very different in brightness are sharpened. For instance, in illustration ㉗, a high threshold means that only the sharp line in the beak would be sharpened. A low threshold means that the gray feathers in the lower right corner would also be sharpened.

4. Drag the Pixel Radius slider or type in the field to set the number of pixels around the edge that have the sharpening effect applied.

5. Check Preview to see the effects of the blur on the selected object.

6. Click OK. The name of the effect appears in the Effect panel as the effect is applied.

TIP High Unsharp Mask settings with a high sharpen and low threshold settings can cause an unwanted halo or glow around objects ㉘.

㉖ *The* **Unsharp Mask** *dialog box.*

㉗ *The effect of applying the* **Unsharp Mask** **effect** *to an image.*

㉘ *The Unsharp Mask effect at a* **high sharpen and low threshold** *can create an unnatural glow around details in an image.*

Original | Find Edges and Invert effects

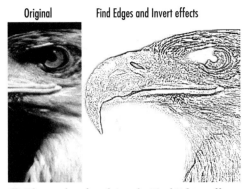

㉙ *The results of applying the* **Find Edges effect** *and then the* **Invert effect** *to an image.*

Original | Convert to Alpha effect

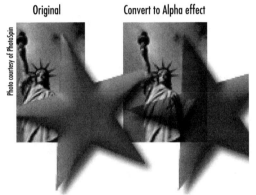

Photo courtesy of PhotoSpin

㉚ *The results of applying the* **Convert to Alpha** *effect.*

Applying the Find Edges Effect

The Find Edges effect changes the colors of the pixels of an image so that a line appears where there was an edge.

To apply the Find Edges effect:

◆ Choose Find Edges from the Other menu of the Effect pop-up list. The image is converted and the name of the effect appears in the Effect panel.

TIP Use the Invert effect *(see page 144)* after the Find Edges effect to convert the image to black on white **㉙**.

Using the Convert to Alpha Effect

The Convert to Alpha effect converts an object or image into a grayscale or alpha channel version. This lets you create see-through effects based on the colors of an image.

To apply the Convert to Alpha effect:

◆ Choose Convert to Alpha from the Other menu of the Effect pop-up list. The image is converted and the name of the effect appears in the Effect panel **㉚**.

TIP Alpha areas that are white allow the images underneath to be seen. Alpha areas that are dark hide the images underneath.

TIP The Convert to Alpha effect is very similar to masking using the grayscale values of an image.

Find Edges Effect; Convert to Alpha Effect

Applying the Adjust Color Effects

Fireworks also has a set of effects that alter certain aspects of the appearance of colors in objects and images, such as brightness, contrast, and tonal relationships. These effects are similar to those found in image editing programs such as Adobe Photoshop.

To apply the Auto Levels effect:

◆ Choose Auto Levels from the Adjust Color menu of the Effect category pop-up list. This applies a preset adjustment of the Levels effect *(see page 144)* to the tones of the object ❹.

TIP Because there are no user controls for the Auto Levels effect, the command is not often used except for those unwilling to learn the other commands.

Brightness and Contrast are the simplest ways to adjust the light and dark areas in an image. The brightness and contrast settings shift all the values of the image.

To apply the Brightness/Contrast effect:

1. Choose Brightness/Contrast from the Adjust Color menu of the Effect category pop-up list. The Brightness/Contrast dialog box appears ❺.

2. Use the Brightness slider to increase or decrease the lightness of the image.

3. Use the Contrast slider to increase or decrease the contrast of the image.

4. Check Preview to see how the controls affect the image.

5. Click OK. The name of the effect appears in the Effect panel.

TIP Brightness and Contrast are extremely rudimentary controls. Most designers use the more sophisticated Curves *(see next page)* and Levels *(see page 144)* controls.

Original   Auto Levels effect

Photo courtesy of PhotoSpin

❹ *The result of applying the* **Auto Levels effect** *to an image.*

❺ *The* **Brightness/Contrast** *dialog box.*

Applying the Adjust Color Effects

Modification point   Eyedroppers

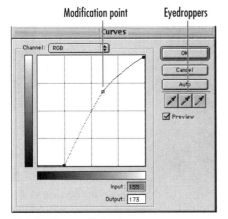

❸❸ *The* **Curves** *dialog box.*

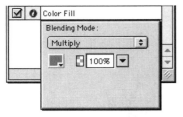

❸❹ *The* **Color Fill** *dialog box.*

The Curves effect uses a tonal graph to change the appearance of an image. Each position on the graph corresponds to a value in the red, green, or blue channels of the image. Moving points on the curve changes the values in the image.

To apply the Curves effect:

1. Choose Curves from the Adjust Color menu of the Effect category pop-up list. The Curves dialog box appears **❸❸**.

2. Set the channel list to RGB to change the red, green, and blue channels together.

   or

   Choose a specific channel to change.

3. Drag a point on the graph to change the straight line to a curve. Move the curve up to lighten the area. Move the curve down to darken the area.

4. Use the Eyedroppers to choose the image's black, neutral, and white points.

5. Check Preview to see how the controls affect the image.

The Color Fill effect allows you to easily tint or change the color of scanned images.

To apply the Color Fill effect:

1. Choose Color Fill from the Adjust Color menu of the Effect category pop-up list. The Color Fill dialog box appears **❸❹**.

2. Use the Color Well to choose a color.

3. Use the Opacity control to set the transparency of the color.

   TIP If you want to change an object's color, it is easier to just change the fill color. However, the Color Fill effect is more helpful when animating objects so they change from one color to another. *(See Chapter 16, "Animations")*

Applying the Adjust Color Effects

The Invert effect reverses selected images, turning them into negatives.

To apply the Invert effect:

◆ Choose Invert from the Adjust Color menu of the Effect category pop-up list. The colors of the image are reversed ③⑤ and the name of the effect is added to the Effect panel.

TIP The Invert command can be used if you want to turn photograph negatives into positive images. It can also be used for dramatic interactive effects.

Original   Invert effect

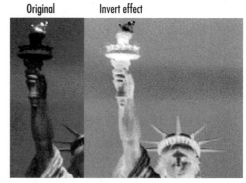

③⑤ *The result of applying the* **Invert** *effect to an image.*

The Levels effect gives you a set of controls for changing the values of an image. These controls let you move the black, white, and midpoint values of the image.

To apply the Levels effect:

1. Choose Levels from the Adjust Color menu of the Effect category pop-up list. The Levels dialog box appears ③⑥.

2. Set the channel list to RGB to change the red, green, and blue channels together.

   or

   Choose a specific channel to change.

3. Drag the Black point, Midpoint, or White point sliders to adjust the tonal range of the image.

   or

   Use the Eyedroppers to select the black, white, and neutral points on the image.

4. Drag sliders for the output ramp to change the appearance of the image.

Black point   Midpoint   White point Eyedroppers

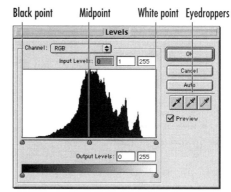

③⑥ *The* **Levels** *dialog box.*

Applying the Adjust Color Effects

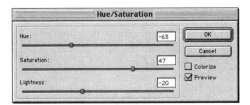

⑰ *The* **Hue/Saturation** *dialog box.*

The Hue/Saturation effect lets you shift the color values as well as tint images.

To apply the Hue/Saturation effect:

1. Choose Hue/Saturation from the Adjust Color menu of the Effect category pop-up list. The Hue/Saturation dialog box appears **⑰**.

2. Use the Hue slider to change the range of colors in the image. As you move the slider, the colors are shifted.

3. Use the Saturation slider to increase or decrease the saturation of the colors in the image. The higher the saturation the more intense the colors appear.

4. Use the Lightness slider to increase or decrease the lightness of the image. Increasing the lightness is similar to adding white to the image.

5. Click Colorize to convert the image to monotone. The Saturation slider can then be used to tint the image with a specific color.

6. Click Preview to see the effects of the controls on the image.

7. Click OK. This applies the Hue/Saturation effect to the image.

Applying the Adjust Color Effects

Using the Eye Candy Filters

Fireworks 4 also ships with three gifts for you—free filters from Alien Skin Software's Eye Candy 4000 collection. These filters are automatically installed as part of the regular Fireworks application.

To work with the Eye Candy interface elements:

- View the original object in the Original Preview window ❸❽.

- View the preview of the effect in the Effect Preview window.

- Press and drag with the Hand tool to move image within the Effect Preview window. This helps you see different areas of the image within the limited area of the Effect Preview window.

- Use the Zoom tool to increase the size of the image within the Effect Preview window.

- Hold the Opt/Alt key while using the Zoom tool to decrease the size of the image within the Effect Preview window.

- Click the OK button to apply the effect and exit the Eye Candy dialog box.

The Bevel Boss effect is a more sophisticated version of the Fireworks inner and outer bevel effects ❸❾.

To set the Bevel Boss effect:

1. Choose Bevel Boss from the Eye Candy 4000LE menu of the Effect category pop-up list. The Bevel Boss dialog box appears.

2. Use tabs to choose the Basic, Lighting, and Bevel Profile controls as described in the following exercises.

Hand Tool
Original Preview   Zoom Tool   Effect Preview

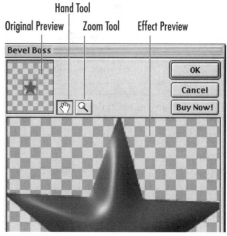

❸❽ *The Eye Candy* interface elements.

❸❾ *Various bevel effects created with the Eye Candy Bevel Boss effect*

The Rest of the Eye Candy 4000 Effects

There are other Eye Candy effects available from Alien Skin Software. They are:

Antimatter, Chrome, Corona, Cutout, Drip, Fire, Fur, Glass, Gradient Glow, HSB Noise, Fractal Roughness, Jiggle, Melt, Shadowlab, Smoke, Squint, Star, Swirl, Water Drops, Weave, and Wood.

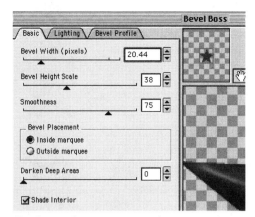

⑩ The **Bevel Boss Basic** *panel.*

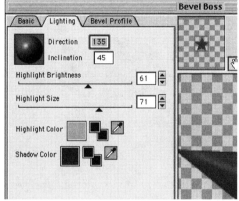

⑪ The **Bevel Boss Lighting** *panel.*

The Basic tab of the Bevel Boss displays the general controls for the bevel **⑩**.

To set the Bevel Boss Basic controls:

- **Bevel Width** sets the width, in pixels, of the bevel.

- **Bevel Height Scale** controls how tall the bevel should be.

- **Smoothness** takes out any roughness that may appear in the bevel.

- **Bevel Placement** positions the bevel inside or outside the object.

- **Darken Deep Areas** adds black to the deep areas of the bevel.

- **Shade Interior** adds shading to interior sections of the bevel.

The Lighting tab displays the controls for how light affects the bevel **⑪**—how much light, its color, how focused or diffused, and the reflection of the light on the surface of the object.

To set the Bevel Boss Lighting controls:

- **Direction** sets the angle of the light. The settings correspond to 360 degrees of a circle.

- **Inclination** positions the ligh. Zero (0) positions the light over the top or bottom of the image. Ninety (90) positions the light over the center of the image.

TIP Drag the small light above the preview ball to move both the direction and inclination

- **Highlight Brightness** increases the amount of highlight in the image.

TIP Increasing the brightness makes the surface look shinier.

- **Highlight Size** increases the size of the highlight in the image.

TIP Increasing the size of the highlight makes the light look stronger or closer.

Using the Eye Candy Filters

The Bevel Profile tab displays the controls for carving the shape of the bevel **42**.

To set the Bevel Boss Bevel Profile controls:

1. Choose one of the presets at the top of the panel.

2. Click on the profile graph to add or move points on the profile.

TIP Each of the points in the graph corresponds to a change in the angle of the bevel.

3. Click Sharp corner to make the point create an abrupt change in the direction of the bevel.

The Marble effect lets you create the look of different types of marble **43**. (*See the first exercise on page 146 for how to work with the Eye Candy interface elements and apply the effect.*)

To apply the Marble effect:

♦ Choose Marble From the Eye Candy 4000LE menu of the Effect category pop-up list, choose Marble. The Marble dialog box appears **44**.

To apply the Marble effect:

- **Vein Size** sets the length of the segments of the vein.

- **Vein Coverage** sets how much of the surface the veins cover.

- **Vein Thickness** sets the width of each vein.

- **Vein Roughness** increases or decreases the jaggedness of the veins.

- **Bedrock** and **Vein** colors set the background and vein colors.

- **Seamless Tile** arranges the marble so that it can be used in a pattern.

- **Random Seed** rearranges the randomness of the marble.

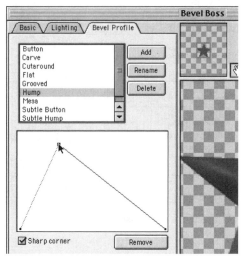

42 The **Bevel Boss Bevel Profile** *panel.*

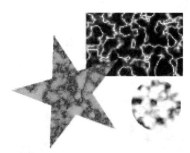

43 *Various marble effects created with the Eye Candy Marble effect.*

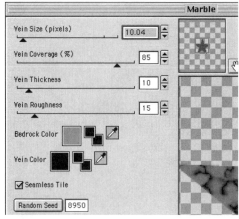

44 *The **Marble** dialog box.*

45 *Various motion trail effects created with the Eye Candy Motion Trail effect.*

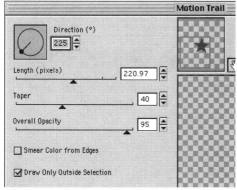

46 *The* **Motion Trail** *dialog box.*

The Motion Trail effect (my favorite!) lets you create special blurred trails that simulate the look of objects moving through space **45**. *(See the first exercise on page 146 for how to work with the Eye Candy interface elements and apply the effect.)*

To apply the Motion Trail effect:

◆ From the Eye Candy 4000LE menu of the Effect category pop-up list, choose Motion Trail . The Motion Trail dialog box appears **46**.

To set the Motion Trail effect:

- **Direction** sets the angle of the motion trail.
- **Length** sets how long the trail should be.
- **Taper** sets how fast the trail should pinch inwards.
- **Overall Opacity** sets the transparency of the motion trail.
- **Smear Color from Edges** controls what image of the original is used to create the trail.
- **Draw Only Outside Selection** keeps the trail from obscuring the original image.

Using the Eye Candy Filters

Working with the Effect Panel

Once you have applied effects to objects, you can use the Effect panel to change the effects, temporarily turn them off, or change the order the the effects.

To modify an effect:

1. Click the information icon in the Effect panel **⑰**. This opens the effect controls.

TIP If the effect is set by a dialog box, such as the Gaussian Blur, clicking on the information icon opens its dialog box.

2. Make whatever changes you want.

3. Click the name of the effect in the panel to apply the new control settings.

To change the display of an effect:

◆ Click the Preview icon in the Effect list **⑰**. This turns the effect on and off.

To delete an effect:

◆ Drag the name of the effect onto the Delete Effect icon.

   or

   Use the Delete Effect command in the Effect panel menu to delete the selected effect.

To apply multiple effects:

◆ Add as many effects as you want from the Effect pop-up list.

TIP Drag the effects up or down in the list to change the order that the effect modifies the image **⑱**.

TIP Each effect is applied in the order that it appears in the Effect list **⑲**.

TIP If you have many effects, use the All On or All Off commands in the Effect panel menu to turn all the effects on and off at once **⑳**.

Preview Information   Save effect Delete effect

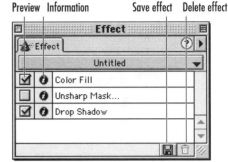

⑰ *The* **Effect panel** *with multiple effects.*

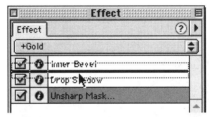

⑱ Drag an effect to a new position *in the Effect list to change how the effect is applied.*

⑲ *The difference between positioning the Drop Shadow effect above the Inner Bevel in the Effect list (left) or positioning the Drop Shadow below the Inner Bevel (right).*

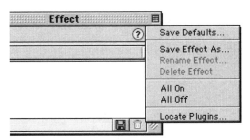

50 *The* Effect panel menu.

51 Saved effects *appear in the pop-up list in the Effect panel.*

Applying Multiple Effects: Fixing the Bug

There is a bug in Fireworks 4 that may cause bad results when trying to apply multiple live effects to objects. For instance, if you apply a Bevel and Motion Trail, you will not get a good result.

Although I hope Macromedia releases a bug-fix, there is a work-around: Apply the first effect, such as the Bevel. Then group the object and apply the second effect to the group.

This allows you to apply multiple effects correctly.

Once you apply effects to objects, you can save the settings so that you can easily reapply the effect to other objects in other documents. This saves all the effects currently in the Effect list as a preset that can be applied from the Effect pop-up list.

To save an effect:

1. Apply the effects you want to an object.

2. Choose Save Effect As from the Effect panel menu **50**. The Save Effect dialog box appears.

3. Type the name of the new effect and click OK. The new effect appears as one of the effect presets **51**.

TIP Use the Rename Effect command in the Effect panel menu to change the name of an effect.

You can also change the setting for the default effects used with the Use Defaults command *(see page 132)*.

To set the default effects:

1. Apply a certain set of effects to an object.

2. Choose Save Defaults from the Effect panel menu. An alert box appears, asking you to confirm that you want to save these settings as the new defaults.

3. Click OK. The next time you choose Use Defaults, the new effects will appear.

Third Party Plug-ins

In addition to the Eye Candy filters, Fireworks also supports many third party plug-ins such as those in Adobe Photoshop and Kai's Power Tools. These appear in the Effect panel **52** and the Xtras menu *(see page 220)*. This allows you to apply those filters and adjust them later, just as you do with the effects that ship with Fireworks.

TIP At this time, Fireworks 4 is unable to use the Photoshop 6 plug-ins. It can use the filters in Photoshop 5.5. Check the Macromedia Web site for any updates that will allow you to use the Photoshop 6 plug-ins.

To add third party plug-ins using the Effect panel:

1. Choose Locate Plug-ins from the Effect panel menu.

2. Use the dialog box to navigate to the folder that contains the plug-ins.

3. Select the folder. An alert box informs you that the next time you launch Fireworks, the plug-ins will be available in the Effect panel.

TIP This technique also adds plug-ins to the Xtras menu *(see page 220)*.

To add third party plug-ins using Preferences:

1. Choose **Edit** > **Preferences** to open the Preferences dialog box **53**.

2. Choose Folders from the tab at the top of the Preferences dialog box.

3. Choose Photoshop® Plug-ins.

4. Click the Browse button.

5. Use the dialog box to navigate to the folder that contains your Photoshop plug-ins.

6. Select the folder.

7. Quit and re-launch Fireworks to see the plug-ins in the Effect panel.

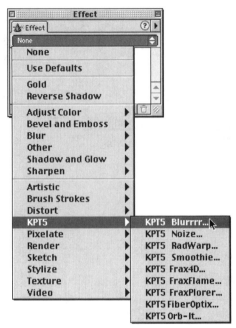

52 Plug-ins *from Adobe and other companies appear in the Effect panel list.*

53 *Use the* Preferences dialog box *to select the folder that contains the additional plug-ins.*

TEXT 10

Whoever said a picture is worth a thousand words underestimated by several hundred kilobytes. Pictures and graphics create much bigger Web files than ordinary HTML text. This means that pages with graphics take much longer to appear on the viewers' computer screens.

All text created in Macromedia Fireworks is eventually exported onto Web pages as graphics. There are perfectly good reasons why someone would convert fast-downloading text into slow-downloading graphics.

It might be to create labels, create a banner design, or just make sure the text looks the same no matter what fonts or system the viewer has. Whatever the reason, Fireworks has many features for working with text.

Typing Text

You access text in Fireworks by using the Text tool. You should find working with text similar to the methods you have used in any graphics or page-layout program.

❶ *The* **Text tool** *in the Tools panel.*

To use the Text tool:

1. Choose the Text tool in the Tools panel **❶**.

2. Click inside the document area or drag to create the area where you want the text to stay inside. This opens the Text Editor **❷**.

To use the Text Editor:

1. Type the text inside the Preview area.

TIP You can copy text from another application and paste it into the Text Editor.

2. Use any of the ordinary text techniques to select text, make corrections, or insert new text within the Preview area.

3. Click Show Font and Show Size & Color to see the text as it will appear in the document.

TIP Turn off the Show Font and Show Size & Color options if you find it difficult to read the text within the Text Editor. For instance, the text may be too small to be read in the Text Editor.

4. Click Apply to see the formatting changes without leaving the Text Editor.

5. Click OK to apply the changes and close the Text Editor.

To reopen the Text Editor:

Select a text block and choose **Text** > **Editor**.

or

Double-click the text block.

❷ *The* **Text Editor.**

Using Specialty Fonts

Even when you work with editable text, the final images posted on the Web do not actually contain any text information at all.

That's because when you convert a Fireworks file to a GIF or JPEG, there are no longer any fonts used in the file. The text shapes are all converted into pixels.

This means that you can use a special font, such as Bonnie Bold, in your Fireworks document without worrying if your viewers will have the font when the graphic is posted to the Web.

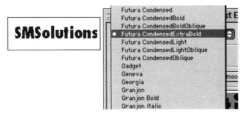

❸ *As you choose a typeface in the Text Editor,* **the side area of the font list** *shows a preview of how the text will look in the selected typeface.*

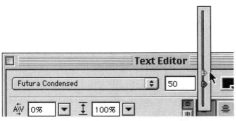

❹ *The* **point size** *control in the Text Editor.*

❺ *The* **styling** *controls in the Text Editor include the buttons for applying bold, italic, and underline style to text.*

Setting the Text Attributes

Once you have opened the Text Editor, you can control the various text attributes. Fireworks also lets you add bold or italic styling to text. You can also apply different text attributes within the Text Editor.

To set the font:

1. Use the font pop-up list ❸ to choose the typeface.
2. Type text inside the Preview area.
3. Use the font pop-up list to change to a different typeface.

TIP You can change text in the Text Editor by dragging across the text to select it and then making any changes.

TIP A small area appears next to the font list that displays a representation of the selected typeface.

To set the point size:

◆ Use the point size slider or type in the field ❹ to change the point size.

To add styling:

1. Select the text.
2. Click the bold or italic buttons to change text ❺.

TIP Styling is discarded if you convert the text into paths *(see page 164)*.

To apply different text attributes:

1. As you are typing the text, make whatever changes you want. The next text you type will reflect those changes.

   or

   Select the text you want to change.
2. Apply the changes to that text.

Setting the Text Attributes

Kerning is adjusting the space between two letters. Fireworks lets you kern text within the Text Editor.

To kern the text:

1. Click between the two letters you want to kern.

2. Use the Kern slider or type in the field **6** to kern the text closer together or further apart. Negative values decrease the space; positive values increase the space **7**.

TIP Click Auto-Kern in the Text Editor to have Fireworks use the built-in kerning pairs from the typeface.

TIP The Preview does not show the effects of kerning. To see those effects, position the Text Editor outside the document area and then use the Apply button to see how the text changes as you enter the kerning amounts.

Range kerning is kerning applied to a selection of text. (Range kerning is sometimes called *tracking* in other programs.)

To set the range kerning:

1. Drag across a selection of the text.

2. Use the Range Kerning slider or type in the field to change the range kerning for the text **8**. Negative values decrease the space; positive values increase the space **9**.

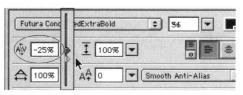

6 *The* **kerning** *controls in the Text Editor.*

People Inc.
People Inc.

7 *The result of kerning to close up the space between the letters* **Pe**, **pl**, *and* **le**.

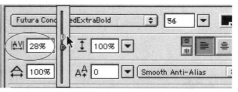

8 *The* **range kerning** *controls in the Text Editor.*

People Inc.
People Inc.

9 *The result of applying range kerning to increase the spaces between the characters.*

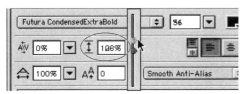

⑩ *The* **leading** *controls in the Text Editor.*

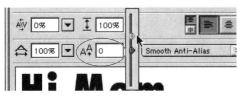

⑪ *The* **baseline shift** *controls in the Text Editor.*

People Inc.
People Inc.

⑫ *The results of applying a positive baseline shift to the characters nc. (The baseline is indicated by the dashed line.)*

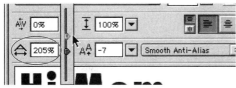

⑬ *The* **horizontal scale** *controls in the Text Editor.*

People Inc.
People Inc.

⑭ *The result of applying horizontal scale to the letter* P.

Leading (pronounced "ledding"), or *line spacing*, is the space between multiple lines of text. (Leading is so called after the metal pieces of lead that were inserted in early typesetting equipment.) If your text consists of only a single line you do not have to worry about setting leading.

To set the leading:

Use the Leading slider or type in the field to change the leading for the text **⑩**.

TIP Fireworks measures leading as a percentage of the point size. A setting of 100% means the space between the lines of text is the same as the point size.

TIP Leading is applied to an entire paragraph, not individual characters.

Baseline shift is the technique of raising or lowering text from its *baseline*, or the line that the text sits on.

To add a baseline shift:

1. Select the text.
2. Use the baseline slider or type in the field **⑪** to raise or lower the text in points from the baseline.

TIP Positive numbers raise the text. Negative numbers lower the text **⑫**.

Text can also be distorted using a technique called horizontal scaling. This changes the width of the text without changing the height.

To change the horizontal scale:

1. Select the text.
2. Use the Horizontal Scale slider or type in the field **⑬** to increase or decrease the horizontal scaling. Amounts lower than 100% make the text width smaller. Amounts higher than 100% make the text wider **⑭**. *(See the sidebar on the following page for a discussion on using the horizontal scale controls.)*

Setting the Text Attributes

Setting the Text Attributes

You can also align text within a text block in a wide variety of ways. The text can be set either horizontally or vertically. Horizontal text reads from left to right.

To set the horizontal alignment:

1. Select the text.

2. Click one of the five alignment settings ⓯:

   - **Left** aligns the text so that it sits on the left side of the text block and creates irregular line breaks along the right side of the text.
   - **Right** aligns the text so that it sits on the right side of the text block and creates irregular line breaks along the left side of the text.
   - **Centered** aligns the text so that the middle of the line of text is positioned in the middle of the text block. There are irregular line breaks on both the left and right sides of the text.
   - **Justified** aligns the text so that it sits on both the left and right side of the text block. Justified alignment increases the range kerning so the line fills the width of the text block ⓰.
   - **Stretched** aligns the text so that it sits on both the left and right side of the text block. Stretched alignment distorts the shape of the text as it increases the horizontal scale, so the line fills the width of the text block ⓱. This could cause typographic purists to cringe *(see the sidebar on this page)*.

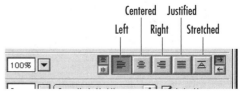

Centered   Justified

Left   Right   Stretched

⓯ *The* **alignment** *controls in the Text Editor.*

People Inc.

People Inc.

⓰ *The results of the* **justified alignment.**

People Inc.

People Inc.

⓱ *The results of the* **stretch alignment.**

Should You Use Horizontal Scale?

Typography purists (such as your outspoken author) disdain the look of electronically scaled type. We say it causes ugly distortions to the look of the original typeface.

We also say that if you need to fit text into a specific area you should use the proper condensed or expanded typeface. However, even the purists cannot always tell if small amounts have been applied.

Horizontal   Vertical

⑱ *The* Horizontal and Vertical dreection *buttons.*

Normal   Reversed

⑲ *The* text flow *controls.*

S M S C
C S M S

⑳ Text reversed *to read from right to left.*

㉑ The Anti-Alias settings *pop-up menu.*

No Anti-Alias
Crisp Anti-Alias
Strong Anti-Alias
Smooth Anti-Alias

㉒ *The effects of the anti-alias settings on text.*

Ordinarily, text reads horizontally—from left to right. However, you can change the text direction so the letters flow from top to bottom. This is very useful for creating vertical buttons.

To set the text direction:

1. Select the text.

2. Click the Horizontal direction button to have the text read horizontally.

or

Click the Vertical direction button **⑱** to have the text read from top to bottom.

TIP Vertical alignment does not show in the Text Editor. Use the Apply button to see the actual vertical alignment.

Another special effect you can create is to have the text read from right to left.

To reverse the text flow:

♦ Click the Reversed button **⑲**. All the text in that text block changes so that the letters flow from right to left **⑳**.

TIP The Reverse text setting can be used with foreign language typefaces.

Text that is displayed as part of Web pages may need to be softened around the edges so it appears less jagged. This is called anti-aliasing.

To set the Anti-Aliasing amount:

1. Select the text.

2. Choose the Anti-Alias setting from the pop-up menu **㉑**.

TIP Anti-aliasing does not show in the Text Editor. Use the Apply button to see the effect **㉒**.

Working with Text Blocks

Once text is in a text block, you do not have to open the Text Editor to make certain formatting changes. You can change the text attributes, fill, stroke, or effects applied to the text block as a whole.

To modify text inside a text block:

1. Drag any of the text block handles to rewrap the text within the block **23**.

2. With the text block selected, choose any of the following commands:
   - **Text > Font** lets you change the typeface.
   - **Text > Size** lets you change the point size.
   - **Text > Style** lets you apply one of the electronic styles such as bold or italic.
   - **Text > Alignment** lets you apply one of the horizontal or vertical alignment settings.

   TIP You cannot apply the changes to just some of the text, only to the entire block.

   TIP You can also select multiple text blocks and apply changes to them all.

To change the appearance of the text:

1. With the text block selected, use any of the Color Wells for fill or stroke to change the color of the text block.

2. Use the Fill, Stroke, or Effect panels to change all the appearance settings of the text block.

As you are typing and formatting text in the Text Editor, you can still reposition the text block on the page without clicking OK and closing the Text Editor.

To reposition text while in the Text Editor:

1. Move the cursor from inside the Text Editor to the canvas area.

2. Drag the text block anywhere on the page **24**.

23 Drag the text block handles *to change the way the text wraps within the block.*

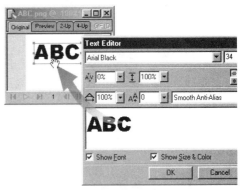

24 *You can reposition a text block as you are working inside the Text Editor.*

㉕ *The result of applying the skew distortion to text.*

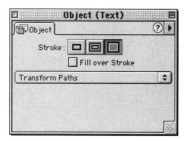

㉖ *The* **Object** *panel when a text block is selected.*

The transformation tools create spectacular results when applied to text.

To transform text in a text block:

1. Select the text block.

2. Use any of the the Transform tools *(see pages 88–93)* to distort the text within the block **㉕**.

TIP The transformation tools change the size of the text by distorting the text, not by changing the point size.

TIP Choose **Modify** > **Transform** > **Remove Transformations** to restore the text to its original formatting.

When you distort text, you have a choice as to how the text is distorted. This is controlled by the object properties for text.

To set the object properties for a text block:

1. Select the text block.

2. Choose **Window** > **Object** to open the Object panel **㉖**.

3. Choose Transform Paths or Transform Pixels.

TIP Transform Paths results in distortions that preserve crisp text. Transform Pixels results in distortions in which the text may be blurred.

Working with Text Blocks

Working with Text on a Path

One of the most popular effects in graphics is to attach text so it flows along a path.

To attach text to a path:

1. Select the text block.
2. Select the path.
3. Choose Text > **Attach to Path**. The text automatically aligns to the path **㉗**.

TIP Text attached to a path can still be edited using the Text Editor *(see page 154)*.

㉗ *The results of* **attaching text to a path.**

Once you have text on a path you can change the alignment, or the position where the text appears on the path.

To change the alignment of text on a path:

1. Select the path that has the text attached to it.
2. Choose Text > **Align** and then choose one of the alignment settings from the submenu. This changes where the text is positioned **㉘** on the path.

   or

   Use the alignment settings in the Text Editor.

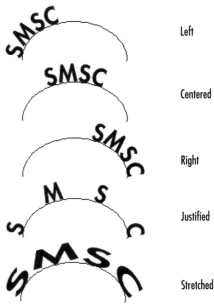

㉘ *The results of* **applying the different alignment settings** *to text on a path.*

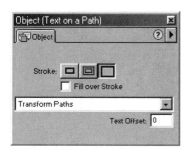

㉙ *The Object panel for* **text attached to a path.**

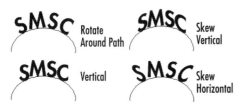

㉚ *The effects of adding a 20 pixel* **Text Offset** *to shift the text along a path.*

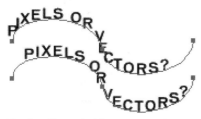

㉛ *The results of applying the* **different orientation settings** *to text on a path.*

㉜ *The results of applying the* **Reverse Direction** *command settings to text on a path.*

You can also control where the text is positioned along the path. This is called the *text offset.*

To change the text offset along a path:

1. Select the text that has been attached to the path.

2. Choose **Window>Object** to show the Object panel **㉙**.

3. Change the amount in the Text Offset field and then click Apply or OK. The text moves along the path **㉚**.

You can also change how the individual characters of the text are positioned in relation to the angle of the path. This is called the *orientation* of the text.

To change the orientation of the text:

Choose **Text>Orientation** and then choose one of the orientation settings to change how the text is positioned on the path **㉛**.

• **Rotate Around Path** keeps the text in a perpendicular orientation as it moves around the path.

• **Vertical** makes each character stand up straight no matter how the path curves.

• **Skew Vertical** maintains a vertical rotation but distorts the characters' shapes as the text follows the path.

• **Skew Horizontal** exaggerates the text's horizontal tilt up to a 90° rotation and distorts the characters' shapes as the text follows the path.

You can also flip the text to the other side of the path.

To reverse the direction of text on a path:

◆ Choose **Text>Reverse Direction** to flip the text so that it flows on the other side of the path **㉜**.

Font Management

The text in a text block or attached to a path is called editable text. This means that you can work with the text—change the font or the letters—at any time. However, there are some effects—such as changing the shapes of letters—that require that the text be converted into paths.

To convert text to paths:

1. Select the text block or text on a path.

2. Choose Text > **Convert to Paths**. This converts the text into grouped paths.

3. Use Subselection tool to manipulate the paths ③③.

TIP Once you convert text to paths, you can no longer edit it in the Text Editor; you can then edit it only as path objects.

You may receive a Fireworks document from someone who uses different fonts from the ones installed in your system. In that case you need to handle the missing font message that appears when you open that Fireworks file.

To change missing fonts:

1. Open the file. A dialog box appears that tells you which fonts are missing ③④.

2. To change all the missing fonts, click the Change All listing under the Change Missing Fonts heading.

   or

   To change a single font, click the name of that particular missing font.

3. Choose the font you want to substitute from the To: list on the right side of the dialog box.

4. Click OK to make the changes.

People Inc.
People Inc.

③③ *The results of* converting text to paths *and then manipulating the converted paths.*

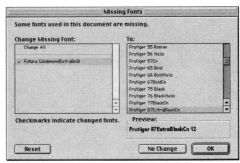

③④ *The* **Missing Fonts** *dialog box allows you to substitute installed fonts for the ones that are missing from the document.*

MASKS AND INTERACTIONS | 11

Objects in Macromedia Fireworks don't exist all alone on the canvas area. You can set one object to interact with other objects in many different ways.

For instance, you can set one object to be partially transparent so you can see through it to other objects below.

You can use the shape of one object as an electronic cookie cutter that punches a hole in another object.

One object's path can be used to form a mask or boundary so that other objects can only be seen within the mask. A mask can also be used as a filter that changes the opacity of other objects.

Finally, you can set the blending modes of objects so that the colors of one object merge or change depending on the colors of any objects below.

This interactivity and masking gives you far more choices than ordinary fills, strokes, and effects.

Applying Transparency

One way to have an object interact with other objects is to the object's transparency or opacity. Transparency—or lack of opacity—allows you to see through an object to the objects underneath.

To change an object's transparency:

1. Choose **Window** > **Layers** to open the Layers panel ❶.

2. Select the object you want to change.

3. Drag the Opacity slider or type a new percentage in the Opacity field ❷.

TIP The Opacity controls in Fireworks are similar to the layer opacity controls in Adobe Photoshop. However, in Fireworks, each object on a layer can have its own opacity setting. In Photoshop all objects on a layer share the same opacity setting.

You can also use one vector object to punch a hole in another vector object so that what's behind shows through.

To create a hole in an object:

1. Select two or more objects.

2. Choose **Modify** > **Join**. The areas where the objects overlap are transparent ❸.

TIP Text characters that have holes, such as the letters *D*, *B*, *o*, or *g*, are automatically joined when you convert the text to paths (*see page 164*).

To fill the hole in an object:

1. Select the joined objects.

2. Choose **Modify** > **Split**.

TIP (Win) You can also use the Join and Split icons on the Modify toolbar to easily change objects.

❶ *The* **Opacity** *slider of the Layers panel.*

100% opacity

50% opacity

❷ *The effect of changing the* **opacity** *of the front object.*

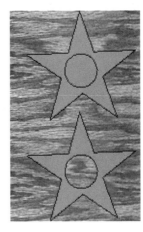

❸ *The* **Join** *command creates a hole where the circle and the star overlap.*

❹ *Select and cut the topmost object to be pasted as a mask.*

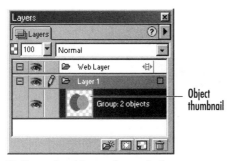

❺ *Group the objects to be masked by the Paste as Mask command.*

Object thumbnail

❻ *The* **Paste as Mask** command *turns the cut object into a mask for the grouped objects.*

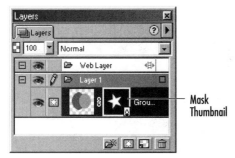

Mask Thumbnail

❼ *The* **Mask Thumbnail** *shows the object used as the mask.*

Creating Masks

Masking is the technique that uses the shape of one object as a contour to crop— or clip—other objects. Only those parts of the objects in the mask are visible. A stencil is a type of mask that allows you to add color within the mask. *(See "Bitmapped or Grayscale Masks" on page 214 for another way of working with masks.)*

TIP Masks don't have to be limited to single objects. The compound objects created by the Join command can also be used as masks.

The easiest way to create a mask in Fireworks is to use the two menu commands. The Paste as Mask command is usually used when the masking element is the topmost object.

To paste an object as a mask:

1. Position the objects to be masked below the object that is to act as the mask.

2. Select the object to be used as the mask ❹.

3. Choose **Edit** > **Cut**. The object disappears from the document.

4. Select the objects to be masked.

5. Choose **Modify** > **Group**. This combines all the objects onto one thumbnail in the Layers panel ❺.

6. Choose **Edit** > **Paste as Mask**. The bottom object is visible only inside the masking object ❻.

TIP The pen icon inside the Mask Thumbnail indicates that the mask is a vector object ❼. You can also use bitmap images as masks *(see page 214)*.

TIP You can still use the Paste as Mask command even if the masking object is not positioned above the other objects. It still masks all objects below.

Another simple way to create a mask is to use the Paste Inside command. This command is used when it is easier to select and cut the objects to be masked, rather than the masking object.

To paste objects into a mask:

1. Position the objects to be masked above the object that is to act as the mask.

2. Select the objects that are to be masked ❽.

3. Choose **Edit** > **Cut**. The object disappears from the document.

4. Select the object to be used as the mask ❾.

5. Choose **Edit** > **Paste Inside**. The objects are automatically grouped and appear inside the mask ❿. The Layers panel shows the new grouped object and its mask ⓫.

TIP You can still use the Paste Inside command even if the masking object is not positioned below the other objects.

TIP You can use also a text object as a mask. Not only that, but you can still edit the text in the Text Editor.

❽ *Select and cut the stripes—the objects to be masked by the Paste Inside command.*

❾ *Select the question mark text—the object to be used as a mask.*

❿ *The Paste Inside command displays the cut objects—the stripes—within the contours of the question mark mask.*

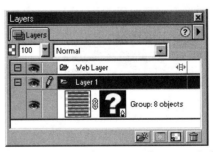

⓫ *The* **Paste Inside command** *automatically groups the cut objects and displays them within the contours of the mask.*

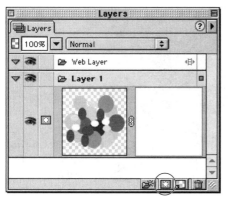

⑫ *Click the* **Add Mask icon** *to add a Mask Thumbnail to the right of the Object Thumbnail in the Layers panel.*

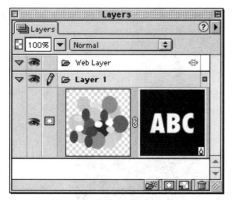

⑬ *With the Mask Thumbnail active, you can add or paste objects to act as a mask.*

You can also create a mask using the Layers panel. This approach makes it easier to visualize what happens when objects are masked. It is also more familiar for anyone who has created a Layer Mask in Adobe Photoshop.

To mask objects using the Layers panel:

1. Select and cut the object to be used as the mask.

2. Select the objects to be masked. If they are not grouped, choose **Modify > Group**. This combines all the objects onto one thumbnail in the Layers panel.

TIP You can also select the grouped objects by clicking the Object Thumbnail in the Layers panel.

3. Click the Add Mask icon in the Layers panel to add an empty Mask Thumbnail next to the Object Thumbnail **⑫**.

TIP A Yellow square around the Mask Thumbnail indicates that you are now working on the mask. In addition, a yellow and black stripe appears around the edge of your document.

4. Choose **Edit > Paste**. The cut object appears in the Mask Thumbnail **⑬**.

To release a mask:

1. Select the mask and the objects being masked.

2. Choose **Modify > Ungroup**. This releases the mask and leaves it positioned on top of the objects that were being masked.

TIP This technique works with all types of masks regardless of what kind of objects they are and how the mask was created.

Creating Masks

Bitmap or Grayscale Masks

You can also use Fireworks objects to mask bitmap images. This lets you create a vignette or a non-rectangular shape around the scanned image. *(For more information on working with scanned images, see Chapter 13, "Working with Pixels.")*

To use objects to mask a scanned image:

1. Choose **Modify > Exit Bitmap Mode**. This ensures that you are working with the image as an object, not as a bitmap image .

2. Create the items you want to act as the mask.

TIP Use the Feather command in the Fill panel to add a softer edge to the mask.

3. Select the items and choose **Edit > Cut**.

4. Use the Pointer tool to select the image.

5. Choose **Edit > Paste as Mask**. The scanned image appears inside the mask .

You can also use the grayscale values of a vector object to create the mask. Dark colors make the mask more transparent. Lighter colors make the mask less transparent.

TIP Use this technique with gradient fills to create an image that fades from full strength to invisible.

To create a vector object grayscale mask:

1. Position the vector object to be used as a mask on top of the objects to be masked.

2. Select all of the objects.

3. Choose **Modify > Mask > Group as Mask**. This sets the top object as a grayscale mask and groups the other objects 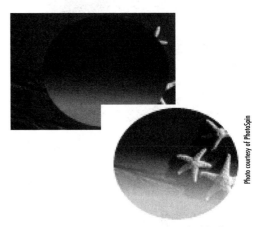.

⓮ *An object can also be used to mask a scanned image.*

Photo courtesy of PhotoSpin

⓯ *The feathered edge of the mask makes the edge of the scanned image fade.*

Photo courtesy of PhotoSpin

⓰ The **Grayscale Appearance** *uses the black and white areas of the gradient inside the ellipse as the mask of the starfish image.*

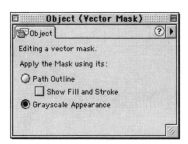

⑰ *The* **Vector Mask settings** *in the Object panel.*

⑱ *The effect of using a bitmapped image as a mask. Here the image of the clock is used as the grayscale mask for the image of the building.*

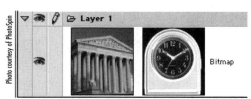

⑲ *A* **bitmapped image as a mask** *as seen in the Layers panel. The mask thumbnail shows that the image is automatically inverted.*

Just because you originally created a mask set to Path Outline doesn't mean it has to stay that way.

To convert a mask into a grayscale mask:

1. Use the Pointer tool or click the Mask Thumbnail to select the mask.

2. Choose **Window**>**Object** to open the Object panel.

3. Check Grayscale Appearance **⑰**. The grayscale values of the image control the visibility of the masking objects.

Just as you can use a gradient's grayscale values as a mask, you can also create a very sophisticated effect by using a bitmap image's grayscale values as a mask **⑱**. *(For more information on working with bitmap images, see Chapter 13 "Working with Pixels.")*

To mask to an image's grayscale value:

1. Position the bitmap image you want to use as the grayscale mask over the objects or images that you want to be masked.

2. Select all the objects.

3. Choose **Modify**>**Mask**>**Group as Mask**. This sets the top object as a grayscale mask and groups the other objects The bitmapped image appears in the Mask Thumbnail **⑲**.

Stop Destroying Innocent Pixels

One of the most important reasons to mask a scanned image, rather than cutting or cropping, is that you preserve the original pixels in the image. The benefit of the mask is that you still have the original image to go back to—not so if you delete.

Bitmap or Grayscale Masks

There's one last option for using a bitmap image as a mask—use the alpha channel transparency as the mask shape. This is very useful when you have a bitmap image with a unique shape on a transparent background. You can use the image's shape to mask other objects.

To mask to an image's alpha channel:

1. Position the image you want to use as the grayscale mask over the objects that are to be masked 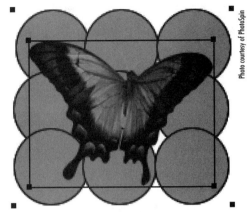.

2. Choose **Modify > Mask > Group as Mask**. This converts the image as a mask set for Grayscale Appearance.

3. Click the Mask Thumbnail in the Layers panel. This selects the bitmap image.

4. Choose Alpha Channel in the Object panel ❷❶. The transparency outline of the image acts as a mask for the objects below ❷❷.

❷⓪ *A bitmap image is positioned over objects in preparation for creating an alpha channel mask. Notice there is an alpha channel transparency around the shape of the butterfly.*

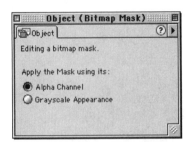

❷❶ *The* **Alpha Channel setting** *lets you use the transparent areas of a bitmap image as a mask.*

❷❷ *The result of applying the* **Alpha Channel as a mask.** *Notice that the objects can be seen only within the shape of the bitmap image.*

Bitmap or Grayscale Masks

Masking Chart

As you have seen, there are many different ways to create masks. Depending on which command you choose, you will get different settings for the mask object. The following chart shows the results of applying the different commands to vector objects or bitmap images types of objects.

Type of Object Used as Mask	Command Chosen	Result in Object Panel
Vector object	Paste as Mask	Path Outline selected Show Fill and Stroke turned off
Vector object	Paste Inside	Path Outline selected Show Fill and Stroke turned on
Vector object	Group as Mask	Grayscale Appearance selected
Bitmap object	Paste as Mask	Grayscale Appearance selected
Bitmap object	Paste Inside	Alpha Channel selected
Bitmap object	Group as Mask	Grayscale Appearance selected

Masking Chart

Editing and Manipulating Masks

Once you have created a mask, you can still make changes to both the mask and the object being masked.

The Layers panel makes it easy to select either the mask or the objects being masked.

To select the mask or the masked objects:

◆ Click the Object Thumbnail of the Layers panel to select the objects being masked **❷❸**.

or

Click the Mask Thumbnail of the Layers panel to select the mask.

Vector objects used as a mask are usually invisible — they only serve to outline the masking elements. However, you can change the settings so that you can see any fill or stroke that has been applied to the vector object.

TIP This technique is very helpful if you need to fill in gaps between the masked objects or you want to add a stroke to the final image.

To apply a fill or stroke to a mask:

1. Use the Pointer tool or click the Mask Thumbnail to select the mask.

2. Choose **Window**>**Object** to open the Object panel.

3. Check Show Fill and Stroke **❷❹**. Any fill or stroke applied to the mask will now be visible **❷❺**.

TIP If you use the Paste Inside command to create a mask, the Show Fill and Stroke setting is automatically turned on.

TIP If you use the Paste as Mask command, the Show Fill and Stroke setting is turned off.

Object Thumbnail   Mask Thumbnail

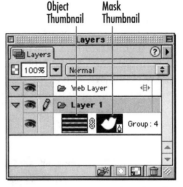

❷❸ *You can click either thumbnail to select the mask or the objects being masked.*

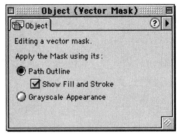

❷❹ *The* **Show Fill and Stroke setting** *in the Object panel.*

Photo courtesy of PhotoSpin

❷❺ *The Show Fill and Stroke command as applied to a mask.*

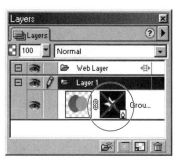

㉖ *The red cross over the Mask Thumbnail indicates that the mask has been temporarily disabled.*

㉗ *A new object can replace a mask or be added to a mask.*

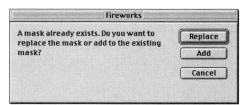

㉘ *Click* **Replace or Add** *to change the masking objects.*

㉙ *The result of adding an object to a mask.*

Sometimes it is easier to work if you don't have a mask to deal with. Fortunately, you can temporarily disable a mask.

To temporarily hide a mask:

1. Click the listing for the mask and the masking object in the Layers panel.

2. Choose Disable Mask from the Layers panel menu. A red cross appears over the Mask Thumbnail **㉖**. The effects of the mask are disabled.

To re-enable a mask:

♦ Click the Mask Thumbnail. This re-activates the effects of the mask.

A mask can consist of single or multiple objects. You can add to or replace the objects in a mask at any time.

To replace or add an object to a mask:

1. Create the object you want to add to the mask in the position where it should be when added to the mask **㉗**.

2. Select the object and choose **Edit > Cut** to send the object to the clipboard.

3. Click the Object Thumbnail in the Layers panel to select the object being masked.

4. If the object being masked is a bitmap image, choose **Modify > Exit Bitmap Mode**. This keeps the images selected as an object.

5. Choose **Edit > Paste as Mask**. A dialog box appears asking if you want to replace the current mask or add to it **㉘**.

6. Click Replace to delete the current mask and replace it with the object on the clipboard.

   or

   Click Add to add the object on the clipboard to the mask **㉙**.

Photo courtesy of PhotoSpin

Editing and Manipulating Masks

Ordinarily, a mask and the contents of the mask will move together. However, you may want to move the items separately to reposition either the mask or the objects being masked.

To move only the objects being masked:

1. Click the Object Thumbnail to select just the objects being masked. A cloverleaf mask handle appears.

2. Drag the mask handle **30**. This moves the objects being masked without disturbing the position of the mask.

To move only the mask:

1. Click the Link icon between the Object Thumbnail and the Mask Thumbnail **31**. This unlinks the mask from the objects being masked.

2. Use any of the object selection tools to move the mask.

TIP Once a mask has been unlinked from its objects, you can use any of the transformation tools or commands to change the objects being masked.

Photo courtesy of PhotoSpin

30 *Drag the* **cloverleaf mask handle** *to move the contents of the mask separately from the mask itself.*

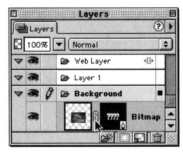

31 *Click the* **Link icon** *to allow you to move or transform the mask without disturbing the contents of the mask.*

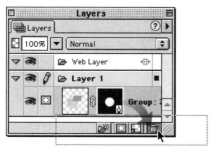

③② Drag the Mask Thumbnail *to apply or discard the mask.*

③③ *Drag the Mask Thumbnail below its listing to* **remove it as an object.**

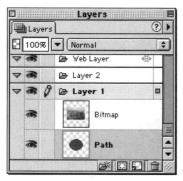

③④ *The mask object as it appears after being removed as an object.*

Applying and Discarding Masks

The beauty of a mask is that it hides objects without destroying any objects or pixels. There may come a time when you want to apply the mask to permanently change the appearance of the masked objects.

To apply a mask to its contents:

1. Drag the Mask Thumbnail into the Delete icon of the Layers panel **③②**. A dialog box appears asking how you want to apply the mask.

2. Choose Apply to delete those areas of the contents that were outside the boundaries of the mask. If the pixels of the underlying image had been altered in appearance by a grayscale mask, those pixels will be permanently changed.

TIP If the mask contains vector objects, the dialog box will state that applying the mask will convert the objects into a bitmapped image. If you do not want a bitmapped image, do not apply the mask. Instead, remove the mask as an object and then use the Crop command as described on page 99.

To discard a mask from its contents:

1. Drag the Mask Thumbnail into the Delete icon of the Layers panel. A dialog box appears asking how you want to apply the mask.

2. Choose Discard to delete the mask without changing its contents.

To remove a mask as an object:

♦ Drag the Mask Thumbnail below its listing in the Layers panel **③③**. This removes the mask and places it as an object on the document **③④**.

Using the Blending Modes

The Object panel lets you change how the colors of one object interact with objects below. This is similar to the layer blending modes in Adobe Photoshop.

To change the object blending mode:

1. Select the top object you want to change.
2. Use the blending mode pop-up list to choose the blending mode ⑤.

⑤ *The* **Blending mode** *pop-up list.*

For a color print-out of the blending modes shown in figures ㊱–㊽, *see the color pages.*

The Normal Blending Mode

Choose **Normal** ㊱ to have the top object not interact with the objects below it.

The Multiply Blending Mode

Choose **Multiply** to add the colors of the top object to the objects below ㊲. This is similar to the result of overprinting one object on top of another.

The Screen Blending Mode

Choose **Screen** to subtract the colors of the top object from the objects below ㊳. This is similar to the result of bleaching out one image from the other.

The Darken Blending Mode

Choose **Darken** to have the colors of the top object visible only where they are darker than the objects below ㊴.

The Lighten Blending Mode

Choose **Lighten** to have the colors of the top object visible only where they are lighter than the objects below ㊵.

㊱ *The result of the* **Normal** *blending mode.*

㊲ *The result of the* **Multiply** *blending mode.*

㊳ *The result of the* **Screen** *blending mode.*

㊴ *The result of the* **Darken** *blending mode.*

㊵ *The result of the* **Lighten** *blending mode.*

41 *The result of the* **Difference** *blending mode.*

42 *The result of the* **Hue** *blending mode.*

43 *The result of the* **Saturation** *blending mode.*

44 *The result of the* **Color** *blending mode.*

45 *The result of the* **Luminosity** *blending mode.*

46 *The result of the* **Invert** *blending mode.*

47 *The result of the* **Tint** *blending mode.*

48 *The result of the* **Erase** *blending mode.*

The Difference Blending Mode

Choose **Difference** to have the colors of the top object create an inversion between them and the objects below. The greater the difference, the lighter the color **41**.

The Hue Blending Mode

Choose **Hue** to have the hue of the top object applied to the objects below **42**.

The Saturation Blending Mode

Choose **Saturation** to have the saturation of the top object applied to the objects below **43**.

The Color Blending Mode

Choose **Color** to have both the hue and saturation of the top object applied to the objects below **44**.

The Luminosity Blending Mode

Choose **Luminosity** to have the lightness information of the top object applied to the objects below **45**.

The Invert Blending Mode

Choose **Invert** to have the shape of the top object reverse the colors of the objects below. For instance, black becomes white and green becomes red. The object's color has no effect on the Invert blend **46**.

The Tint Blending Mode

Choose **Tint** to have the color of the top object tint the objects below **47**.

The Erase Blending Mode

Choose **Erase** to have the top object hide the objects below. Only objects outside the top object are visible. The color of the top object has no effect on the results **48**.

Using the Blending Modes

AUTOMATION FEATURES 12

One of the challenges of creating Web graphics is that a typical Web site has hundreds of different images for graphics, buttons, and navigational elements. Once you've created those items, you may find it necessary to repeatedly change the look of many different elements.

Sure, you could open each file for the different elements and make the changes manually, but would you want to? Maybe if you were being paid by the hour, but not if you're trying to get the job done quickly.

Fortunately, Macromedia Fireworks provides you with many ways to automate creating objects and making changes. Some of these automation features, such as styles, should be prepared before you do too much work. Others, such as Find and Replace are useful in making changes to existing artwork. But no matter when you use these features, they all help you work faster and more efficiently.

Paste Attributes

If you have created an object with a certain set of intricate fill settings—for instance a special gradient, feathering, and texture—it might be cumbersome to reapply all those settings to another object created later. Rather, you can copy the settings from one object to another.

TIP Paste Attributes include stroke, fill, and effect settings. Paste Attributes from text objects will include font, size, style, and range kerning.

To paste attributes from one object to another:

1. Select the object with the attributes you want to copy.

2. Choose **Edit > Copy**.

3. Select the object with the attributes you want to change.

4. Choose **Edit > Paste Attributes**. The second object takes on all the settings of the first ❶.

TIP Changes made to gradients or patterns using the vector controls (*see page 113*) are not saved when copying and pasting attributes.

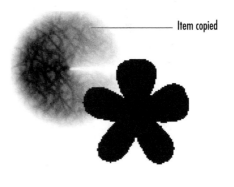

Item copied

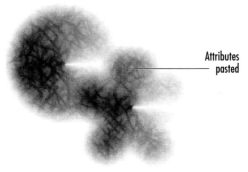

Attributes pasted

❶ *The result of applying the* **Paste Attributes** *command of the fill attributes, including color, feathered edge, and texture, of the circle object applied to the flower shape.*

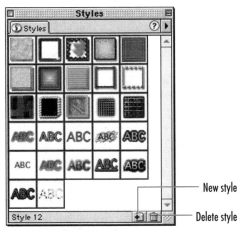

New style

Delete style

❷ *The* **Styles** *panel stores previews of the styles. These styles all come preset with Fireworks.*

❸ *The* **Edit Style dialog box** *lets you name the style and select which properties are included as part of the style.*

Using Styles

Styles are simply a way to store all the information about the fill, stroke, effect, or text settings. You can then easily apply the style to other objects without applying all the settings one by one. The Styles panel comes with an assortment of object and text styles that you can use. There are still more styles located on the Fireworks CD. However, most likely you will want to define your own styles.

To define an object style:

1. Open the Styles panel by choosing **Window**>**Styles** ❷.

2. Select an object and use the Fill, Stroke, and Effect panels to give the object any look you want.

3. With the object selected, click the New Style button at the bottom of the Styles panel. The Edit Style dialog box appears ❸.

4. Name the style.

5. Check the boxes for the properties you want the style to control.
    *   **Fill Type** controls a pattern, gradient, or Web dither.
    *   **Fill Color** controls the color of a fill.
    *   **Effect** controls the effect.
    *   **Stroke Type** controls the size and type of stroke.
    *   **Stroke Color** controls the color of a stroke.

6. Click OK to store the style in the Styles panel.

TIP The preview in the Styles panel is always a square, regardless of the shape that was used to define the style.

Using Styles

In addition to styles for objects, you can also define styles that apply text properties. Once you have defined a style, it is easy to apply that style to objects.

To define a text style:

1. Select a text block and use the Text Editor as well as the Fill, Stroke, and Effect panels to format the text.

2. With the formatted text block selected, click the New Style icon at the bottom of the Styles panel. The Edit Style dialog box appears ❹.

3. Use the Name field to name the style.

4. In addition to the object properties described on the previous page, check the boxes for which text properties you want the style to control.
   - **Text Font** controls the font.
   - **Text Size** controls the point size ❺.
   - **Text Style** controls styling such as Bold or Italic.

5. Click OK to store the style in the Styles panel.

TIP The preview in the Styles panel is always *ABC*, regardless of the text that was used to define the style.

To apply a style to objects:

1. Select the object or objects to which you want to apply the style.

2. Click the preview of the style ❻. The object changes according to the definition of the style.

TIP Unlike the styles in Macromedia FreeHand or other programs, Fireworks styles can't be used to update objects. Changing the definition of the style doesn't change the objects that have had the style previously applied to them.

❹ *The* **Edit Style** *dialog box lets you name the style and set which properties are included as part of the style.*

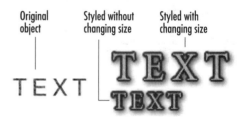

❺ *The difference between applying a style that affects the text size and one that does not.*

❻ *Click the* **style preview** *(circled) to apply a style to a selected object.*

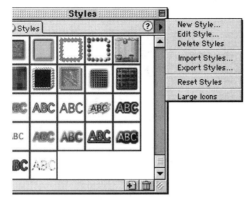

❼ *The* Styles panel menu.

Managing Styles

As you create more styles, the Styles panel can get pretty crowded. You can use the Export Styles, Delete Styles, and Import Styles commands to help manage your styles.

For instance, use the Export Styles command for all the styles that relate to a specific project. Then use the Delete Styles command to delete those styles.

Later, when you are working on that project, use the Import Styles command to add those styles back to the Styles panel.

This method helps keep your styles focused on your current project.

Once you define a style, it continues to appear in the Styles panel where you can access it for other documents. You can also save styles and export them to share with other people working on the same project.

To export styles:

1. In the Styles panel, select the style you want to export.

2. Select additional styles by holding the Command/Ctrl key and clicking the styles.

   TIP To select adjoining styles, select the style at one end of the group, hold down the Shift key, and click the style at the other end of the group. All styles between the first and last style are selected.

3. Choose Export Styles from the Styles panel menu ❼. A dialog box appears.

4. Use the dialog box to name the document that contains the styles and click Save.

To import styles:

1. Choose Import Styles from the Styles panel menu ❼.

2. Navigate to find the document that contains the styles you want to import.

3. Choose Open. The styles appear in the Styles panel.

If you have many styles in the panel, you can delete the ones you do not need.

To delete styles:

1. Select the styles you want to delete.

2. Click the Delete Styles button at the bottom of the Styles panel.

   or

   Open the Styles panel menu and choose Delete Styles.

Using Styles

Once you have defined a style, you can edit which properties of the style are applied to objects. For instance, you can turn off the effect and only have the fill and stroke applied to objects.

To edit styles:

1. Choose Edit from the Styles menu. This opens the Edit Style dialog box.

2. Make whatever changes you want and click OK.

You have two choices as to how the styles are displayed in the Styles panel. The large icons show more details in the styles but take up more room than the small icons.

To change the Styles panel views:

1. Choose Large Icons from the Styles panel menu. This increases the size of the preview in the Styles panel.

2. If Large Icons is already chosen, choose it again to change the previews to the small icons ❸.

If you have added and deleted styles, you can reset the Styles panel to the original styles that shipped with Fireworks.

To reset the styles to the defaults:

1. Choose Reset Styles from the Styles panel menu.

2. Click OK when the dialog box asks for confirmation.

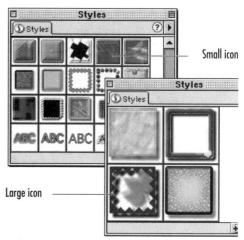

Small icon

Large icon

❸ *The difference between the* **small icons** *and the* **large icons** *in the Styles panel.*

◉ *The* **Find and Replace** *panel.*

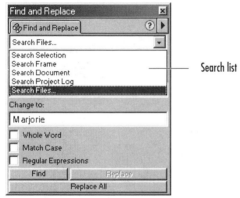

Search list

⑩ *The* **Search choices** *for Find and Replace.*

Working with Find and Replace

The Find and Replace panel lets you quickly change the formatting of vector and text objects. For example, you can find all instances of a certain font or color and then change them to something else.

TIP Find and Replace only works with vector and text objects.

To use the Find and Replace panel:

1. Choose **Window** > **Find and Replace** to open the Find and Replace panel **◉**.

2. Use the Search list as described below to specify the locations where the Find and Replace commands should search.

3. Choose which type of attributes, as described on pages 188.

4. Use the Find, Replace, and Replace All buttons as described on page 191 to control which elements should be replaced.

To set the Find and Replace search location:

1. Choose **Window** > **Find and Replace** to open the Find and Replace panel **◉**.

2. Open the Search list **⑩** and choose a place for the Find and Replace to occur as follows:

   - **Search Selection** searches among the currently selected items.
   - **Search Frame** searches in the current frame of the document. *(For more information on working with Frames, see Chapter 16, "Animations.")*
   - **Search Document** searches throughout the current document.
   - **Search Project Log** searches within all the files listed in the Project Log. *(For information on adding files to the Project Log, see page 193.)*
   - **Search Files** searches within a specific list of files.

3. If you choose Search Files, use the operating system dialog box to navigate to add files from different locations.

To set the search attributes:

◆ Choose one of the five attributes from the Find list ⑪.

- **Find Text** searches for specific words and changes them to others.
- **Find Font** searches and changes text attributes such as font, style, and point size.
- **Find Color** searches and changes colors of Fireworks objects.
- **Find URL** searches and changes the URLs within a document. *(For more information on working with URL links, see Chapter 17, "Hotspots and Links.")*
- **Find Non-Web 216 Colors** searches and changes colors so that they are part of the Web 216 palette.

TIP You can only search for one attribute at a time. So you can search and change all red objects and change them to green, but you can't search for red Courier text and change it to green Helvetica.

To find and replace text attributes:

1. Choose Find Text from the Attribute list. The text attributes appear ⑫.

2. In the Find field, type the text you want to locate.

3. In the Change to field, type the replacement text.

4. Check Whole Word to make sure the text only appears as a whole word and not part of another word.

5. Check Match Case to make sure the upper-case and lower-case letters match the text exactly as typed.

6. Check Regular Expressions to use special control characters in your find and replace text strings.

TIP For instance, entering the regular expression tag *s$* searches for the letter *s* that appears only at the end of a word or line.

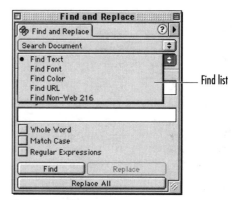

⑪ *The* **Find list** *in the Find and Replace panel allows you to specify the type of search.*

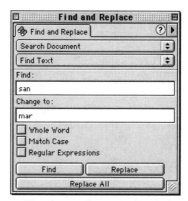

⑫ *The* **text attributes** *in the Find and Replace panel.*

Regular Expressions

Regular expressions are special symbols that can be added to change how the Find & Replace commands work. They work like the special symbols and wild card characters in word processing and page layout programs.

There are hundreds of different regular expressions—more than can be covered here. You can find more information on regular expressions at *http://developer. netscape.com/docs/manuals/communicator/ jsguide/regexp.htm.*

Character	Looks for	Example
^	The beginning of the input or line	^H finds the H in **Help** but not **FreeHand**
$	The end of the input or line	s$ finds the s in **Fireworks** but not **wish**
*	The preceding character that appears zero or more times	es* finds the es in **best** or the ess in **mess** or finds the e in **bet**
+	The preceding character that appears one or more times	es+ finds the es in **best** or the ess in **mess** but does not find the e in **bet**
?	The preceding character that appears zero or one times	st?on finds the **ston** in **Redstone** or the **son** in **Davidson** but does not find anything in **Littleton** or **Emerson**
.	Any single character except for the newsline character	.ealthy finds both **healthy** and **wealthy**
|	Either the characters before the | or the characters after the |	www|http finds both **www** or **http**
(n)	The preceding character when it occurs n number of times	e(2) finds ee in **sleep** or **keep** but not k**ept**
(n,m)	The preceding character when it occurs at least n times but not more than m times	FF(2,4) finds FF in **FF0000, FFF000** or **FFFF00**
[abc]	Any of the characters in the brackets	[abc] finds **a**, **b**, or **c**
[a-c]	Any of the characters in the range of the characters between the hyphen	[a-e] finds **a**, **b**, **c**, **d**, or **e**
[^abc]	Any character not enclosed in the brackets	[^aeiou] finds the **d** in **adapt** and the **c** in **ouch**
[^a-c]	Any of the characters not in the range of characters between the hyphen	[a-s] finds the **t** in **text** or **u** in **ugly**, but not the **a** in **apple**
\d	Any numerical character from 0 to 9	\d finds the 2 in **H20** or the 7 in **7th Heaven**
\D	Any non-numerical character (same as [^0-9])	\D finds the **th** in **7th** or the **rd** in **3rd**
\n	Line feed character	
\r	Carriage return	
\s	Any white space character such as a tab, form feed or line feed	\spress finds the **press** in **Peachpit press** but not **depressed**
\S	Any single non–white-space character	\Spress finds the **press** in **depressed** but not **Peachpit press**
\t	A tab character	
\W	Any non-alphanumeric character	\W finds characters such as the **&** in **Big & Tall** or the **@** in **@mindspring.com**

To find and replace Font attributes:

1. Choose Find Font from the Attribute list. The font attributes appear **13**.

2. Choose the typeface to search for from the Font list in the Find controls.

3. Set the replacement typeface from the Font list in the Change controls.

4. Set the type style to locate from the Style list in the Find controls.

TIP Use Any Font or Any Style to include all fonts or all styles in the search.

5. Set the replacement type style from the Style list in the Change controls.

TIP Use Same Style to retain the type style in the search.

6. Set a range of point sizes to be changed by entering minimum and maximum amounts in the Min and Max fields in the Find controls.

TIP To set a single point size to change, delete any amount in the Min field and enter an amount in the Max field.

7. Set the point size to be changed by entering the amount in the Size list in the Change controls.

To set the Color attributes:

1. Choose Find Color from the Attribute list. The color attributes appear **14**.

2. Use the Find Color Well to select the color to change.

3. Use the Change to Color Well to set the replacement color.

4. Use the Apply to list **15** to set which properties should change.
   - **Fills & Strokes** changes the fills and strokes but not effects.
   - **All Properties** changes the fills, strokes, and effects.
   - **Fills**, **Strokes**, or **Effects** changes just one of those attributes.

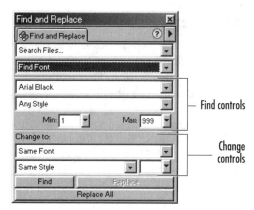

13 *The* **Find Font attributes** *in the Find and Replace panel.*

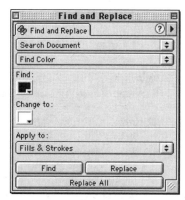

14 *The* **Find Color attributes** *in the Find and Replace panel.*

15 *The* **Apply to** *list for the attributes changes.*

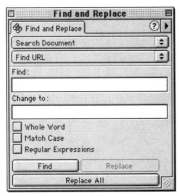

⑯ *The* URL attributes *in the Find and Replace panel.*

⑰ *The* Non-Web 216 attributes *in the Find and Replace panel.*

⑱ *The* Find, Replace, *and* Replace All *buttons in the Find and Replace panel.*

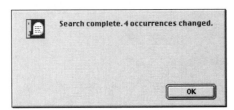

⑲ *The* Search complete *dialog box tells you the results of the Find and Replace command.*

To find and replace URL attributes:

1. Choose Find URL from the Attribute list. The URL attributes appear **⑯**.
2. In the Find field, type the URL to search for.
3. Type the replacement URL in the Change to field.

TIP Set the Whole Word, Match Case, and Regular Expressions as described on page 189.

You can also use the Find and Replace controls to change all non-Web-safe colors to their closest Web-safe equivalent.

TIP This command only works on native Fireworks objects, not scanned or bitmap images.

To search for Non-Web 216 Colors:

1. Choose Find Non-Web 216 from the attribute pop-up list. The Non-Web 216 attributes appear **⑰**.
2. Use the Apply to list to set which properties should change *(see the description on the previous page)*.

To use the Find, Replace, and Replace All buttons:

1. Click Find **⑱** to select the first object that meets the search criteria.
2. Click Replace **⑱** to change that one instance.

   or

   Click Replace All **⑱** to change all the elements that meet the search criteria.

TIP If you choose Replace All, a dialog box appears telling you when the search is complete and how many changes were made **⑲**.

Working with Find and Replace

It's not enough to make changes to multiple files. You also need to control what happens to the original files when you make those changes. To do so, you need to set the Replace Options.

To set the Replace Options:

1. Choose Replace Options from the Find and Replace panel menu ⓴. This opens the Replace Options dialog box ㉑.

2. Choose Save and Close Files to automatically save and close the files as they are changed.

3. Choose one of the options from the Backup Original Files list:
   - **No Backups** overwrites the original file with the changed file.
   - **Overwrite Existing Backups** makes a backup copy of the file, but then further changes will overwrite those backup files.
   - **Incremental Backups** makes backup files each time the changes are made, numbering each of the backups.

You can keep a record of what files have been changed and when the changes were made by adding the files to the Project Log.

To add the changed files to the Project Log:

◆ Choose Add Files to Project Log from the Find and Replace panel menu.

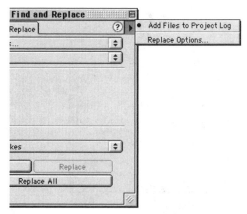

⓴ *The* Find and Replace panel menu.

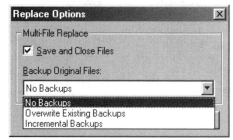

㉑ *The* Replace Options dialog box.

Frame   Date and Time

㉒ *The* **Project Log** *panel.*

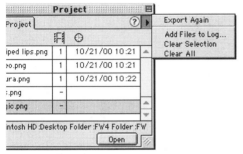

㉓ *The* **Project Log** *menu.*

Using the Project Log

It may be difficult to remember all the files associated with a Web site or project. The Project Log gives you an easy way to organize these files into groups. You can also use the Project Log as part of a Find and Replace routine *(see pages 187–192).*

To add or delete Project Log files:

1. Choose **Window** > **Project Log** to open the Project Log panel **㉒**.

2. Choose Add Files to Log from the Project Log menu **㉓**.

3. Use the operating system dialog box to navigate to select the files to be added to the Project Log.

4. Select an item or items in the Project Log and then choose Clear Selection to delete the selected files from the Project Log.

   or

   Choose Clear All to delete all the files from the Project Log.

TIP The Project Log frame and date columns show which frames have been altered and the most recent modification date using Find and Replace.

The files in the Project Log can also be exported using the current export settings.

To export files from the Project Log:

1. Set the Export defaults as desired. *(See Chapter 20, "Exporting," for setting the Export defaults.)*

2. Select the files in the Project Log that you want to export.

3. Choose Export Again from the Project Log menu. This lets you save each of the exported files.

Scripting Commands

At its simplest function, the History panel acts as a list from which you can undo and redo commands *(see page 45)*. It can also be used as part of JavaScript commands that can automate complex actions.

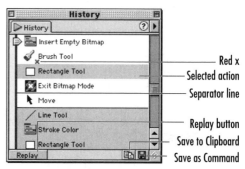

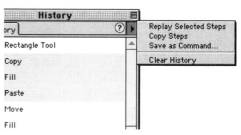

❷❹ *The* **History** panel *allows you to replay actions and turn them into scripts.*

To replay a set of actions:

1. If the History panel is not visible, choose **Window>History** to open the History panel **❷❹**.

2. Use the Shift key to select the range of actions you want to replay.

TIP The History panel displays a red *x* or separator line between actions that cannot be replayed together. For instance, you cannot replay drawing with the Paintbrush.

3. Click the Replay button.

   or

   Choose Replay Selected Steps from the History panel menu **❷❺**.

❷❺ *The* **History** panel menu.

To store actions as a script:

1. Select a range of actions in the History panel.

2. Use the Shift key to select the range of actions you want to replay. Use the Cmd/Ctrl key to select non-contiguous actions.

3. Click the Save as Command button.

   or

   Choose Save as Command from the History panel menu **❷❺**.

4. Use the Save Command dialog box **❷❻** to name the command. The command automatically appears under the Commands menu.

TIP Commands are JavaScript (.jsf) files stored in the folder Fireworks 4: Configuration: Commands.

❷❻ *The* **Save Command** *dialog box allows you to name a command created by the History panel.*

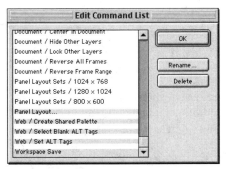

27 *The* **Edit Command List** *dialog box allows you to rename or delete commands that appear in the Commands menu.*

Sharing Commands with Dreamweaver

Macromedia Dreamweaver also uses .jsf commands. This makes it possible to have a command in Dreamweaver that also controls actions in Fireworks.

Many of these commands are available as free downloads at the Macromedia Dreamweaver Exchange: *www.macromedia.com/exchange/dreamweaver.* This includes commands such as Joseph Lowery's BulletBuilder which converts the bullets of an unordered list to a graphic, generated by Fireworks.

Fireworks Commands

You can also download over a hundred free, Fireworks commands at: *http://comharsa.com/firefaq.*

These include animations, batch processing, and special effects.

Once you save a command, it appears under the Command menu in the menu bar. You can run these commands any time.

To play back commands:

◆ Choose the command listed under the Commands menu.

TIP Fireworks ships with several commands that make it easier to perform several commonly used tasks. These commands are listed under the Commands menu.

You can also create commands that will automatically rearrange your onscreen panels back into your own favorite positions. This is extremely helpful for those people who open and close panels; move them around; and then can't find the panel they need to work with.

To save a panel layout:

1. Arrange the panels and toolbars in the configuration you want to save.

2. Choose **Commands**> **Panel Layout**.

3. Name the layout and click OK. The panel layout appears under the Panel Layouts Sets submenu in the Commands menu.

To use the Panel Layout command:

◆ Select the panel arrangement from the **Commands** >**Panel Layout Sets** submenu.

To edit the commands list:

1. Choose **Commands** >**Edit Command List**. The dialog box appears **27**.

2. Select the command you want to edit.

3. Click Rename to rename a command.

4. Click Delete to delete commands you no longer want on the list.

TIP The Delete command cannot be undone so make sure you have chosen the right command.

As mentioned, the Fireworks commands are written in a Web-scripting language called JavaScript. This is the same language many people use to program commands for Web sites. This means you can write your own commands for Fireworks actions.

TIP Learning the JavaScript necessary to write your own Fireworks commands is well beyond the scope of this book. However, the following exercise gives you the steps you need to take to write the JavaScript command.

To write your own JavaScript command:

1. Start a new document in a text editor or word processing program.

2. Open one of the commands that ship with Fireworks or type your own commands.

3. Make any changes to the command.

   or

   Type your own JavaScript commands.

4. Save the file as a text file with the extension .jsf.

5. Place the file in the Fireworks 4: Configuration: Commands folder. The command will then be available under the Fireworks Commands menu.

TIP You can create a sub-folder in the Commands folder to hold your own scripts.

Understanding a Command JavaScript

One way to begin learning how to write JavaScripts is to examine the commands that ship with Fireworks. Here's a step-by-step breakdown of what's going on inside the command labeled, "Center in Document."

The first part checks to make sure there is a selected object. If not, the script won't run.

```
if (fw.selection != null && fw.selection.
length > 0) {
```

The script gets the document size.

```
var docWidth = fw.getDocumentDOM().
width;
var docHeight = fw.getDocumentDOM().
height;
var docLeft = fw.getDocumentDOM().left;
var docTop = fw.getDocumentDOM().top;
```

This section does the math to find the coordinates of the middle of the document. Notice it uses values obtained in the previous section.

```
var middleWidth = docWidth/2;
var middleHeight = docHeight/2;
```

Next, the script gets the size of the selected objects.

```
var selectBounds = fw.getDocumentDOM
().getSelectionBounds();
var selectLeft = selectBounds.left;
var selectTop = selectBounds.top;
var selectRight = selectBounds.right;
var selectBottom = selectBounds.bottom;
```

The script then does the math to find the middle of the selection.

```
var selectMiddleWidth = (selectRight -
selectLeft)/2;
var selectMiddleHeight = (selectBottom -
selectTop)/2;
```

Next the script finds where to move the selection.

```
var moveToX = docLeft + middleWidth -
selectMiddleWidth - selectLeft;
var moveToY = docTop + middleHeight -
selectMiddleHeight - selectTop;
```

Finally, the script moves the selection!

```
fw.getDocumentDOM().moveSelectionBy({
x:moveToX, y:moveToY}, false, false);}
```

㉘ *The first* **Batch Process** *dialog box lets you select the files for batch processing.*

The Power of Batch Processing

A typical Web site can contain hundreds, even thousands, of images. When you need to make changes, you don't want to have to open and modify each file one by one.

Combining the different options together makes Fireworks's batch processing commands a very powerful tool. You choose the files you want to change, pick the changes you want to make, and let Fireworks do the rest.

Fireworks opens the files, makes the changes, exports them, and closes the originals automatically.

Batch Processing Changes

Batch processing allows you to combine exporting, scaling, find and replace, renaming, and commands together into one super-command that can be applied to many files at once.

To set the batch processing options:

1. Choose **File > Batch Process**. The Batch Process (Mac) or Batch (Win) dialog box appears **㉘**.

2. Set the files for batch processing as described in the next exercise.

3. Set the Batch Options as described on the next page.

4. Set the renaming controls as described on page 199.

5. Set the destination controls as described on page 200.

TIP You can batch process any native Fireworks file as well as any other file that Fireworks can open. This includes scans or FreeHand files.

There are several different ways to set which files should be part of batch processing.

To choose the files for batch processing:

1. In the Batch Process dialog box **㉘**, use the navigation controls to select the files for batch processing.

2. Click the Add, Add all, or Remove buttons to add or delete the files for batch processing.

3. Choose Include Files from Project Log to batch process those files listed in the Project Log.

4. Choose Include Current Open Files to batch process the files that are currently open.

Once you have selected the files for processing, you can choose what commands you want to apply to the files.

To set the commands for batch processing:

1. Click the Next button in the Batch Processing dialog box to open the second dialog box **⑳**. This is where you can set which commands should be made part of the batch processing.

2. Choose an option from the list under Batch Options. (These options are described in the following exercises.)

3. Use the Add button to add that option to the right side.

4. Use the up or down arrows to set the order that the option should run.

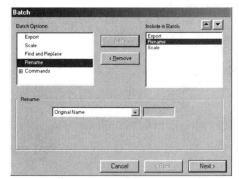

⑳ *Choose which of the* **Batch Options** *should be included in the batch processing.*

The export controls let you choose how the file should be optimized for viewing on the Web. *(For more information on the export commands, see Chapter 20, "Exporting.")*

To set the controls for the Export option:

◆ Use the Settings list to choose one of the export options **㉚**.

or

Click the Edit button to open the Export Preview dialog box which lets you create a new set of export options.

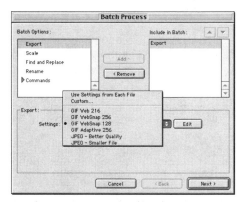

㉚ *The* **Export controls** *of batch processing.*

The scale controls let you choose the final size of the images.

To set the controls for the Scale option:

◆ Use the Scale list to choose one of the scaling options **㉛**:

- **No Scaling** leaves the images at their original size.
- **Scale to Size** lets you set a specific pixel dimensions.
- **Scale to Fit Area** lets you set a maximum height or width.
- **Scale to Percentage** lets you set the percentage of change.

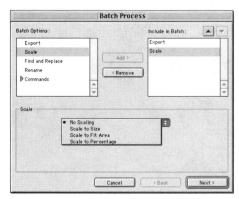

㉛ *The* **Scale controls** *of batch processing.*

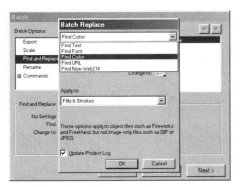

32 *The* Batch Replace controls.

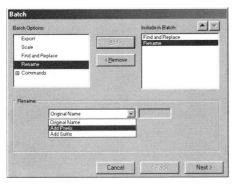

33 *The* Rename controls *of batch processing.*

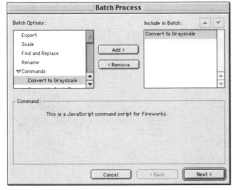

34 *The* Commands controls *of batch processing.*

The Batch Replace controls let you look for certain attributes in a file and replace them with others.

To set the Batch Replace controls:

◆ Use the Batch Replace panel to change the various options in the file **32**. *(These are the same controls found in the Find and Replace panel covered on page 187.)*

You can also control the naming conventions used for the new files. For instance, you may want to add a suffix to indicate the new files are different from the old ones.

To set the Rename controls:

◆ Use the Rename pop-up list to choose to add a prefix or suffix to the changed files **33**.

The Commands controls let you add your own custom JavaScript commands as part of the batch processing.

To set the Commands controls:

◆ Choose one of the JavaScripts listed under the Commands section **34**.

Batch Processing Changes

Finally, you use the Saving Files controls to set where you want the new files to be saved 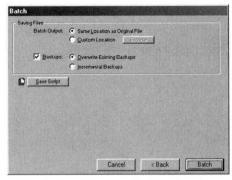.

To set destination options for batch processing:

1. Set the Batch Output for the Same Location as Original File.

   or

   Choose Custom Location and then click the Browse button to choose a new location for the files.

2. If desired, check the Backups option to make backups of the original files.

3. If you choose Backups, you can choose Overwrite Existing Backups to have any new backups erase older ones.

   or

   You can choose Incremental Backups to add to the backups by making numbered copies of the originals.

4. Click the Batch button to run the complete batch processing.

㉟ *The* **Saving Files** *controls of batch processing.*

Once you have made all the settings for the batch processing, you can then save them as a JavaScript that can be run over and over. For instance, if you receive a large number of scans every month that need to be scaled and exported, you can run the batch process script rather than have to reset the batch options.

To save the batch settings as a script:

◆ Click the Save Script button. A dialog box lets you choose where to save the .jsf file.

WORKING WITH PIXELS | 13

It is the vector objects in Macromedia Fireworks that make it so easy to use. But what if you want to use images such as photographs or scanned art that cannot be created by vector objects?

Fortunately there is an alter ego to the vector side of Fireworks—a complete set of features for creating, importing, and working with pixel-based artwork. This is similar to the pixel-editing features found in programs such as Adobe Photoshop, Jasc Paint Shop Pro, and Corel Painter.

Although technically the correct term for these graphics is pixel-based or raster images, Macromedia calls them *bitmap images.*

Please note that the title of this chapter, *Working with Pixels,* has nothing to do with my cat, Pixel, even though she would like to think I wrote an entire chapter all about her.

Switching to the Bitmap Mode

If you want to work with photographs, scans, or other pixel images, you must switch to the bitmap mode.

To use the bitmap mode features:

◆ Choose **File > Open** and choose a scanned or pixel-based image. The image automatically opens in the bitmap mode, unless you have changed the bitmap preferences *(see page 219)*.

TIP The thick striped line around the image indicates that the bitmap mode tools are available **❶**.

or

Double-click a bitmap image with either the Pointer or Subselection tools.

To switch back to vector drawing:

◆ Choose **Modify > Exit Bitmap Mode**. This brings you back to the normal vector-drawing mode.

or

Click the Exit Bitmap Mode button **❶**.

To create a bitmap image from scratch:

1. Choose **Insert > Bitmap Image**. The striped line appears around the edge of the image, indicating you are working in the bitmap mode.

2. Use any of the tools in their bitmap mode to paint or modify the area inside the empty image **❷**.

TIP All the vector tools are available in the bitmap mode except the Pen tool.

3. Choose **Modify > Exit Bitmap Mode**. The area of the empty image shrinks to the size of the area that was painted or modified.

TIP Artwork created in the bitmap mode is not as versatile as artwork created in the vector drawing mode.

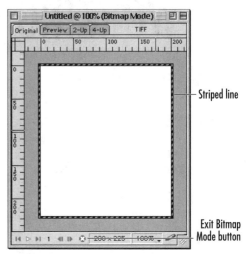

— Striped line

Exit Bitmap
— Mode button

❶ *The* **striped line** *indicates the artwork can be edited using the bitmap mode tools.*

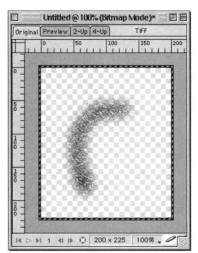

❷ *Inserting a* **bitmap image** *allows you to use any of the bitmap mode tools, such as the Brush tool shown here, to paint inside the area.*

❸ *The* **import pointer** *for imported artwork.*

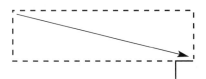

❹ *Dragging the import pointer places the imported artwork at a specific size. (The arrow indicates the direction of the drag.)*

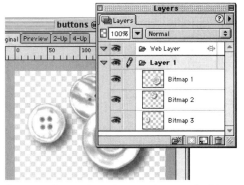

❺ Layers from Photoshop *are imported with each of the Photoshop layers as their own bitmap image in Fireworks.*

Importing Bitmap Images

You can insert bitmap images into Fireworks files. These can be files created by programs such as Adobe Photoshop or Corel Painter.

To import bitmap images:

1. With a file open, choose **File** > **Import** or **Insert** > **Image** and navigate to find the file you want to import.

2. Click OK. A small import pointer **❸** indicates the file is ready for placing on the currently selected Fireworks layer.

3. Click to simply place the image at its original size.

    or

    Drag the import pointer to draw a rectangle that scales the image to fit **❹**.

You can also open bitmap images as a Fireworks document.

To open bitmap images:

1. Choose **File** > **Open**.

2. Navigate to find the bitmap image file and click OK.

3. The file opens as a Fireworks document.

    TIP If the Photoshop file contains layers, each of the layers appears in its own layer as a bitmap image **❺**.

Manipulating Bitmap Images

If you have bitmap images in your Fireworks files, you may want to crop those images to eliminate pixels you don't need.

To crop bitmap images:

1. Select a pixel image.

2. Choose **Edit** >**Crop Selected Bitmap**. A bounding box with handles appears around the image ➏.

3. Drag the handles so that they surround the area you want to keep.

4. Double-click inside the bounding box. The excess image is deleted.

You can also combine bitmaps, turn vector objects into bitmaps, or add vector objects to bitmaps.

To combine or convert objects:

1. Select the objects you want to combine or convert ➐.

TIP Select a single vector object to convert it to a pixel-based image object.

2. Choose **Modify** >**Convert to Bitmap**. Vector objects are converted to pixels and separate bitmap images are combined into a single bitmap ➑.

TIP If you convert vector objects into image objects, you lose the ability to edit the paths that defined the vector objects.

➏ The **crop handles** let you discard portions of imported images.

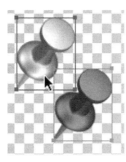

➐ Two imported images can be moved or manipulated as separate images.

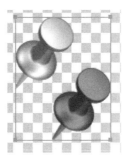

➑ The **Convert to Bitmap** command combines the two imported images into one image object.

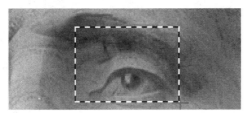

❾ *The* **Marquee tools** *in the Tools panel.*

❿ *The* **marching ants** *of the marquee surround the selected area.*

Width   Constraints list

⓫ *The* Marquee Tool Options *panel.*

Height

Edge list

Selecting Pixels

The basic bitmap selection tools are the two Marquee tools, rectangle and ellipse, and the two Lasso tools, regular and polygon.

TIP As you start to use the Marquee tools, you automatically switch to the bitmap mode.

To use the Marquee tools:

1. Press the Marquee tool in the Tools panel and choose either the rectangular or elliptical shape **❾**.

2. Move the cursor over the image area and drag diagonally to create a selection. A series of moving dashes (called *marching ants*) indicates the selected area **❿**.

TIP Press the mouse and then hold the Opt/Alt key to draw the selection from the center outward, instead of from the corner.

TIP Hold the Shift key to constrain the selection to a square or circle.

The marquee tool styles let you set specific sizes or proportions for the selected area.

To change the Marquee tool constraints:

1. Double-click either of the marquee tools in the Tools panel to open the Marquee Tool Options panel **⓫**.

2. Choose one of the following from the Styles list:

   - **Normal** creates a marquee without any constraints on its size.
   - **Fixed Ratio** constrains the marquee to the sizes in the width and the height fields.
   - **Fixed Size** constrains the marquee to the pixel amounts in the width and height fields.

Selecting Pixels

You can also change the appearance of the edges of a marquee selection.

To change the Marquee tool edges:

1. In the Marquee Tool Options panel, choose from the Edge list 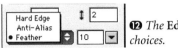.

   - **Hard Edge** gives the selection a solid or jagged edge 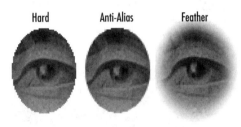.
   - **Anti-Alias** gives the selection a smoother edge .
   - **Feather** blurs the edges of the selection .

2. If you choose Feather, set the amount of the blur with the control slider or type the amount of the feather (in pixels) in the field.

12 *The Edge list choices.*

13 *The effects of changing the edge choices of a selection.*

You might want to select shapes besides rectangles and ellipses. To do so, you can use either of the Lasso tools.

To use the Lasso tools:

1. Press the Lasso tool in the Tools panel and choose either the regular or the polygon lasso 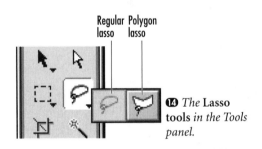.

2. Use the Edge list in the Options panel to choose among Hard Edge, Anti-Alias, or Feather.

3. With the regular lasso, drag around the area you want to select **15**.

   or

   With the polygon lasso, click the cursor around the area you want to select. Each click creates a point of the polygon that selects the area **15**.

   TIP The regular lasso is useful for following the curved contours of images. The polygon lasso is best for creating selections with straight sides.

14 *The Lasso tools in the Tools panel.*

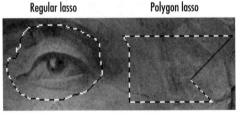

15 *A comparison of the Regular lasso and the Polygon lasso.*

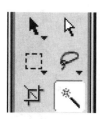

⑯ *The* **Magic Wand** *in the Tools panel.*

Edge list

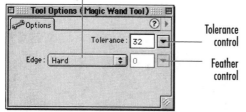

Tolerance control

Feather control

⑰ *The* Magic Wand Tool Options.

⑱ *The* area selected with the Magic Wand.

You can also select areas by their color. To do this, you use the Magic Wand.

To use the Magic Wand:

1. Choose the Magic Wand in the Tools panel **⑯**.

2. In the Magic Wand Tool Options panel **⑰**, use the Tolerance control to set how many colors the Magic Wand selects.

3. Use the Edge list in the Tool Options panel to choose among Hard Edge, Anti-Alias, or Feather (*see the previous page*).

4. Click the area you want to select. The marching ants indicate the selected area **⑱**.

After you finish working with a selection, you can deselect the selected area.

To deselect a selected area:

◆ Click outside the selection with one of the Marquee or Lasso tools.

   or

   Choose **Edit** > **Deselect**.

TIP You cannot deselect with the Magic Wand tool by clicking outside the selection. This only selects a different area.

To hide the marching ants around a selection:

◆ Choose **View** > **Hide Edges** to hide the display of the marching ants around a selection.

TIP The selection remains in effect, you just don't see the marching ants that define its boundaries.

Setting the Tolerance

Tolerance controls how many similar colors the Magic Wand selects that are adjacent to the original point where you click. The lowest tolerance, 0, selects only one color, the exact color of the pixel clicked with the Magic Wand. As you increase the tolerance, up to 255, the Magic Wand selects a greater range of colors.

Selecting Pixels

You can change a selected area by using modifier keys with any of the selection tools.

To change the shape of selections:

With an area selected, use any of the selection tools.

- Hold the Shift key to add to the selected area. A plus (+) sign indicates you are adding to the selection **⓳**.

- Hold the Opt/Alt key to delete from the selected area. A minus (–) sign indicates you are subtracting from the selection **⓴**.

TIP You can switch tools at any time. For instance, if the original selection was created by the Magic Wand, you can use the Lasso to modify it.

TIP The additional selection does not have to touch the original. For instance, you can select the top and bottom of an image, leaving the middle untouched.

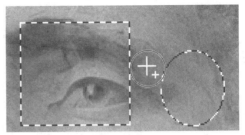

⓳ *Hold the Shift key to* **add** to a selection.

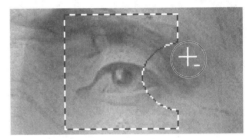

⓴ *Hold the Opt/Alt key to* **delete from a** selection.

Rather than use marquee, lasso, or Magic Wand tools, you can also use menu commands to select pixels. Because these commands have keyboard shortcuts, the shortcuts make it easier to select and deselect areas.

To use the Selection commands:

- Choose **Edit** > **Select All** to select all the pixels in the image.

- Choose **Edit** > **Deselect** to deselect the pixels enclosed by the marching ants.

- Choose **Modify** > **Marquee** > **Select Inverse** to swap the status of the selected pixels, that is, deselect the selected pixels and select everything else.

㉑ *Before the* **Select Similar** *command (top), only the color the the letter K is selected. After the* **Select Similar** *command is applied (bottom), other areas with a similar color are selected.*

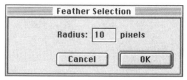

㉒ *The* **Feather Selection** *dialog box.*

Glow indicates feathering

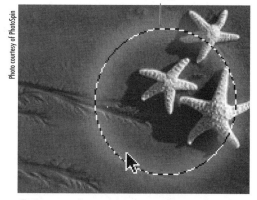

㉒ *Press on the marching ants to see a glow that indicates the area that is feathered.*

Once you have selected a certain area with the Magic Wand, you might not want to keep clicking to select similar colors.

To use the Similar command:

With an area selected, choose **Modify > Marquee > Select Similar**. This selects all the areas of the image that have the same color **㉑**.

TIP The Select Similar command uses the tolerance set for the Magic Wand.

TIP You can also use the Select Similar command on selections created by the Marquee or Lasso tools.

To feather a selection:

1. With the area selected, choose **Edit > Feather** to open the Feather Selection dialog box **㉒**.

2. Enter the number of pixels that you want to blur along the edge of the selection and then click OK.

TIP To see the feathering, position the Pointer tool over the marching ants and press the mouse button. The feathering is displayed as a glow in the image **㉓**.

Selecting Pixels

Once you have made a selection, you can change the size or shape of the selection using the Marquee commands:

To expand the size of a selections:

1. With an area selected, choose **Modify** > **Marquee** > **Expand**. This opens the Expand dialog box ㉔.

2. Set the size (in pixels) of how much to increase the marquee area.

3. Click OK. The size of the selection increases ㉕.

To contract the size of a selections:

1. With an area selected, choose **Modify** > **Marquee** > **Contract**. This opens the Contract dialog box ㉔.

2. Set the size (in pixels) of how much to decrease the marque area.

3. Click OK. The size of the selection decreases ㉕.

To create a border around a selections:

1. With an area selected, choose **Modify** > **Marquee** > **Border**. This opens the Border dialog box ㉔.

2. Set the size (in pixels) of the radius of the border.

3. Click OK. The selected area is converted into a border ㉕.

To smooth the edges of a selections:

1. With an area selected, choose **Modify** > **Marquee** > **Smooth**. This opens the Smooth dialog box ㉔.

2. Set the size (in pixels) of how big an area should be smoothed.

3. Click OK. The shape of the selection changes ㉕.

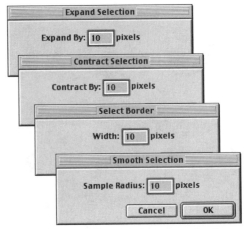

㉔ *The* Expand Selection, Contract Selection, Select Border, and Smooth Selection *dialog boxes.*

Original selection

Photo courtesy of PhotoSpin

Expand Selection   Contract Selection

Select Border   Smooth Selection

㉕ *The results of applying the* Expand Selection, Contract Selection, Select Border, and Smooth Selection *commands to a selection.*

Working with Selections

Move Selection cursor

Photo courtesy of PhotoSpin

㉖ *A selection can be moved without disturbing the pixels of the image inside the selection.*

Cut Selection cursor

㉗ *A selection and its contents can be cut from its image.*

Copy Selection cursor

㉘ *A selection can be moved while making a copy of the contents.*

Working with Selections

Once you made a selection, there are all sorts of things you can do with it. For instance, you might want to move the selection, so that it is exactly over a certain area, without disturbing the pixels beneath it. You can move both the selection and the image. Finally, you can simultaneously move the selection and copy the image.

To move a selection:

1. With one of the bitmap selection tools chosen, move the cursor within the marching ants selection. The cursor changes to the move selection cursor **㉖**.

2. Drag the selection to a new position.

To move a selection and the image:

1. With one of the bitmap selection tools chosen, hold the Cmd/Ctrl key and move the cursor within the marching ants selection. The cursor changes to the cut selection cursor **㉗**.

2. Drag the selection and image to the new position.

To move a selection and copy the image:

1. With one of the bitmap selection tools chosen, hold the Cmd+Opt (Mac) or Ctrl+Alt (Win) keys and move the cursor within the marching ants selection. The cursor changes to the copy selection cursor **㉘**.

2. Drag the selection and image to the new position.

   TIP Copying a selection adds it to the currently chosen bitmap. *(See the next page for how to copy a selection as a separate bitmap.)*

You can delete the image within a selection.

To delete the image inside a selection:

◆ With the selection active, press the Delete (Backspace) key.

Using a combination of the selection commands, you can create a vignette (faded cropping) of an image.

To create a vignette:

1. Use any of the bitmap selection tools to select the area that should appear inside the vignette. For example, use the elliptical marquee to create an oval vignette.

2. Choose **Modify** > **Marquee** > **Feather** to apply a soft blur to the edge of the selection.

TIP You can also apply the feather to the selection using the Options panel for the selection tool.

3. Choose **Modify** > **Marquee** > **Select Inverse**. This selects the area that should be deleted **㉙**.

4. Press Delete/Backspace to delete the area outside the original selection **㉚**.

You can also copy the image inside a selection and then paste it into a separate bitmapped image in the same Fireworks document or a new document.

To copy a selection into a new bitmapped image:

1. Use any of the bitmap selection tools to select the area that should appear inside the vignette.

2. Choose **Edit** > **Copy**.

3. Click the Add Layer icon in the Layers panel.

4. Choose **Edit** > **Paste**. The area inside the selection appears on the new layer.

㉙ *To vignette an image, select the area that you want to delete.*

㉚ *Press the Delete/Backspace key to delete the selected area from the image.*

Working with Selections

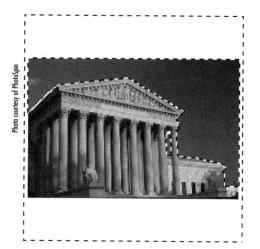

Photo courtesy of PhotoSpin

31 *The shape of a selection can be stored with a document.*

Saving and Restoring Selections

Selections are fragile little creatures. If you deselect the selection, or exit the bitmap mode, you lose the marching ants that you worked so hard to shape just so. Fortunately, you can save the shape of the selection. Once you have saved a selection, you can reapply it at any time.

To save a selection shape:

♦ With the area selected **31**, choose **Modify > Marquee > Save Selection**. The shape of the selection is stored with the document.

TIP Only one selection is saved at a time. If you save another selection you delete the previously saved selection.

To reapply a stored selection shape:

♦ In the bitmap mode, choose **Modify > Marquee > Restore Selection**. The shape of the selection is reapplied.

TIP The saved selection is stored inside the document and can be applied even after the document is closed and reopened.

Save the Pixel!

I hate to lose pixels. They're much too valuable to just throw away.

So instead of permanently destroying the pixel data by deleting a selection, I'd rather use a mask to hide the area inside a selection. *(See To Save a Selection as a mask on the next page.)*

Saving and Restoring Selections

Another way to save a selection is to convert the shape into a mask. This converts the shape of the marching ants into a grayscale mask. *(For more information on working with masks, see Chapter 11, "Masks and Interactions.")*

To save a selection as a mask:

1. Create a selection around the area that you want to hide.

2. Click the Add Mask icon at the bottom of the Layers panel. A mask is created that follows the contours of the marching ants **32**.

   or

   Choose **Modify** > **Mask** > **Hide Selection** to create a mask that follows the contours of the marching ants **33**.

To save an inverted selection as a mask:

1. Create a selection around the area that you want to keep visible.

2. Choose **Modify** > **Mask** > **Reveal Selection**. This creates a mask that shows the object within the contours of the marching ants **34**.

To convert a mask into an image:

♦ Drag the Mask Thumbnail in the Layers panel below the image to convert it into a bitmap object.

Add Mask icon

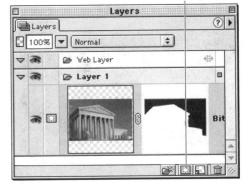

32 *When a selection is active, click the the* **Add Mask icon** *to automatically convert the selection into a grayscale image that masks the original image.*

33 *The* **Hide Selection** *command creates a mask that hides the selected area.*

34 *The* **Reveal Selection** *command creates a mask around the area that is not selected.*

35 *The* **Rubber Stamp** *in the Tools panel.*

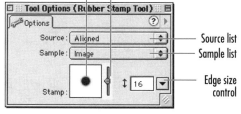

36 *The* **Rubber Stamp Tool Options** panel.

How the Rubber Stamp Works

Digital rubber stamps (such as the ones found in Fireworks or Photoshop) simply copy the image from one area and paint it onto another. This lets you paint part of one image onto another.

However, the Rubber Stamp tool does not recognize specific shapes or items. If you drag with the Rubber Stamp in a large enough area, you copy the image from one area to another.

Using the Pixel Tools

Most tools, such as the Paint Brush and Pencil, have both vector and pixel-based modes. The Rubber Stamp tool, however, works only on pixel images, not vector objects. The Rubber Stamp tool acts like a paintbrush, but instead of painting with a solid color, you paint with an image.

To set the Rubber Stamp options:

1. Choose the Rubber Stamp tool in the Tools panel **35**.

2. In the Rubber Stamp Tool Options **36**, how to control the source:

   TIP The source is where the Rubber Stamp tool samples the image.

   - **Aligned Source** keeps the source positioned along with the movements of the mouse.

   TIP Use Aligned Source when you want to be able to release the mouse button but not lose the position you are copying.

   - **Fixed Source** returns the source to the original click point when you release the mouse.

   TIP Use Fixed Source when you want to make multiple copies of a part of the image.

3. Use the Sample list to choose:
   - **Image** samples only the area inside the image.
   - **Document** samples anywhere inside the document.

   TIP Document sampling lets you sample vector objects to paint them as pixels.

4. Use the Edge size control to specify the size of the Rubber Stamp brush.

5. Use the Edge softness control to change the softness of the Rubber Stamp edge.

Using the Pixel Tools

To use the Rubber Stamp tool:

1. Position the Rubber Stamp tool over the area that you want to copy.

2. Opt/Alt-click. A circle appears that indicates the source point.

3. Move the Rubber Stamp cursor where you want to paint with the sample and press and drag. The source point follows your movements as the Rubber Stamp paints the image where its cursor is ❸❼.

4. To change the sampled area, Opt/Alt-click.

5. Then paint with the Rubber Stamp tool with the new sampled area.

As mentioned on the previous page, you can set the Sample list to Document. This allows you to use the Rubber Stamp tool to sample the fill of a vector object and then paint it onto a bitmapped image.

To paint the image of a vector object:

1. Set the Rubber Stamp Sample to Document.

2. Switch to the bitmap mode.

3. Position the Rubber Stamp tool over the vector object.

4. Opt/Alt-click to define the source or the area that you want to copy.

5. Move the Rubber Stamp tool to the area where you want to copy the vector image.

6. Press and drag with the Rubber Stamp. The source circle follows your movements as the Rubber Stamp paints the image elsewhere ❸❽.

7. To change the source, hold the Opt/Alt key and click a new area. Then paint with the Rubber Stamp tool with the new source area.

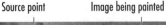
Source point   Image being painted

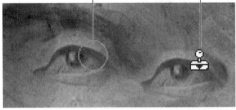

❸❼ *Painting with the Rubber Stamp.*

Vector being sampled

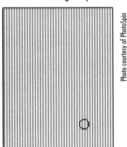

❸❽ *Sampling the document allows you to use a fill, such as a pattern, inside a vector to paint onto a bitmapped image.*

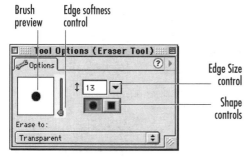

39 *The* **Eraser** *in the Tools panel.*

Brush preview   Edge softness control

Edge Size control

Shape controls

40 *The* **Eraser Tool Options** *panel.*

41 *The effects of the* **Transparent setting** *for the Eraser tool.*

42 *The* **Eyedropper** *in the Tools panel.*

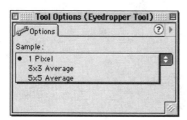

43 *The* **Eyedropper Tool Options** *control the size of the area sampled by the Eyedropper.*

In the bitmap mode, the Knife tool turns into the Eraser tool. This lets you paints with a color or deletes pixels from an area.

To set the Eraser options:

1. Choose the Eraser in the Tools panel **39**.

2. In the Eraser Tool Options panel **40**, choose the round or square shape.

3. Use the edge size control to set the size of the Eraser.

4. Use the Edge softness control to change the appearance of the Eraser edge.

5. Use the Erase to list to control the effect of the Eraser.

   - **Transparent** removes the pixels from the image allowing the underlying image to show through **41**.
   - **Fill Color** uses the Fill color set in the Tools panel.
   - **Stroke Color** uses the Stroke color set in the Tools panel.
   - **Canvas Color** uses the color of the canvas.

The Eyedropper allows you to choose colors by sampling them from images.

To use the Eyedropper:

1. Choose the Eyedropper tool in the Tools panel **42**.

2. Use the Eyedropper Tool Options panel **43** to set the size of the area the Eyedropper uses to judge the color.

   - **1 Pixel** picks up the color from the single pixel directly underneath the Eyedropper.
   - **3×3 Average** picks up the color averaged from 9 pixels within the 3×3 pixel area.
   - **5×5 Average** setting picks up the color averaged from the 25 pixels within the 5×5 pixel area.

TIP Use the Average settings to get the overall color of the areas of a scanned image.

Using the Pixel Tools

With image objects, the Paint Bucket acts as a speedy way to fill an area with a color.

To set the Paint Bucket options:

1. Choose the Paint Bucket tool in the Tools panel ④.

2. In the Paint Bucket Tool Options panel ④, use the Tolerance control to set the size of the area filled ④.

3. Use the Edge list to set the edge of the area filled by the Paint Bucket to Hard Edge, Anti-Alias, or Feather.

4. If the edge is set to Feather, use the Feather amount to set the width of the feathered border.

TIP The Fill Selection Only option causes the Paint Bucket to fill all of a selection regardless of the tolerance.

TIP Turn on the Mouse Highlight to have the Paint Bucket indicate which vector object it is about to fill.

To use the Paint Bucket:

1. Choose the Paint Bucket tool in the Tools panel.

2. Click the Paint Bucket over the image. This fills the area with the currently selected Fill color.

TIP If a selection is active, the Paint Bucket fills only within the marching ants.

The Pencil, Brush, and Paint Bucket tools can be set so that they don't affect the transparent areas of the image.

To work with the Preserve Transparency setting:

1. Double-click the tool in the Tools panel to open the options for the Brush, Pencil, or Paint Bucket.

2. Choose Preserve Transparency.

3. Paint with the tool in the Image Editing mode. The tool will work only on the existing areas of the image, not in the transparent areas ④.

④ *The* **Paint Bucket** *in the Tools panel.*

Edge list

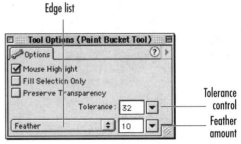

Tolerance control

Feather amount

④ *The* **Paint Bucket Tool Options.**

50 100

④ *At a setting of 50, the Paint Bucket fills a small area of color. At a setting of 100, the Paint Bucket fills a larger area of color.*

④ *The Brush tool set to* **Preserve Transparency** *draws only on the image.*

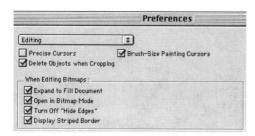

48 *The* **When Editing Bitmaps** *settings let you change how you work in the Bitmap mode.*

49 *Turn off the* **Expand to Fill Document** *setting to limit the effect of the bitmapped tools to only the current pixel area of the image.*

Setting Bitmap Preferences

Fireworks also lets you set preferences for how to work with bitmap images.

To set the When Editing Bitmaps preferences:

1. Choose **Edit > Preferences**.
2. Choose Editing from the list.
3. In the When Editing Bitmaps area, set the controls as described below **48**.

To control the editing area of the image:

◆ Select Expand to Fill Document to automatically add space around a bitmapped image.

TIP When this setting is turned off, the effect of any of the bitmap tools is limited to just the original area of the bitmap image **49**.

To control how images are opened:

◆ Select Open in Bitmap Mode to automatically open bitmapped images or files containing only bitmapped images in the bitmap mode.

TIP When this setting is not chosen, you have to switch to the bitmap mode to edit bitmap images *(see page 202)*.

To change the status of the Hide Edges command:

◆ Select Turn off "Hide Edges" to display the marching ants when you create a new selection even if you have chosen the Hide Edges command.

TIP When this setting is not chosen, you do not see the marching ants even when you create a new bitmap selection.

To change the Bitmap Mode display border:

◆ Select Display Striped Border to show the striped border when working in in the Bitmap mode.

TIP Turn this option off to hide the border.

Applying Xtras

Some of the commands in the Effect panel *(see Chapter 9)* can also be applied to pixel images. When applied to pixel images, these effects are called Xtras **50**.

TIP Some Photoshop compatible plug-ins that are not available as effects, are available as Xtras. The disabled plug-ins file, located at Fireworks4:Configuration:Xtras, lists the disabled plug-ins and whether or not they are disabled for Xtras, effects, or both.

To apply Xtras to bitmap images:

1. Use any of the techniques to switch to the bitmap mode *(see page 202)*.

2. Choose an Xtra from the Xtras menu.

3. If the Xtra has a dialog box, adjust the settings as desired. *(See Chapter 9, "Effects" for details as to use the settings for each of the Xtras.)*

3. Click OK to apply the settings.

To apply Xtras to vector objects:

1. Select one or more vector objects.

2. Choose an Xtra from the Xtras menu. A dialog box appears indicating that the image will be converted into a pixel image **51**.

3. Click OK. The object is converted and the Xtra is applied.

To reapply Xtras quickly:

With an object selected, choose **Xtras** > **Repeat [Name of Xtra]**.

TIP The Mac keystroke is Command-Option-Shift-X.

TIP The Win keystroke is Ctrl-Alt-Shift-X.

50 *The outside area of this image was selected by creating a feathered ellipse and then inverting the selection. The Gaussian Blur and Brightness/Contrast Xtras were then applied to the selection.*

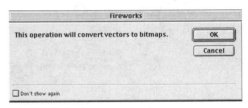

51 *This dialog box appears when you want to apply an Xtra to a vector object.*

Using Xtras Instead of Effects?

Unlike effects, which can be edited or turned off, once you apply Xtras, you can't go back later to change the values or remove the results. So why would anyone want to use Xtras?

Xtras allow you to apply an effect to only a portion of an image object.

They require less computer processing than effects and do not have to be re-drawn every time a document is opened or manipulated.

Some third party plug-ins work only as Xtras.

IMPORTING 14

As the poet John Donne wrote, "No man is an island, entire of itself." So, too, with Macromedia Fireworks. Although it boasts a wealth of tools, fills, and effects, it is not a software island unto itself. It is very likely that you will need to work with other programs along with Fireworks.

For instance, you probably have scanned images from pixel-based programs such as Adobe Photoshop directly from scanner software. Or you may have used Photoshop or Corel Painter to create artwork with special effects.

You might have logos and other artwork created in vector-drawing programs such as Macromedia FreeHand, CorelDraw, or Adobe Illustrator.

Fortunately, you can open or import files created in all of these programs in Fireworks.

Working with Scanned Artwork

If you have a scanner, you can scan images directly into Fireworks. You can also open or insert scans created by other programs into existing Fireworks. The scans can be TIFF, GIF, JPEG, PNG, BMP, or PICT (Mac) files.

To scan an image directly into Fireworks:

1. Choose **File > Scan** and then use the TWAIN module or Photoshop Acquire plug-in that matches your scanner.

2. Follow the scanner software instructions to scan the image. The image opens as a native Fireworks document.

To open a scanned image:

1. Choose **File > Open** and then choose the scan you want to open.

2. Click OK. The scan opens ready for image editing ❶.

TIP The document opens at the same resolution and size as the original scan.

To import scans as image objects:

1. Choose **File > Import** or **Insert > Image** and then find the scan you want to import. Click OK. The import pointer indicates the file is ready for placing on the currently selected Fireworks layer.

2. Drag the import pointer to draw a rectangle that scales the image to fit.

   or

   Click to place the scanned image at the original size.

3. The scan appears as bitmap image on the currently selected object layer ❷. *(For more information on working with bitmap images, see Chapter 13, "Working with Pixels.")*

TIP Use the Import command to add scans to other artwork.

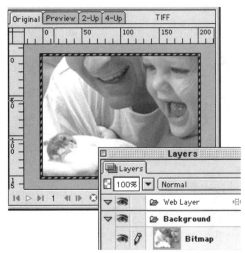

❶ *A scan opened in the* **Bitmap mode** *on the background layer of a Fireworks document.*

❷ *A scan imported as a* **bitmap image** *on a* **layer** *of a Fireworks document. Notice the extra canvas area around the bitmap image.*

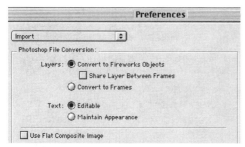

❸ *The* **Photoshop File Conversion Preferences** *control how Photoshop documents are imported.*

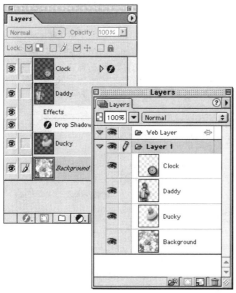

❹ *The layers from a Photoshop document (left) can be converted into Fireworks bitmapped objects (right).*

Working with Photoshop Files

Macromedia knows how popular Adobe Photoshop is. So Fireworks lets you import and open Photoshop files. You can control how features such as layers, layer masks, and layer effects are imported. You use the Layers settings to control how layers are converted from Photoshop into Fireworks.

Before you open Photoshop files in Fireworks you need to set the Photoshop File Conversion options.

To set the Photoshop File Conversions:

1. Choose **Edit > Preferences**.

2. Choose Import from the pop-up menu (Mac) or click the Import tab (Win) to show the Photoshop File Conversion settings **❸**.

3. Use the following exercises to control how Photoshop elements are converted.

To set the Layer options:

◆ Set the Photoshop File Conversion options for Layers as follows:

- **Convert to Fireworks Objects** converts Photoshop layers into individual bitmap objects **❹**. This is the most common option.
- **Share Layer Between Frames** sets the Photoshop layers as Fireworks shared layers. This can be useful in creating animations. *(See Chapter 16, "Animations.")*
- **Convert to Frames** converts each layer into a Fireworks frame. This can help when creating animations.
- **Use Flat Composite Image** imports Photoshop files as an image with only one layer.

TIP You can also use the Import command to place a single bitmapped image into a Fireworks document.

You use the Text settings to control how text is converted from Photoshop into Fireworks.

To set the Text options:

- Set the Photoshop File Conversion options for Layers as follows:
  - **Editable** keeps the Photoshop text as Fireworks text.
  - **Maintain Appearance** converts the Photoshop text into a Fireworks bitmapped image.

TIP The version of Fireworks 4 available at this writing cannot import text from Photoshop 6 and maintain its editability. All text from Photoshop is converted into bitmaps. However, text created in Photoshop 5.5 and earlier versions is imported as editable text!

Photoshop allows you to add layer masks, shadows, glows, and bevels to images. Wherever possible Fireworks tries to maintain these effects.

To open Photoshop files with layer effects:

- In the Photoshop File Conversion Preferences choose Maintain Layers. Photoshop layer effects are converted into the nearest Fireworks effect.

TIP Although Fireworks can convert effects such as Drop Shadow and Bevel, other Photoshop features such as Satin or Pattern Overlay do not have an equivalent in Fireworks and are discarded when imported. *(See the sidebar on this page.)*

Working with Photoshop

Fireworks 4 helps you make the transition from Photoshop to Fireworks as easy as possible. However, there are some features in Photoshop 6 that have no equivalent in Fireworks.

For instance, there is no equivalent to the Satin, Pattern, Gradient Overlay, and Stroke layer effects. Fireworks discards these effects when opening Photoshop files. Adjustment layers are also discarded.

Fireworks converts Photoshop's layer clipping paths into bitmapped masks. However, if a layer has both a layer mask and a clipping path, Fireworks cannot convert both.

Finally, although Fireworks does have an equivalent to Photoshop's Drop Shadow, there are controls in the Photoshop Drop Shadow that that do not exist in Fireworks. Those features are discarded when the file is opened in Fireworks.

For more details on the equivalent and different features in Fireworks and Photoshop, see Chapter 21, "Compared to Photoshop."

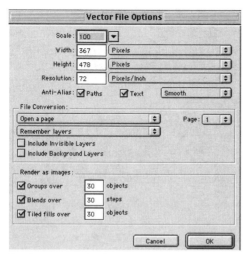

⑤ *The* Vector File Options *dialog box.*

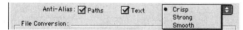

⑥ *The* Anti-Alias options *let you control the look of paths and text separately.*

Working with Anti-Aliasing

Anti-aliasing adds to the number of colors in GIF images. Turning off the anti-aliasing helps keep the file size down.

Next, at very small point sizes, text with anti-aliasing set to Smooth or Strong may become difficult to read. Using the Crisp setting or turning off anti-aliasing entirely may improve the legibility of the text.

Remember, regardless of how you set the anti-aliasing of imported artwork, you can always change those settings later in the Fill panel or Text Editor. *(See pages 117 and 159 for how to control anti-aliasing.)*

Importing Vector Objects

Fireworks can also open artwork created in vector-drawing programs such as Macromedia FreeHand, Adobe Illustrator and CorelDraw. This lets you use the more sophisticated tools in the vector-drawing programs; the vector artwork you then import into your Fireworks document retains its editability.

To set the size of imported vector artwork:

1. Choose **File** > **Open** and navigate to choose the vector file. The Vector File Options dialog box appears **⑤**.

2. Use the Scale control to import the art at a specific size relative to its original size.

   or

   Adjust the width and height fields to change the size of the art to fit a space.

   or

   Choose the resolution from the default setting of 72 pixels per inch to change the size of the art.

   TIP The same choices are available if you choose **File** > **Import** to add vector files into an existing Fireworks document.

The Vector File Options let you control the anti-aliasing around paths and text.

To set the Anti-Alias options for paths and text:

1. Check Anti-Alias: Paths to set a soft edge around the paths **⑥**. *(See page 117 for an illustration of how anti-aliasing affects paths.)*

2. Check Anti-Alias: Text to set a soft edge around text **⑥**.

3. If you set text to Anti-Alias, choose Crisp, Strong, or Smooth in the pop-up menu **⑥**. *(See page 159 for an illustration of each of these settings.)*

Importing Vector Objects

If your artwork has multiple pages or layers, you can specify how those pages or layers are opened.

To set which pages of vector artwork to open:

◆ In the Vector File Options dialog box, choose the following options for opening multi-page documents:

- **Open a page** opens a specific page. If you choose this option, use the Page list to choose which page is imported ❼.

  or

- **Open Pages As Frames** from the Open As list to open each of the pages as a Fireworks frame ❼.

TIP Open Pages As Frames was designed to allow you to import FreeHand pages as Fireworks frames. This is useful for creating animations. Unfortunately a bug in Fireworks 4 has broken this feature. I sincerely hope that Macromedia releases an updater that fixes this problem. *(For more information on working with animations, see Chapter 16, "Animations.")*

To set the layers of opened vector artwork:

1. In the Vector File Options dialog box, choose the following layer options ❽:
   - **Remember layers** imports the layers as Fireworks layers.
   - **Ignore layers** imports the artwork onto one Fireworks layer.
   - **Convert layers to frames** opens each of the layers as a Fireworks frame ❾.
2. Check **Include Invisible Layers** to bring in artwork on the layers that are not visible in the vector program.
3. Check **Include Background Layers** to bring in artwork on the background layers in FreeHand.

❼ The **Page options** *for importing vector artwork from a program that lets you specify multiple pages.*

❽ The **Layer options** *for importing vector artwork.*

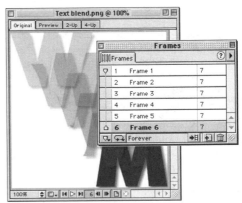

❾ *Individual layers in vector artwork can be converted into individual frames in Fireworks.*

Fireworks lets you convert those elements in a vector file that contain hundreds of elements into bitmap images. This helps avoid importing files that create hundreds of individual Fireworks objects.

To convert imported vector art into pixel images:

◆ In the Vector File Options dialog box, choose one of the following Render as images options ⑩:

- **Groups over_ objects** controls how groups should be converted.
- **Blends over_steps** controls how blends are converted.
- **Tiled fills over_objects** controls how tiled fills or patterns are converted.

TIP Rendering vectors as pixels turns all the objects into a bitmapped image ⑪.

⑩ *The* **Render as images options** *control whether objects are imported as vector objects or pixel-based images.*

Vector objects   Bitmapped image

⑪ *The difference between importing as vector objects or pixel-based images. Notice that the bitmap image has a white background while the vector objects do not.*

When to Rasterize Vector Objects?

As you have guessed by now, I would much rather work with vector objects than bitmap images. So when might I want to render groups, blends, or patterns into bitmap images?

If I have grouped artwork for simple logos, maps, or illustrations I usually turn off the option for groups. I want the ability to edit the individual elements in the group.

With blends, I usually set the number to 30. This lets me use morphing blends for animations but rasterizes the blends that are simply gradients.

Finally, I always rasterize tiled fills. I've yet to find a time I need to edit pattern elements in Fireworks.

Importing Vector Objects

Importing EPS Files

Fireworks can open EPS files. If the files are rasterized EPS images, such as those created by Photoshop, the EPS File Options dialog box appears.

To open EPS files:

1. Choose **File** > **Open** and then find the EPS file you want to open. Click OK. The EPS File Options dialog appears **⑫**.

2. Set the Width and Height fields.

3. Set the Resolution amount.

4. Check Constrain Proportions to keep the width and height in proportion to each other.

5. Check Anti-aliased to soften the edges of the artwork.

TIP Vector EPS files created in programs such as FreeHand and CorelDraw will be rasterized when they are opened. Save the file without the EPS information to open them as a vector file.

TIP Some vector EPS files created by Adobe Illustrator are opened using the vector options covered in the previous section. *(See the sidebar on this page for a discussion of which vector EPS files can be opened.)*

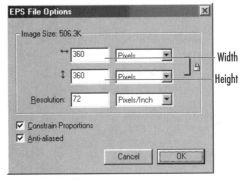

⑫ *The* **EPS File Options** *let you open EPS files as rasterized images.*

What about Vector EPS Files?

Vector EPS files are those files created by Macromedia FreeHand, Adobe Illustrator, or CorelDraw. They are actually vector drawings with a special EPS header that allows them to be placed in print page layout programs such as QuarkXpress or Adobe InDesign.

For the most part, Fireworks will open these vector EPS files as if they are rasterized EPS files. That is, Fireworks will convert all the vectors into one solid bitmap image—most likely *not* what you want to happen!

If you want to open these files as vectors, you need to open them in the program they were created in and re-save the file as a native FreeHand or CorelDraw file.

The exception is Adobe Illustrator EPS files. Thanks to John Ahlquist and Jeff Doar, Fireworks is able to open some versions of Illustrator EPS files using the vector file options. These are usually files saved in early versions of Illustrator such as Illustrator 88 or Illustrator 3.

Importing EPS Files

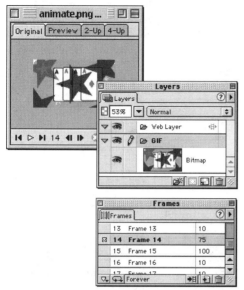

 GIF Animations import into Fireworks with each of the animation images on its own Fireworks frame.

Importing GIF Animations

Fireworks can open and convert GIF animations into Fireworks frames. This makes it easy to convert your old GIF animations into new Fireworks animations. *(For more information on creating animations in Fireworks, see Chapter 16, "Animations.")*

To open Animated GIF files:

◆ Choose **File** >**Open** and then find the Animated GIF you want to open. Click OK. The animation opens with each image frame of the animation on its own Fireworks frame ⓭.

TIP GIF animations are imported into Fireworks at animation symbols. *(See Chapter 16, "Animations" for more information on working with animation symbols.)*

TIP You can also use the **File** >**Import** or **Insert** >**Image** commands to import Animated GIF files with the same results.

Importing Text

You can also import text saved in the ASCII or RTF formats into Fireworks documents. This is much easier than retyping long documents.

To open text as Fireworks files:

1. Choose **File** > **Import**. Navigate to find an RTF (Rich Text Format) or ASCII text file.

   TIP You can also use the **File** > **Import** or **Insert** > **Image** commands to import text files into existing Fireworks documents.

2. Click to place the text file in a text block the same width as the document **14**.

   or

   Drag to set a specific width for the text block.

   TIP RTF text maintains all the font attributes that are in the Fireworks Text Editor. The character color comes from the first character color in the text file.

3. Use the Text Editor to make any changes to the text.

   TIP You can also open text files as their own Fireworks documents. You can then add any images you want.

14 *RTF or ASCII text can be imported into Fireworks documents.*

OPTIMIZING 15

People who create Web graphics are obsessed—not necessarily with the look of the graphics (although that would be nice)—but with file sizes. They can spend hours working to reduce the size of a graphic from 5.1K to 4.9K.

Why the obsession? While two-tenths of a kilobyte may not seem like much to a single graphic, multiply it across all the graphics on a page and it adds up. That adds to the time that it takes the page to download—time that viewers don't want to waste sitting around waiting for a page to come into view.

Optimizing refers to setting all the controls so that graphics are created in the proper format and in the smallest possible file size. It is often a juggling act to balance reducing the file size while at the same time maintaining the original quality of the image.

Fireworks gives you specialized tools that that make it easy to reduce files while maintaining their appearance.

Following the Optimizing Steps

There are several different parts to optimizing files. Use the steps below as a guide to optimizing files using the document window controls. *(For the equivalent steps using the special Export Preview controls, see page 249.)*

To optimize and export files:

1. Use the tab controls in the Document Window to control the onscreen preview of the file *(see the next page)*.

   TIP The onscreen preview allows you to compare different optimization settings as well as judge how long it will take the file to download.

2. Use the Optimize panel to set the type of file, its compression, and other file characteristics *(see pages 235 and 240)*.

3. If you are optimizing a GIF file, control the colors in the file using the Color Table panel *(see page 237)*.

4. Set the transparency options *(see page 245)*.

5. Choose **File** > **Export** to export the file at the optimization settings. *(See Chapter 20, "Exporting".)*

The Optimize panel or Export Preview?

When Fireworks was first released the only place where you could optimize files was in the Export Preview dialog box. Many people complained that if you needed to make a change as you were setting the optimization controls, you had to switch out of the Export Preview, make the change, and then come back to the document page.

So Fireworks made it possible to set the optimization controls while still working on the document—a better way to work.

However, Macromedia didn't throw out the Export Preview dialog box. You can still use it to optimize images. It is also used to optimize images that are opened using the Launch and Edit feature in Dreamweaver *(see page 250)*.

While there may be some old-time Fireworks users who still use the Export Preview dialog box for optimization, I'd rather use the Optimize panel. The Export Preview dialog box is covered on page 249.

❶ *The* **Preview tab** *in the document window.*

Active panel

❷ *The* **4-Up tab** *lets you compare different optimization settings of the image.*

Controlling the Onscreen Preview

As you optimize images, they can drastically change their appearance from the original artwork. The Preview tabs allow you to see the effects of the optimization settings on the image.

To use the preview tabs:

◆ Click the Preview tab in the document window to see a full-screen preview of the artwork ❶.

or

Click the 2-Up tab to split the window into two sections so you can compare the original artwork to the artwork at the current optimization settings.

or

Click the 4-Up tab to split the window into four sections so you can compare the original artwork to the artwork at three different optimization settings ❷.

TIP Although you can use the zoom and magnification controls to change the size or position of the preview, it is usually better to optimize an image at the 100% view. This lets you see the image without exaggerating or minimizing the effects of the optimization.

The active panel shows the results of the current settings of the Optimize panel. You create different optimization settings for each panel by choosing a new active panel.

To change the active panel:

◆ Click inside one of the panels. A black line appears around the panel. This indicates that panel is active ❷.

By default, Fireworks displays the original file in the left-hand panel in the 2-Up tab and the top-left panel in the 4-Up tab. If you want, you can change that panel so that it displays a preview setting.

To change a panel to show the original file:

1. Press the panel control under the preview image in the panel.

2. Choose Original (No Preview) to see the original image ❸.

TIP When a panel has been set to Original (No Preview), you can use any of the Fireworks editing tools or commands to make changes to the file.

To change a panel to show the export preview:

1. Press the panel control under the preview image in the panel.

2. Choose Export Preview to see the effects of the optimization settings.

TIP When a panel has been set to Export Preview, you can not make changes to the file within that panel.

There is a difference between the brightness, or gamma, of Macintosh and Windows monitors. Fireworks lets you switch your monitor display so you can simulate the gamma of another operating system.

To change the preview gamma display:

♦ Choose View > Windows Gamma or View > Macintosh Gamma to see how your image will appear using a different operating system ❹. (See the color pages for a display of this effect.)

❸ *The panel control under the preview image lets you switch between showing the original image and the export preview.*

❹ *Changing the Gamma display lets you see the differences between Windows (left) and Macintosh (right) monitors.*

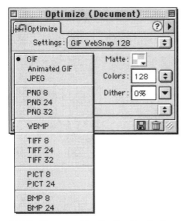

❺ *The* **Format list** *in the Optimize panel.*

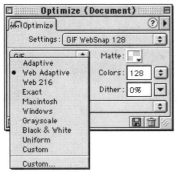

❻ *The* **Palette list** *in the Optimize panel.*

When should you use the GIF format?

Use the GIF format for images with flat or solid areas of color. Type, cartoons, and flat color logos usually look best when saved as GIF images.

You must use GIF images if you need the area around the image to be transparent or for animations. *(See the color pages for a display of the type of images that look best as a GIF.)*

Optimizing GIF Files

One of the most popular types of Web files is the GIF. (Although some people pronounce this format as "jif," I prefer "gif" since I don't like peanut butter on the Web.)

To choose GIF as the optimize format:

1. If the Optimize panel is not visible, choose **Window** > **Optimize**.

2. Choose GIF from the Format list. This changes the panel to the GIF options **❺**.

3. Set the GIF options as described in the following exercises.

GIF files are limited to a maximum of 256 colors. The color palette determines what kinds of colors are included in the file.

To choose a GIF color palette:

◆ Choose one of the following from the Palette list **❻**:

- **Adaptive** samples the colors in your file whether or not they're Web-safe.
- **Web Adaptive** (Mac) or **WebSnap Adaptive** (Win) uses the Adaptive palette, but any color that's within 7 units of a Web-safe color, gets shifted to the nearest one.
- **Web 216** uses only Web-safe colors, replacing non–Web-safe colors with the closest Web-safe color.
- **Exact** uses the Adaptive palette but automatically finds the exact number of colors in the graphic.
- **Macintosh** or **Windows** limits the colors to those in the Macintosh or Windows operating systems.
- **Grayscale** shifts the colors to the range of 256 grayscale values.
- **Black & White** uses just those two colors.
- **Uniform** uses a mathematical palette based on RGB pixel values. There is little use for this on the Web.
- **Custom** lets you open a swatches palette saved from Fireworks *(see page 55)* or from Photoshop.

Most Web designers make GIF files smaller by reducing the number of colors in the color palettes below the maximum number of 256.

To reduce the number of colors in a file:

◆ Use the Number of Colors control to lower the number even further ❼.

TIP Fireworks eliminates colors from the palette based on how often the color appears in the image. You can also use the Color Table panel to delete specific colors in the file *(see the next page)*.

Dithering is a technique that mixes a dot pattern of two colors to create the illusion of a third. Dithering helps maintain the look of GIF files when reducing colors.

To set the dithering of an image:

◆ Use the Dither control to change how much dithering is applied ❽.

TIP Most people don't like the look of dithering. Use the smallest amount of dithering you can.

Another way to lower the file size is to apply a Loss compression which is similar to the compression used on JPEG images *(see page 240)*. This lowers the file size by throwing away some of the details and distorting the image.

To apply Loss to a GIF image:

◆ Use the Loss control to increase the amount of Loss compression in the image ❾. The higher the Loss values the more distortions will be created in the image.

TIP Use low values of the Loss setting to shave small amounts from the file. The higher Loss settings create ugly distortions in the flat colors.

Loss control

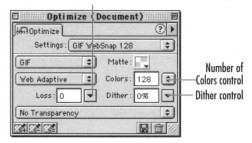

Number of Colors control

Dither control

❼ *The* **Optimize panel** *set for GIF export.*

Dithering applied   No dithering

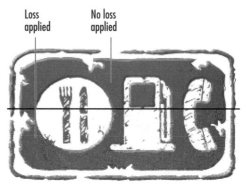

❽ **Dithering** *can help reduce banding, especially when using a reduced number of colors.*

Loss applied   No loss applied

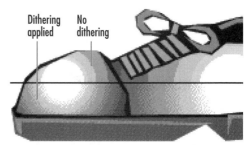

❾ **Adding loss** *reduces the size of a GIF file but can add distortion to the image.*

Selected color

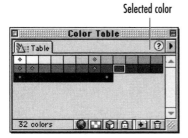

⑩ *The* **Color Table** *panel.*

Locked and
shifted to Web-safe

Locked to
Web-safe

Shifted to
Web-safe

Web-safe

Locked

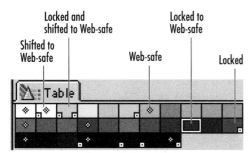

⑪ *The* **Swatch feedback** *in the Color Table gives you information about the status of the colors.*

Adjusting the Color Table

In addition to lowering the number of colors for a GIF image, you can control each individual color in the file with the Color Table panel. *(See the color pages for how the Color Table changes images.)*

To control the colors in the Color Table:

1. If the Color Table panel **⑩** is not visible, choose **Window>Color Table**.

2. Choose Rebuild Color Table from the Color Table panel menu to update the panel.

   TIP The word Rebuild appears at the top of the Color Table whenever the Color Table does not indicate the current optimization settings.

3. Click the swatch in the Color Table to select the color. A highlight appears around the swatch **⑪**.

4. Select additional colors by holding the Command/Ctrl key as you click the color swatch.

   or

   Hold the Shift key to select a range of colors.

5. Use the exercises that follow to change the colors in the table.

   TIP Colors that have been locked or modified can be identified by the swatch feedback symbols in the Color Table **⑪**.

   TIP Deselect Show Swatch Feedback in the Color Table panel menu to hide the swatch feedback symbols.

   TIP Press a swatch in the Color Table to see where that color appears in the image.

Adjusting the Color Table

To edit colors in the table:

◆ Choose Edit Color from the Color Table panel menu **⑫** or click the Edit icon at the bottom of the panel **⑬**. This opens the color picker.

To change the color to a Web-safe color:

◆ Choose Snap to Web Safe from the Color Table panel menu or click the Web icon **⑬**. This forces the color to the closest Web-safe color.

To delete colors from the table:

◆ Choose Delete Color from the Color Table panel menu or click the Delete icon at the bottom of the panel **⑬**.

To lock the color:

◆ Choose Lock Color from the Color Table panel menu or click the Lock icon at the bottom of the panel **⑬**.

TIP Apply the Lock color command again to unlock colors.

TIP Use the Unlock All Colors command from the panel menu to unlock all the colors in the table.

To add colors to the table:

◆ Choose Add Color from the Color Table panel menu or click the Add icon at the bottom of the panel **⑬**. This opens the color picker.

To clear color changes in the table:

◆ Choose Remove Edit from the Color Table panel menu. This restores the swatch to its original value.

TIP Use the Remove All Edits to restore all modified swatches to their original values.

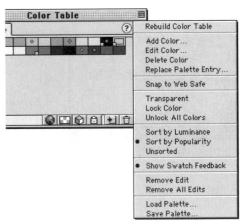

⑫ *The* Color Table *panel menu.*

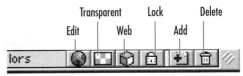

⑬ *The* Swatch icons *in the Optimize panel.*

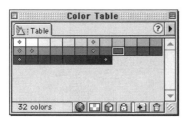

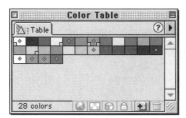

⓮ *Use the* **Sort by Luminance** *command to arrange colors from light to dark.*

⓯ *Use the* **Sort by Popularity** *command to arrange colors in order of their frequency within the file.*

⓰ *How* interlaced or progressive images *appear as they are downloaded into a file.*

You can change the order in which colors appear in the Color Table.

To sort the colors in the Color Table:

◆ From the Color Table panel menu, choose:

- **Sort by Luminance** to arrange the colors from dark to light **⓮**.
- **Sort by Popularity** to arrange the colors from most-used to least-used **⓯**.

If you have spent some time modifying a Color Table, you can save it for later use.

To save the colors in the Color Table:

1. Select Save Palette from the Color Table panel menu. This opens the standard Save As dialog box.

2. Use the Save As dialog box to name and save the palette to a location.

To load colors into the Color Table:

1. Select Load Palette from the Color Table panel menu.

2. Navigate to a saved palette. The palette replaces the swatches in the current Color Table.

TIP You can also load .act files created by Adobe Photoshop or Adobe Image-Ready to create a Fireworks Color Table.

Revealing Images

You can set graphics so they reveal slowly as they download **⓰**. This lets visitors quickly decide if they want to wait to see the complete image.

To create images that appear gradually:

◆ For GIF images, choose Interlaced from the Optimize panel menu.

or

◆ For JPEG images, choose Progressive from the Optimize panel menu.

Adjusting the Color Table; Revealing Images

Optimizing JPEG Files

JPEG is another popular file format for Web graphics. Instead of throwing away colors, JPEG files are *compressed* by throwing away some information. *(See the color pages for an illustration of various compression settings.)*

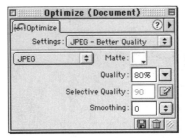

⓱ *The* JPEG settings *in the Optimize panel.*

To choose JPEG as the optimization format:

1. If the Optimize panel is not visible, choose **Window** > **Optimize**.

2. Choose JPEG from the Format list. This changes the panel to the JPEG options **⓱**.

3. Set the JPEG options as described in the following exercises.

You control the file size by changing the Quality setting. The lower the Quality the more compression applied to the image, resulting in a smaller file.

80% Quality

20% Quality

To change the file size of the JPEG image:

◆ Use the Quality control to change the file size—the lower the quality, the smaller the file **⓲**.

TIP Setting the Quality control too low can make the image look coarse or filled with blocks.

TIP There are no industry standards for what the amount of compression stands for. So a Quality setting of 50% in Fireworks may not look the same as the same amount applied in ImageReady or another program.

⓲ Lowering the quality of a JPEG image *degrades the image by deleting details and creating square blocks in the image.*

When should you use the JPEG format?

Because JPEG images can display millions of colors, they are used for photographic images or images with subtle blends. *(See the color pages for a display of the type of images that look best as a JPEG.)*

The art of setting the JPEG controls lies in making the compression artifacts less noticeable.

With smoothing

Without smoothing

⓳ Adding Smoothing *to a JPEG can reduce the coarseness by adding a slight blur.*

Sharpen JPEG Edges on

Sharpen JPEG Edges off

⓴ *The* **Sharpen JPEG Edges setting** *helps keep the flat areas of color, such as type, crisp against the background of an image.*

The more you lower the JPEG quality the more you may notice coarse or blocky areas in the image. Fireworks gives you several tools to reduce that coarseness.

Smoothing works by slightly blurring the details in the image.

To smooth a JPEG image:

◆ Set the Smoothing control to the numbers 0 through 8. The higher the number, the greater the blur applied to the image **⓳**. *(See the color insert for examples of the different JPEG settings.)*

You can also improve the appearance of a JPEG image by applying the Sharpen JPEG Edges command. This setting looks for areas of flat color and sharpens the edges **⓴**.

To sharpen the edges of a JPEG image:

◆ Choose Sharpen JPEG Edges from the Optimize panel menu.

TIP Sharpen JPEG Edges does not affect the entire image, just where there is a flat area of color against a different colored background.

TIP The Sharpen JPEG Edges command is particularly useful for enhancing text that is part of a scanned image. However, if you have text created in Fireworks, the Selective JPEG Compression works even better to improve the look of the image *(see the next page).*

Creating Selective JPEG Files

Another way to improve the look of a JPEG image is to create a Selective JPEG. This allows you to have a low quality for certain parts of the image and a higher quality for areas that you want to look good. For example, you can set a high quality around someone's face but use a low quality for the background.

Creating a Selective JPEG is a two step process. First you mask the part of the image you want to maintain at high quality, then you set the amount of compression to apply to that area.

To create the Selective JPEG mask:

1. Use the bitmap selection tools to select the area to act as the mask.

2. Choose **Modify** > **Selective JPEG** > **Save Selection as JPEG Mask**. A color appears inside the marching ants. This indicates the mask area of the Selective JPEG ㉑.

3. After setting the mask, you can deselect the bitmap selection. The mask is saved as part of the document.

To set the amount of Selective JPEG compression:

1. Click the Selective Quality icon in the Optimize panel ㉒.

   or

   Choose **Modify** > **Selective JPEG** > **Settings**. The Selective JPEG Settings dialog box appears ㉓.

2. Select Enable Selective Quality.

3. Enter an amount in the Quality field.

> **TIP** Once you have enabled the Selective JPEG Quality you can also change the quality from the Optimize panel.

㉑ *The* **Selective JPEG mask** *is shown inside the selection of marching ants. This indicates which area of the image will be compressed by the Selective Quality control.*

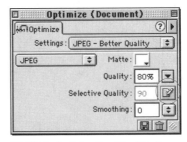

㉒ *Click the* **Selective Quality icon** *(circled) to open the Selective JPEG Settings dialog box.*

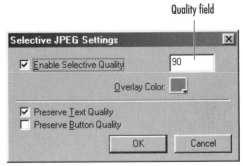

㉓ *The* **Selective JPEG Settings** *dialog box.*

Creating Selective JPEG Files *(side margin)*

㉔ *Even at a very low JPEG quality the* **Preserve Text Quality** *setting maintains a high quality for the Fireworks text in a JPEG image.*

Working with Selective JPEGs

When you first apply the Selective JPEG you may see an increase in the file size. This is because part of the image has less compression applied.

However, you can lower the file size much more because you can then increase the compression applied outside the mask.

If you set the Selective Quality for text or buttons you may see some additional compression outside the text or buttons.

The mask does not change if you apply feathering to the selection. The compression is applied as an absolute value, not a relative one.

You can modify the mask by converting it back into a selection.

To modify the mask:

1. Choose **Modify** > **Selective JPEG** > **Restore JPEG Mask as Selection**. The mask is converted into marching ants.

2. Move or modify the selection using any of the bitmap selection tools *(as covered in Chapter 13)*.

3. Choose **Modify** > **Selective JPEG** > **Save Selection as JPEG Mask** to apply the new selection as the mask.

To remove the Selective JPEG mask:

◆ Choose **Modify** > **Selective JPEG** > **Remove Mask**.

You can also apply Selective JPEG compression to text and buttons.

To apply a Selective JPEG to text or buttons:

1. Set the following in the Selective JPG Settings dialog box:
   • **Preserve Text Quality** applies the Selective JPEG Quality to text created in Fireworks **㉔**.
   • **Preserve Button Quality** applies the Selective JPEG Quality to symbols that act as buttons. *(See Chapter 19, "Behaviors" for more information on creating buttons.)*

You can also change the mask color.

To change the Selective JPEG overlay color:

◆ Use the Overlay Color Well in the Selective JPEG dialog box to set the color of the Selective JPEG mask.

TIP Changing the mask color has no effect on your final image but can help you see the mask over colors in the image.

TIP If you are extremely organized, you can change the color according to the amount of compression applied.

Choosing GIF or JPEG

As a general rule, most people use JPEG for photos and GIF for flat-color artwork. But there are times when that rule does not apply.

Working with Flat Colors

For instance, if you have a photograph with very flat colors, such as a road sign on a white background, you may find that optimizing as a GIF allows you to keep the appearance of the flat colors **25**.

The same image, optimized as a JPEG, may require high amounts of smoothing to overcome distortion in the JPEG compression **25**. Even then, the flat colors may still look distorted.

You may also find that monochromatic images with text, such as the face of a clock, look better when optimized as a GIF **26**. The monochrome colors in the image allow you to use a palette of colors without sacrificing the look of the numbers of the clock.

You may also want to optimize as a GIF since GIF images can support transparency *(see the next page)*.

GIF or JPEG? The lady or the tiger? The choices are not always simple.

25 *Optimizing as a GIF (top) maintains the look of the flat colors in a photograph. Optimizing as a JPEG (bottom) can create distortions in the flat colors.*

26 *The numbers in a monochromatic image may look better when optimized as a GIF (top) rather than as a JPEG (bottom).*

㉗ *The* **Transparency list** *lets you add transparency to GIF images.*

㉘ *The* **Transparency Eyedropper** *lets you select which colors should be made transparent.*

㉙ *The* **Eyedropper** *allows you to select colors in the image that should be transparent.*

Setting Transparency

One of the main advantages of the GIF format is that certain areas of an image can be made transparent. This allows you to have a Web graphic that blends into the background of the page.

To create transparency in a GIF image:

1. Choose GIF in the Optimize panel.

2. Choose either Index Transparency or Alpha Transparency from the Transparency list **㉗**.

TIP See the following exercise to understand the difference between the two types of transparency settings.

3. Use the Transparency Eyedropper **㉘** to click the color in the image that you want to make transparent. The transparent area is indicated with a checkerboard grid **㉙**.

4. Use the Eyedropper with the plus (+) sign to select additional colors to make transparent.

5. Use the Eyedropper with the minus (–) sign to deselect colors.

TIP You can also select colors in the Color Table and click the Transparency icon to make those colors transparent.

Fireworks lets you choose between Index Transparency and Alpha Transparency. Index Transparency makes specific color transparent.

Alpha Transparency uses the outline of the objects on the canvas as the shape of the transparency.

To choose the type of transparency:

◆ Set the Transparency pop-up list as follows:

- **Index Transparency** sets a specific color as transparent.

TIP Index Transparency can create undesirable effects if the transparency color appears within the image itself ⯃.

- **Alpha Transparency** sets the transparent areas of the canvas as transparent ⯄.

TIP The Alpha Transparency is seen only if the canvas color of the image has been set to transparent.

A matte color changes the edges of transparent images so that they look better as they pass over background colors ⯅.

To choose a matte color:

◆ Click the Matte color well in the Optimize panel to choose the color closest to the backgrounds or images that you expect the file to be placed over.

TIP If possible, use the eyedropper to sample the color from another document.

TIP If you do not know the color of the background click the None icon in the panel to specify no matte.

TIP Although there is no actual transparency for JPEG images, you can use the Matte color to set the background color for JPEG images.

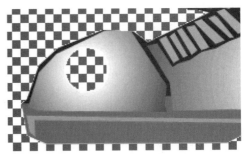

⯃ *An* **Index Transparency** *using the color white created a transparent background but also caused the white in the gradient to become transparent.*

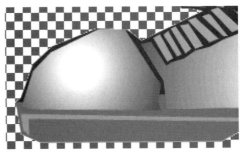

⯄ *An* **Alpha Transparency** *used the outline of the objects as the transparency without causing the white in the shoe to be transparent.*

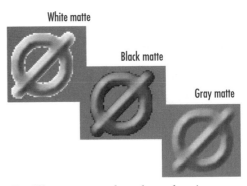

⯅ **Different matte colors** *change how images appear over backgrounds. In this case the gray matte looks best over the gray background.*

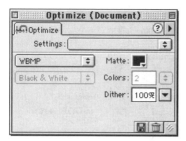

❸ *The* WBMP Optimization settings.

❸ *A* **WBMP image** *is displayed in black and white with dithering to show shading.*

The Web on a Telephone?

Yes, many communications experts agree that in the future most people will access the Web via their cellular telephone. Think about it—a cellular phone is cheaper and more portable than a computer. In fact, I already get text-only Web pages and e-mail on my cell phone.

Of course the Web on a cell phone will be much different from the Web you access on a computer. The colors will be much more limited and there will be far less text.

Creating WBMP Images

In the future, most people will view Web pages on WAP (Wireless Application Protocol) devices such as cellular telephones or personal digital assistants such as Palm Pilots.

Instead of GIF or JPEG, these devices will display WBMP (Wireless BitMap) images. WBMP images display images using only black or white pixels. (My cat, Pixel, is a WBMP image!)

To save files in the WBMP format:

1. Choose WBMP from the format list in the Optimize palette **❸**.

2. Set the amount of dithering applied to the image **❸**. Dithering simulates colors and shades in images.

Optimizing Other Formats

Although Fireworks was designed for Web graphics, Fireworks does convert images for use in print and onscreen presentations.

To export other file formats:

1. Choose among the other file formats in the Optimize panel format list.
   - **Animated GIF** is used for animations. *(See Chapter 16, "Animations.")*
   - **PNG** is used for Web graphics that can be seen with specialized plug-ins. PNG is also used for onscreen presentations such as those created in Microsoft PowerPoint, Macromedia Director, or Macromedia Authorware.
   - **TIFF** is used for graphics inserted into page layout programs such as QuarkXPress or Adobe PageMaker.
   - Choose **PICT** (Mac) or **BMP** (Win) for applications that cannot read any of the other formats.

2. Set the number of colors and matte color according to the previous exercises.

Working with Optimization Settings

Fireworks lets you save the settings in the Optimize panel so they can be applied later.

To save optimization settings:

1. Set the Optimize panel to the settings you want to save.

2. Click the Save Settings icon or choose Save Settings from the Optimize panel menu ❸. A dialog box appears.

3. Give the settings a name and then click OK. This adds the settings to the default settings in the Settings list ❸.

TIP Saved settings automatically appear in the Settings list of the Optimize panel and can be accessed at any time.

TIP Settings are stored in Fireworks4: Configuration:Export Settings folder. They can be moved from one machine to another.

To delete saved settings:

1. Choose the setting you want to delete.

2. Choose Delete Settings from the Optimize panel menu.

   or

   Click the Delete Settings icon.

If you need your graphics to be under a certain size, Fireworks lets you optimize files to a specific size.

To optimize a file to a target size:

1. Set the file type in the Optimize panel.

2. Choose Optimize to Size from the Optimize panel menu. A dialog box appears ❸.

3. Enter an amount in the Target Size field.

4. Click OK. Fireworks changes the optimization settings so that the file is smaller than the target size.

Save settings   Delete settings

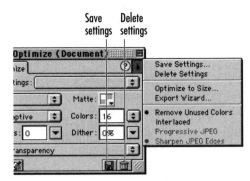

❸ *You can save the settings in the Optimize panel for later use.*

❸ *The* **Settings list** *in the Optimize panel.*

❸ *The* **Optimize to Size** *dialog box lets you set a target size that the optimization settings should be set to.*

③ *The* **Export Preview** *dialog box allows you to optimize and export files.*

Preview Window controls

③ *The* **Preview Window controls** *in the Export Preview dialog box function like the 2-Up and 4-Up tabs in the document window.*

Save Current Settings

④ *The* **Save Current Settings button** *adds the current optimization settings to the Saved Settings list.*

Optimizing in the Export Preview

As mentioned earlier, you can also optimize images in the Export Preview dialog box. You can also export files directly from the Export Preview.

To optimize using the Export Preview:

1. Choose **File** > **Export Preview.** This opens the Export Preview dialog box **③**.

2. Use the Preview Window controls to split the preview area into sections **③**.

3. Use the Format list to choose the type of file format.

4. Set the format options.

5. Use the Transparency options to set any transparency for the file.

6. Click OK to set the optimization and return to the document window.

   or

   Click Export to export the file. *(See Chapter 20, "Exporting" for more information on exporting files.)*

To save settings using the Export Preview:

1. Click Save Current Settings **④** in the Export Preview.

2. Name the settings file.

3. Click OK. The setting appears in the Export Preview Saved Settings list as well as the Optimize panel settings.

Optimizing in Dreamweaver

One of the benefits of using both Fireworks and Macromedia Dreamweaver is that you can make changes to Fireworks files while working in Dreamweaver.

To optimize in Dreamweaver:

1. In Dreamweaver, select the imported graphic.

2. Choose **Commands**>**Optimize Image in Fireworks**.

   or

   Right-click (Win) or Control-click (Mac) to choose the command from the contextual menu.

TIP The Optimize Image in Fireworks command lets you make changes only to the Export Preview settings. If you want to change the content of the image, you need to use the exercise on the following page.

3. A dialog box appears asking which file you want to open 🐽.

   • **Yes** opens the Fireworks PNG file. This is called the source file.

   • **No** to open the file that was exported from Fireworks and then inserted into Dreamweaver. This could be a GIF or JPEG file.

4. Navigate to find the source file or the exported file.

5. Use the Fireworks Export Preview dialog box to make changes to the file 🐽.

6. Click Update. Fireworks makes the changes to and saves the source PNG file. Fireworks then re-exports the file. Dreamweaver updates the inserted image on the page.

TIP If you have made changes to the size of the file, click the Reset Image button in the Dreamweaver Property Inspector to see those changes on the page.

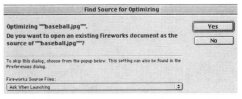

🐽 *Dreamweaver's* **Find Source for Optimizing** *dialog box lets you open the original Fireworks source file or the exported image.*

🐽 *The Fireworks* **Export Preview** *appears as part of the process of optimizing Fireworks files from within Dreamweaver.*

43 *Click the* **Edit button** *(circled) in the Dream-weaver Properties panel to open Fireworks so that you can edit the original source image.*

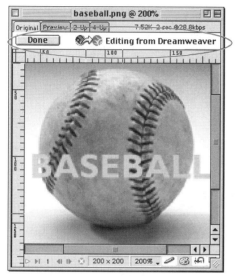

44 *A* **Launch and Edit session** *is indicated by the logos at the top of the Fireworks document window.*

You can also use the special Launch and Edit feature that allows Dreamweaver to signal Fireworks to make changes to images imported into Dreamweaver documents.

To use the Launch and Edit in Dreamweaaver:

1. In Dreamweaver, select the graphic exported from Fireworks and inserted into the Dreamweaver document.

2. Click the Edit button in the Dreamweaver Properties panel **43**. This opens the Fireworks document in a special Launch and Edit session indicated by the Dreamweaver and Fireworks logos at the top of the document window **44**.

TIP You may be asked to locate the Fire-works source (PNG) file used to create the graphic inserted into Dreamweaver.

3. Use the complete range of Fireworks tools to make whatever changes you want to the Fireworks file.

4. Click the Done button at the top of the Fireworks document window. Fireworks re-optimizes the file, closes the original, and inserts the updated file into the Dreamweaver page.

Integrating with Flash

You can also integrate Fireworks with Macromedia Flash with the same sort of automatic updating that happens with Dreamweaver. This gives you the benefit of using Fireworks effects and Photoshop plug-ins in your Flash animations.

TIP Strictly speaking, the integration with Flash isn't optimization since you import the native Fireworks PNG file into Flash.

To import Fireworks files into Flash:

1. In Flash, choose **File**>**Import** and use the import box to select the Fireworks PNG files you want to use.

2. Click the Import button. The Fireworks PNG Import Settings dialog box appears ⓯.

3. Choose Import Editable Objects to use the Fireworks objects as ordinary Flash objects.

   or

   Choose Flatten Image to bring the image into Flash as a single bitmapped image. The image is automatically inserted as a Bitmap symbol in the Flash Library panel ⓰.

4. If you choose Import Editable Objects, choose from the following:
   • **Include Images** to import bitmap images.
   • **Include Text** to import text blocks.
   • **Import Guides** to import the ruler guides.

TIP Importing as editable objects does not allow updating from Fireworks into Flash.

TIP The bitmapped images imported into Flash are linked to the original Fireworks file and can be edited and updated as shown in the next exercise.

⓯ *The* **Fireworks PNG Import Settings** *lets you choose to import Fireworks files as editable objects or a single bitmapped image.*

⓰ *The* **imported Fireworks PNG files** *appear in the Flash Library as Bitmap symbols.*

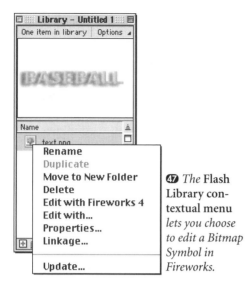

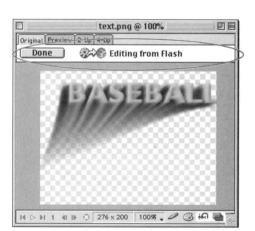

47 *The* Flash Library con-textual menu *lets you choose to edit a Bitmap Symbol in Fireworks.*

48 *A* **Launch and Edit session** *is indicated by the logos at the top of the Fireworks document window.*

Once a Fireworks image is in the Flash Library, you can use Flash to open a special Launch and Edit session of Fireworks and make changes to the image.

To use the Launch and Edit in Flash:

1. In Flash, Control-click (Mac) or Right-mouse-click (Win) the icon of the imported Bitmap Symbol. A contextual menu appears **47**.

2. Choose Edit with Fireworks 4. This opens the original Fireworks document in the Launch and Edit mode **48**.

   TIP You may be asked to locate the Fireworks source (PNG) file used to create the graphic inserted into Flash.

3. Make whatever changes you want within Fireworks.

4. Click Done to close the Fireworks file and automatically update the Flash Bitmap Symbol.

Swatches Palettes

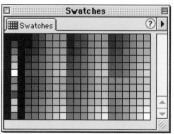

The Swatches panel set to display the Web-safe colors in the **Color Cubes** *arrangement.*

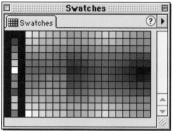

The Swatches panel set to display the Web-safe colors in the **Continuous** *arrangement.*

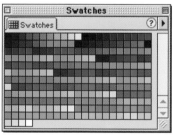

The Swatches panel set to display the **Macintosh colors.**

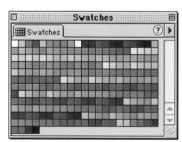

The Swatches panel set to display the **Windows colors.**

Choosing GIF Optimization

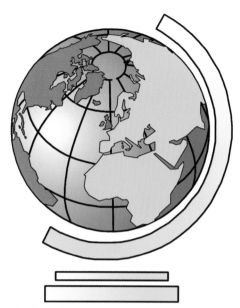

The flat colors and limited blends in this image should be exported as a **GIF** *image.*

Choosing JPEG Optimization

The continuous tones in this photo should be exported as a **JPEG** *image.*

Adding Dithering to Maintain Colors.

The Adaptive palette always is the closest to the original image. As you lower the number of colors, you may need to add dithering to maintain blends.

Using the Web-safe palette almost always changes the look of the artwork. Adding dithering can help maintain blends, but can distort the look of flat colors.

The original art contains more than 256 colors. These colors are easily reproduced in print.

Using all 256 Adapative colors provides the closest equivalent of the original art.

Using 32 Adapative colors without dithering, some of the subtle colors have been changed. The blend in the left block is slightly banded.

Using 32 Adapative colors with a small amount of dithering restores an indication of the blend. Notice, though, some dithering in the flat colors.

Using 32 Web-safe colors without dithering, many of the colors have been shifted, noticeably in top block. There is no indication of the blend.

Using 32 Web-safe colors with dithering restores an indication of the blend but requires much more dithering in the flat colors than the Adaptive palette.

Handling GIF Blends

GIF images with blends need special handling to avoid banding, the abrupt transition from one color to another.

Using 256 colors, there is some banding in the colors of the blend.

Switching to the Web-safe palette creates unacceptable banding.

Adding dithering helps reduce the banding with the 256 colors, and the dithering is hardly noticeable.

Adding dithering to the Web-safe palette helps reduce the banding but is very noticeable.

Color Table

The settings of the Color Table change the look of a GIF image.

The original color table for this image consists of mostly red and gray colors.

When a new color table is loaded, the colors of the image changes to match the new combination of blue colors.

JPEG Comparisons

As you lower the file size of a JPEG image, the image quality decreases. Notice that a small amount of compression is hardly noticeable while the file size is reduced greatly. Notice also how smoothing blurs the image.

JPEG at 100% Quality *creates a 16.58 K image.*

JPEG at 80% Quality *creates a 5.00 K image.*

JPEG at 40% Quality *creates a 2.80 K image.*

JPEG at 40% Quality, Smoothing of 4 *creates 2.52 K image.*

GIF Loss

The Loss control in the GIF Optimize panel decreases the file size while keeping the number of colors constant. However, it can cause distortions in the image.

The original GIF image with no Loss applied has a file size of 9.10K.

With a Loss setting of 10, the file size is reduced to 8.18K. The disortion is hardly noticeable.

With a Loss setting of 50, the file size is reduced to 5.92K, but the distortion is now very noticeable.

Web Palette or Adpative Palette

The differences between an Adaptive palette or a Web palette.

*An **Adaptive palette** maintains as many of the original colors as possible. Notice the subtle shade for the face and hands.*

*A **Web 216 palette** with dithering on creates a pattern of dots in the shirt, face, and hands to simulate non-Web colors. This is unacceptable for flat color art.*

*The **Web 216 palette** with dithering off shifts the colors in the shirt, face, and hands to the closest Web-safe color.*

Gamma Correction

Use the View menu to compare the choosing the Windows or Macintosh gamma on artwork.

Artwork as seen in the **Windows Gamma.** *Notice that the dark letters on the dark background are difficult to read.*

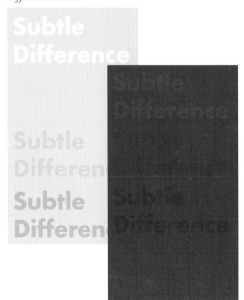

Artwork as seen in the **Macintosh Gamma.** *Notice that the light letters on the light background are difficult to read.*

Web Dither Fill

The Web Dither Fill allows you to use two colors in a checkerboard pattern to create the illusion of a third color.

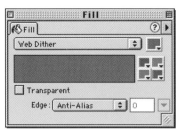

The Fill panel set to Web Dither shows the mixture of the two colors.

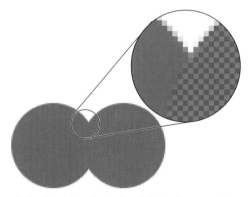

The **Web Dither** *fill in the right circle approximates the purple in the left circle. The blowup shows the color on the right is actually a pattern.*

The Blending Modes

The blending modes control how one color interacts with the colors below it.

*The **Hue** blending mode.*

*The **Normal** blending mode.*

*The **Saturation** blending mode.*

*The **Multiply** blending mode.*

*The **Invert** blending mode.*

*The **Screen** blending mode.*

*The **Tint** blending mode.*

*The **Darken** blending mode.*

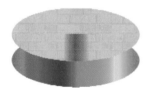

*The **Color** blending mode.*

*The **Lighten** blending mode.*

*The **Luminosity** blending mode*

*The **Difference** blending mode.*

*The **Erase** blending mode.*

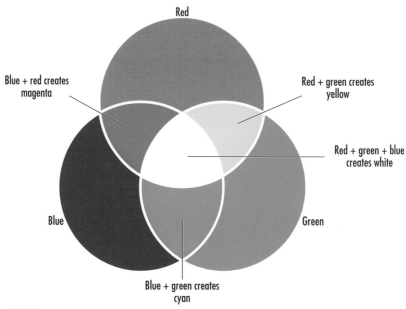

An example of additive colors, sometimes called RGB.

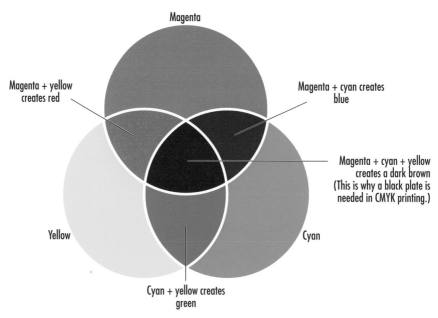

An example of subtractive colors, sometimes called process colors.

ANIMATIONS 16

I t's hard to believe that, just a few years ago, there were very few Web pages with animated images. Today it's hard to find a Web page that doesn't have some type of animated image. Words move up and down or from side to side. One picture turns into another. Images zoom in and out.

Any animation—cartoon, Web graphic, or motion picture—is basically a series of still images that appear in quick succession, giving the illusion of motion. Just like the flip books you played with as a child.

Fireworks gives you an extensive collection of tools and commands to create both GIF animations and Flash (SWF) animations.

I remember how excited I was when I created my first Web animation. Even though I have written and produced many television commercials, it was a real thrill to see my own artwork move around the page. If this is your first experience creating animations, enjoy it!

Working with Frames

Before you can create animations, you need to understand how to work with frames. Each frame of your Fireworks document becomes an image of the animation.

To open the Frames panel:

◆ Choose **Windows** > **Frames**. The Frames panel appears ❶.

Each document contains at least one frame. You can add more frames at any time.

To add individual frames:

1. Click the New/Duplicate icon in the Frames panel. A new frame appears.

TIP The new frame created by clicking the icon is an empty frame that does not contain any artwork.

2. Click the name of the frame to make it the active frame. Any artwork created appears only on that frame.

To add multiple frames:

1. Choose Add Frames from the Frames panel menu. The Add Frames dialog box appears ❷.

2. Use the number control to set how many frames will be added.

3. Click one of the four radio buttons to choose where to insert the new frames.

4. Click OK. The new frames appear.

You can duplicate frames and their artwork by using the Frames panel.

To duplicate frames:

1. Select the frame or frames you want to duplicate.

2. Drag the frames onto the New/Duplicate icon ❸.

Frame number · Frame name

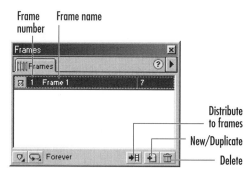

Distribute to frames

New/Duplicate

Delete

❶ *The **Frames** panel. Every new Fireworks document has a single frame.*

❷ *The **Add Frames** dialog box allows you to add many frames at once.*

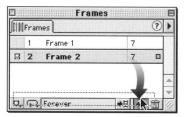

❸ *Drag selected frames onto the New/ Duplicate icon to duplicate those frames.*

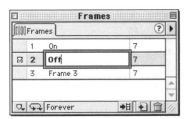

❹ *Double-click to* **rename a frame.**

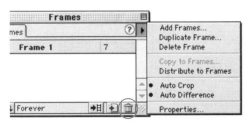

❺ *Use the Frames panel menu or the Delete icon (circled) to delete a frame.*

❻ *Drag selected frames to a new position to reorder a frame.*

Frames are created with the default names Frame 1, Frame 2, and so on. You can change the default names at any time.

To rename a frame:

1. Double-click to highlight the name of the frame **❹**.

2. Type the new name.

3. Press the Return/Enter key to apply the new name.

TIP If you reorder frames, the default names automatically re-number as you change the frame position. Custom names do not change when you reorder frames.

To delete frames:

1. Click to select one frame.

2. Hold the Shift key and click another frame. All the frames between are selected.

   or

   Hold the Command/Ctrl key and click individual frames.

3. Click the Delete icon in the Frames panel.

   or

   Choose Delete Frame from the Frames panel menu **❺**.

To reorder frames:

1. Drag the frame to the new position **❻**.

2. Release the mouse. The frame appears in the new position.

Creating Frame-by-Frame Animations

The most rudimentary way to create animations is to manually place objects on each frame of the document. If you have many objects it may be easier to arrange all the objects on one frame and then let Fireworks automatically place the objects onto new frames.

TIP You can preview how your animation will appear by using the preview controls *(see page 273)*.

To place objects on separate frames:

1. Place the objects on one frame.
2. Add a new frame using the Frames panel *(see previous page)*.
3. Select the new frame.
4. Create the artwork on the new frame.
5. Repeat these steps as many times as is necessary to create the animation.

To automatically distribute objects onto frames:

1. Create a file with all the objects on a single frame.

TIP The order that the objects appear in the Layers panel is the order that they will appear in the Frames panel.

TIP Group objects that you want to stay together on a single frame.

2. Select all the objects and choose Distribute to Frames from the Frames panel menu ❼. New frames are created with each of the objects in the selection on its own frame ❽.

   or

   Click the Distribute to Frames icon at the bottom of the Frames panel.

TIP The number of objects determines the number of frames.

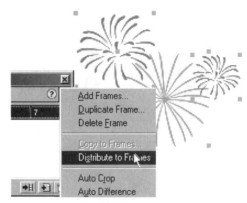

❼ *The* Distribute to Frames *command.*

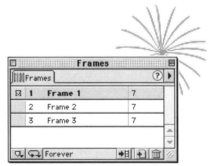

❽ *Distribute to Frames sends each of the grouped objects onto its own frame.*

Creating Frame-by-Frame Animations

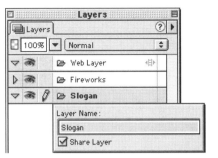

❾ *You can set a layer to be shared across frames.*

❿ *The* **Shared Layer** *icon (circled) indicates that the objects on that layer will be seen on all frames.*

⓫ *The* **Copy to Frames** *dialog box.*

You may want an image to appear on all the frames. Rather than copy the image onto every frame, you can place it on a layer that is shared across frames.

To share a layer across frames:

1. Select the layer that you want to share.

2. Double-click the name of a layer to choose Share Layer **❾**.

    or

    Choose Share Layer from the Layers panel menu. The Shared Layer icon appears next to the layer name **❿**.

TIP When a layer is shared across frames, editing an object on that layer changes the object's appearance on all the frames.

You can also copy an object onto all the frames, or a selected range of frames, of a document.

To copy an object onto frames:

1. Create a file with multiple frames.

2. Place an object on one of the frames that you want to appear on all the frames.

3. With the object selected, choose Copy to Frames from the Frames panel menu. The Copy to Frames dialog box appears **⓫**.

4. Choose All Frames to copy the selected object onto all the frames of the image.

    or

    Use the other selections in the Copy to Frames dialog box to copy an object to a specific frame or a range of frames.

TIP After you copy an object to frames, editing the object changes its appearance only on the frame where you make the changes.

Creating Frame-by-Frame Animations

Importing onto Frames

Although Fireworks has a robust set of drawing tools, you may want to create artwork in programs such as Macromedia FreeHand or Adobe Illustrator . For instance, you can use the blend commands to morph one shape into another. You can then import the artwork and distribute it to frames in Fireworks.

⑫ *A blend created in a vector drawing program can be imported into Fireworks to create an animation.*

TIP Use the Release to Layers command in FreeHand or Illustrator to distribute the blends onto layers.

To distribute vector layers onto frames:

1. Choose File > Import and find a vector file with objects on separate layers. The Vector File Options dialog box opens.

2. Use the Layers pop-up list **⑬** to assign objects on each layer to frames and then click the OK button.

TIP At the time of writing, there is a bug that prevents FreeHand files from importing correctly if you choose this option. You need to import the artwork onto one frame and then use the Distribute to Frames command *(see page 263)*.

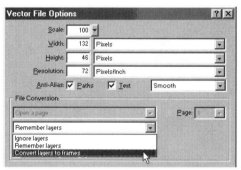

⑬ *The* **File Conversion pop-up list** *lets you move the objects on frames in a vector file onto frames in Fireworks.*

You can also distribute objects on FreeHand's multiple pages onto frames.

To distribute pages onto frames:

1. Choose File > Import and find a FreeHand file with objects on separate pages. This opens the Vector File Options dialog box.

2. Use the Pages pop-up list **⑭** to assign objects on each page to frames and then click the OK button.

TIP Once again there is a bug that prevents FreeHand files from importing correctly. Import each page individually and then use the Distribute to Frames command *(see page 263)*.

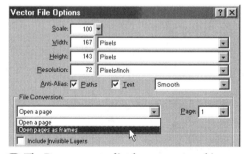

⑭ *The* **Pages pop-up list** *lets you move objects from pages to frames.*

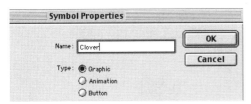

⑮ *The* **Symbol Properties** *dialog box lets you name and choose the type of symbol.*

⑯ *The* **Instance of a symbol** *is indicated by the arrow icon.*

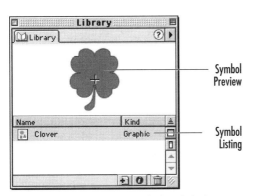

Symbol Preview

Symbol Listing

⑰ *The* **Library** panel *holds the symbols for a document.*

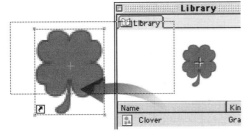

⑱ **Drag a symbol** *from the Library panel to create a new instance.*

Creating Graphic Symbols

Symbols are objects or groups of objects that have the power to control copies of themselves. Copies created from symbols are called *instances*.

There are three types of symbols in Fireworks. *Graphic symbols* are single-frame symbols that can be animated using a technique called *tweening*.

To create a graphic symbol:

1. Select the object or objects that you want to make a symbol.

2. Choose **Insert > Convert to Symbol**. The Symbol Properties dialog box appears **⑮**.

3. Enter the name for the symbol.

4. Choose Graphic as the type of symbol. *(Animation symbols are covered later in this chapter. Button symbols are covered in Chapter 19.)*

5. Click OK. The object on the canvas is converted into an instance of the symbol **⑯**. The symbol appears in the Library panel **⑰**.

You can have as many instances of a symbol as you want on a canvas.

To create additional instances of a symbol:

◆ Copy the instance and paste it on the canvas.

   or

   Opt/Alt-drag to create a new instance.

   or

   Drag the preview or the listing of the symbol from the Library panel onto the canvas **⑱**.

TIP You can drag instances from one document into another. This automatically adds the symbol to the new document's Library panel.

Whatever changes are made to a symbol are automatically applied to all of its instances.

To edit a symbol:

1. Double-click an instance of the symbol. This opens the Symbol Editor **⑲**.

   or

   With an instance selected, choose **Modify** > **Symbol** > **Edit Symbol**.

   or

   Double-click the Symbol Preview or Symbol Listing in the Library panel.

2. In the Symbol Editor, make whatever changes you want to the symbol.

3. Close the window. All instances of the symbol are updated.

TIP Notice that the Symbol Editor does not show the tabs for the Preview options.

TIP If you find it difficult to see the symbol in its window, choose **Modify** > **Canvas Color** to set a separate background color for the symbol.

To create a blank Symbol Editor:

1. Choose **Insert** > **New Symbol**. This opens the Symbol Properties dialog box.

2. Name the symbol.

3. Choose Graphic for the type of symbol.

4. Click OK. A blank Symbol Editor appears.

TIP You can also click the New Symbol icon in the Library panel *(see page 268)* to create a blank Symbol Editor.

To break the link to a symbol:

1. Select the instance.

2. Choose **Modify** > **Symbol** > **Break Apart**. This converts the instance into an ordinary object, no longer controlled by the symbol.

⑲ *The* **Symbol Editor** *is where you can edit the appearance of a symbol.*

Other Uses for Symbols

Although graphic symbols are very helpful in creating animations, they are not limited to only animated images.

You can also use graphic symbols for elements that appear many times in your artwork. Since each instance is governed by the symbol, any changes to the symbol will change all the instances.

For example, if you create a page with the name of the company repeated many times, you can change the typeface or color of the name and see those changes reflected in the instances of that symbol throughout the document.

❷⓿ *The instances created by a graphic symbol can be modified before tweening.*

❷❷ Tweened instances *create frame-by-frame animation.*

Tweening Instances

You can modify two or more instances so that their appearance changes over a series of frames. This is called *tweening*.

To animate instances by tweening:

1. Position the first instance.
2. Position additional instances where you want the instances to move **❷⓿**.
3. Make any changes you want to the instances.

TIP You can scale, rotate, or skew the instances. You can also change the opacity of the instances.

4. Select all the instances and choose **Modify > Symbol > Tween Instances**. The Tween Instances dialog box appears **❷❶**.
5. Set the number of new instances that will be added between the current symbol instances.
6. Select Distribute to Frames to create new frames with each instance on its own frame.

TIP If you do not select Distribute to Frames in the Tween Instances dialog box, you can use the Distribute to Frames icon in the Frames panel (*see page 258*).

7. Click OK. The new instances fill in the space between the original instances **❷❷**.

❷❶ *The* Tween Instances *dialog box lets you set the number of steps between the instances.*

A Bit of History

The term tweening comes from film animation. The artists who drew the animations would draw the main frames of an action. They would then hand the job over to lower-ranking artists, called tweeners, who would fill in the artwork between the frames of the action.

Tweening Instances

One important advantage that tweening has over animation symbols *(see the next page)* is the ability to tween effects. This allows you to change an object's color or apply any of the other effects as part of the animation.

TIP At the time of this writing, there are some bugs that prevent all the effects from being tweened. For example, the drop shadow effect does not tween correctly.

To tween effects:

1. Select an instance of a graphic symbol.
2. Use the Effect panel to add an effect to the instance ㉓. For example, to change the color of an object, you would use the Color Fill effect.
2. Apply the same effect to another instance of the same symbol.

TIP You must apply the effect to both instances. For example, you must have the color effect set for both instances to see a color change.

3. Apply the Tween command. The effect changes across the intermediate steps of the tween ㉔.

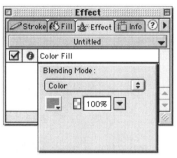

㉓ *Use the* **Color Fill effect** *to change the color of an instance.*

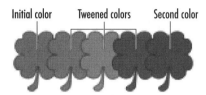

Initial color   Tweened colors   Second color

㉔ *Tweening two instances with the Color Effect applied lets you change the color of an object as part of an animation.*

Tweening versus Animation Symbols

Tweening the instances created by graphic symbols offers some advantages over using animation symbols. *(See the opposite page for more information on working with animation symbols.)*

You can tween multiple objects to move them in different directions. You can apply effects such as changing color. Or you can apply skewing to change the shape of an instance.

However, unlike animation symbols, tweened instances are discreet objects on multiple frames and cannot be easily modified later.

The Symbol Properties dialog box lets you set an animation symbol.

This frame-by-frame animation symbol has the Up graphic on one frame of the symbol and the Down graphic on the second.

Play button

An animation symbol in the Library panel displays a special animation symbol icon (circled).

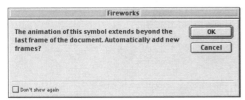

This dialog box adds the extra frames necessary to display an animation symbol.

Creating Animation Symbols

Animation symbols make it easier to animate objects and make changes. You can create an animation symbol that contains frame-by-frame animation.

TIP You can preview how your animation will appear by using the preview controls *(see page 273).*

To create a frame-by-frame animation symbol:

1. Choose **Insert > New Symbol**.

2. In the Symbol Properties dialog box, name the symbol and set the type for Animation 25.

3. Click OK to open the Symbol Editor.

4. In the Symbol Editor use the tools and commands to create the artwork.

TIP To use existing artwork in the animation, cut the artwork from the document window and then paste it into the Symbol Editor.

5. Use the Frames panel to add the frames to the animation Symbol Editor.

6. Create the artwork for each frame of the animation.

TIP For instance, to animate text that changes, you would put one text block on the first frame and another text block on a second frame 26.

7. Close the Symbol Editor. The new symbol you just created appears in the Library panel 27.

TIP Click the Play button in the Library panel to see a preview of the animation.

8. Drag the symbol from the Library panel to add it to your document.

TIP If you see a dialog box asking you to add frames, click OK 28. The animation symbol will not play properly without the extra frames.

Creating Animation Symbols

The Animate selection command automatically converts an object into an animation symbol. These automatic controls let you set the motion, direction, scaling, opacity, and rotation of the symbol.

To set the automatic animation controls:

1. Select the artwork you want to animate.

2. Choose **Modify** > **Animate** > **Animate Selection**. This opens the Animate dialog box 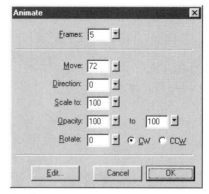.

3. Use any combination of the settings to control the animation as follows **30**:

   - **Frames** sets the number of frames that the animation will use.
   - **Move** sets the distance (in pixels) that the object will move.
   - **Direction** sets the angle that the object will move.
   - **Scale** to sets the final size of the object.
   - **Opacity** sets the beginning and end opacity of the object.
   - **Rotate** sets the degrees that the object will rotate and the direction of rotation as clockwise (CW) or counterclockwise (CCW).

4. Click OK to close the dialog box and return to the document window. The selected object is added to the Library panel. An instance of the symbol replaces the artwork originally selected.

TIP If you set an amount in the Motion field, a motion control line extends out from the instance **31**. *(See page 271 for how to manually adjust the control.)*

TIP Using the Animate Selection command skips the Symbol Properties dialog box. So, if you want to change the name of the symbol, you need to open the Symbol Properties.

29 *The* **Animate dialog box** *lets you set the controls for automatic animation.*

30 *Using a combination of the animation controls, this text was set to move, fade in, scale up, and rotate over ten frames.*

31 *The* **motion control** *extends out from the animation symbol.*

32 *Automatic animation controls moved and rotated the arrow. Frame-by-frame animation created the motion lines around the arrow.*

Nesting Symbols

If you have used graphic and animation symbols in Macromedia Flash, you should be familiar with the concept of nesting symbols—using the instance of a graphic symbol as the artwork for an animation symbol.

For instance, let's say you create a graphic symbol of a star.

You can then drag an instance of that star from the Library panel into the Symbol Editor of a frame-by-frame animation.

Next, you can use two or more frames to create the effect of the star blinking on and off or changing color.

Finally, you can add the automatic animation controls to make the blinking star rotate and move across the page.

The benefit of all this is, if you want to change the shape or color of the star, you only need to edit the original graphic symbol and all the other instances will update.

You can also convert existing artwork into a frame-by-frame animation symbol.

To convert artwork into a frame-by-frame animation symbol:

1. Select the artwork you want to animate.
2. Choose **Insert > Convert to Symbol**. This opens the Symbol Properties dialog box.
3. Name the symbol and set the type for animation and click OK. This opens the Animate dialog box.
4. Click Edit in the Animate dialog box. This opens the Symbol Editor which contains the selected artwork.
5. Use the frame-by-frame techniques described on pages 258–259 to create the animation.
6. Close the Symbol Editor. The new symbol appears in the Library panel. An instance of the symbol replaces the artwork that was selected.

Finally, you can create an animation symbol that uses a combination of automatic animation and frame-by-frame techniques **32**.

To create a combination of animation controls:

1. Select the artwork you want to animate.
2. Choose **Modify > Animate > Animate Selection**.
3. Set the Animate options as described on the previous page.
4. Click Edit to open the Symbol Editor and set the frame-by-frame animation.
5. Close the Symbol Editor. The new animation symbol appears in the Library panel and the animation instance replaces the selected artwork.

TIP Combining the two types of animation allows you to move artwork on the page while at the same time changing the image inside the artwork.

Working with Symbols

Creating symbols isn't enough; you will also want to edit them. You can change the name of a symbol or convert to a different type of symbol by opening the Symbol Properties dialog box.

To open the Symbol Properties dialog box:

◆ Double-click the listing of the symbol in the Library panel.

or

Choose Properties from the Library panel menu. ➌➌.

or

Click the Properties icon in the Library panel.

You can edit the artwork or frames of a symbol by opening the Symbol Editor.

To open the Symbol Editor:

◆ Double-click a graphic or animation symbol.

or

Choose Edit Symbol from the Library panel menu ➌➍.

or

Double-click the symbol preview in the Library panel.

or

Click the Edit button in the Symbol Properties dialog box.

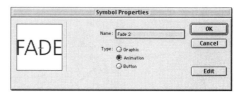

➌➌ *The* **Symbol Properties** dialog box *for an existing symbol.*

New Symbol   Symbol Properties

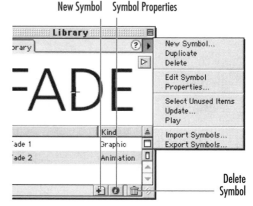

Delete
Symbol

➌➍ *The* **Library panel** *displays and controls the symbols in a document.*

WARNING: Saving Symbols

The Save command does not work when you are working inside the Symbol Editor. You must close the window and then apply the Save command to save your work.

Working with Symbols

You may notice two commands in the Library panel for Exporting Symbols and Importing Symbols.

This makes it possible for you to use symbols throughout many different Fireworks documents. Then, if you change the appearance of a symbol in the main document, you can update all the instances in other documents.

Although it is perfectly fine to use these commands with graphic and animation symbols, it's more likely that you will want to export button symbols to other documents. Exporting and importing symbols are covered in Chapter 19, "Behaviors."

Of course, the techniques described here for editing, naming, duplicating, deleting, and managing graphic and animation symbols also apply to button symbols.

To create a blank Symbol Editor:

◆ Click the New Symbol icon in the Library panel **34**.

or

Choose New Symbol from the Library panel menu.

To duplicate a symbol:

◆ Drag the symbol listing onto the New Symbol icon in the Library panel **34**.

or

With the symbol selected choose Duplicate from the Library panel menu.

To delete a symbol:

1. Select the symbol or symbols you want to delete.

2. Click the Delete icon in the Library panel **34**.

or

Drag the symbols onto the Delete icon.

or

Choose Delete from the Library panel menu.

TIP If you delete a symbol that is in use you will see a dialog box alerting you that this will also delete any instances of that symbol in the document.

TIP You may also want to clean up your files by deleting symbols which are not in use. Use the Select Unused Items in the Library panel menu so you can then delete them.

Modifying Animations

Fireworks uses a technique called *onion skinning,* which allows you to see a lower opacity version of the objects on other frames 35.

TIP For those who are wondering, I turned on onion skinning to create the animation images in this chapter.

To turn on Onion Skinning:

1. Open the Onion Skinning controls in the Frames panel 36.

TIP You can turn on onion skinning in either the Document window or a Symbol Editor.

TIP If you turn on onion skinning in the Document window, you need to turn it on separately in a Symbol Editor.

2. Choose one of the following options:
   - **Show Next Frame** displays the frame after the selected frame.
   - **Before and After** shows the frames before and after the selected frame.
   - **Show All Frames** displays all the frames in the document.

TIP Onion skinning also shows the individual steps of automatic animation symbols.

35 *An example of how* **onion skinning** *lets you see the frames of an animation.*

36 *The* **Onion Skinning** *menu in the Frames panel.*

Still More History

Once again a term in computer animation comes from traditional film animation. Onion skinning comes from the days when film animators used vellum sheets to plot their animations. When the sheets were layered, the artists could see through them like the layers of an onion.

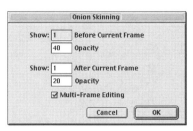

37 *The* Onion Skinning *dialog box.*

38 *Move the* Onion Skinning controls *in the Frames panel to customize which frames should be displayed. Here frames 1–6 have onion skinning turned on.*

39 Multi-frame editing *allows you to select and modify objects on different frames.*

Green dot (start)   Red dot (end)

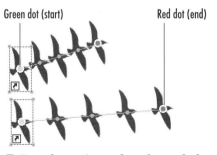

40 Drag the motion path *to change the length and direction of an animation symbol.*

To customize onion skinning:

1. Choose Custom from the Onion Skinning controls menu. The Onion Skinning dialog box appears **37**.

2. Change the number of frames that should be visible.

3. Change the opacity of the visible frames.

TIP Click to move the onion skinning icons to the frames you want displayed **38**.

Multi-frame editing allows you to work with objects that are on different frames.

To edit multiple frames of a window:

1. Make sure onion skinning is turned on.

TIP The frames available for multi-frame editing are limited to the frames visible through onion skinning.

2. Choose Multi-Frame Editing from the Onion Skinning menu of the Frames panel.

3. Use any of the tools or commands to select objects on any of the visible frames **39**.

You can change the length and direction of an animation by changing its motion path.

To edit an animation symbol motion path:

1. Drag the green dot of the motion path to position the start of the animation **40**.

2. Drag the red dot to position the end of the animation.

TIP If there is no motion path, only a green dot, you need to add frames using the Object panel or choose **Modify** > **Animate** >**Animate Settings**.

To edit the attributes of an animation symbol:

◆ Use the Object panel to change the number of frames, scaling, opacity, or rotation ❹❶.

or

Choose **Modify** >**Animate** >**Settings** to open the Animate dialog box.

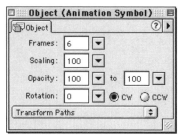

❹❶ *The* **Object panel for an animation symbol** *lets you change the automatic animation controls.*

The number of frames assigned to an animation symbol can be extended. This allows you to create a symbol that loops or repeats during the animation ❹❷.

To create a repeating animation symbol:

1. Create a frame-by-frame animation symbol *(see page 265)*. For instance, you can create a star that blinks on two separate frames.

2. Place the instance of the symbol on the canvas.

3. Use the Object panel to increase the number of frames for that instance of the symbol ❹❶. For example, if symbol has two frames, setting six frames in the Object panel repeats the animation three times.

❹❷ **Increase the frames for an animation symbol** *to repeat the animation. Here the two frames of the blinking star repeat three times across six frames.*

Two instances of the same animation symbols can start on different frames of the document. This causes the instances to display their images on staggered frames ❹❸.

To stagger the animation display:

1. Create a frame-by-frame animation symbol. For instance, you can create a star that blinks on two separate frames.

2. Place one instance of the symbol on the first frame of the document.

3. Use the Object panel to extend the number of frames.

4. Place another instance on the next frame. When the animation plays, each instance displays a different image in each frame.

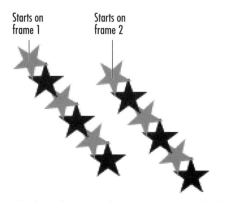

❹❸ **Place the start of an animation symbol on different frames** *to stagger the appearance of the animation.*

Modifying Animations

First frame Play/ Stop Last frame Current frame Previous frame Next frame

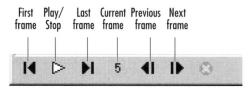

❹❹ *The* **Animation Controls** *in the Document window.*

❹❺ *The* **Animation Controls** *in the Export Preview dialog box.*

Don't Overload Your Animations

As exciting as it is to create an animation, watch out. If you create a large image with many colors and many frames your animation will take too long to download.

Previewing Animations

As you create animations, you may want to see how the frames look in sequence. Fireworks lets you preview animations in the Document window.

To preview animations in the document window:

◆ Use the animation controls at the bottom of the Document window **❹❹**.

- **Next frame** or **Previous frame** move one frame at a time.
- **First frame** or **Last frame** jump to the beginning or end of the animation.
- **Play** runs the animation.
- **Stop** halts the play of the animation.

TIP If you want to see the animation with the Preview tab selected, make sure you have set the Optimize panel to Animated GIF. If not, the animation will play extremely slowly. *(For more information on using the Optimize panel and Preview tab, see Chapter 15, "Optimizing.")*

You can also preview animations in the Export Preview dialog box although it is much easier to preview in the Document window.

To preview animations in Export Preview:

1. Choose **File** > **Export Preview**.

2. Use the animation controls at the bottom of the preview area **❹❺**.

Previewing Animations

Frame Controls

Just as in comedy, in animation timing is everything. Fireworks lets you control the frame timing, or how long each frame remains visible.

To set the frame timing in the document window:

1. Double-click the number in the Frame Delay column of the frame in the Frames panel. This opens the Frames Properties controls **46**.

   or

   Select the frame and choose Properties from the Frames panel menu.

   TIP Use the Shift key to select more than one frame at a time.

2. Enter a number in the Frame Delay field. The higher the number, the longer the frame remains visible.

3. Press the Return/Enter key to apply the changes and close the Frames Properties control.

If you use the Export Preview dialog box to optimize and export your images, you can set the animation timing using the animation controls in the Export Preview.

To set the frame timing in Export Preview:

1. Choose File > **Export Preview**.

2. Click the Animation tab to display the Frame list.

3. Enter a number in the Frame Delay field **47**.

   TIP The bottom of the animation area in the Export Preview shows the total running time of the animation.

Frame Delay column

46 *The Frames Properties controls let you set the frame delay for each frame.*

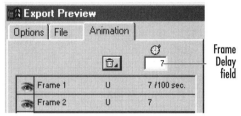

Frame Delay field

47 *Set the frame delay in the Export Preview to control how long a frame is visible during an animation.*

Timing Secrets

Here are a few of my favorite timing tricks for animations.

If you set the animation to loop many times, set the last frame of an animation to run longer than the other frames. This gives your viewer's eyes a chance to rest on the final frame.

If objects move in the animation, increase the frame delay as the animation progresses. This gives the effect of the objects slowing down as they move.

Decrease the frame delay as the animation progresses to give the effect of speeding up the motion.

Stagger the timing of frames to make the objects more natural looking.

Frame Controls

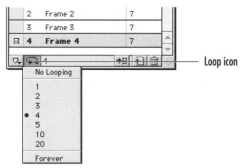

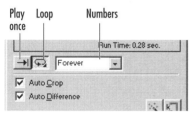

Loop icon

48 *The* **Loop** *controls in the document window.*

Play Loop   Numbers
once

49 *The* **Looping** *controls of the* *Export Preview.*

You can set how many times the animation repeats using the *looping* controls.

TIP Some Web sites require banner ads to repeat only a certain number of times and then stop.

To set looping in the document window:

1. Click the Loop icon to open the Loop list **48**. Set the list as follows:
   - **No Looping** sets the animation to play once.
   - The numbers specify how many times the animation repeats.
   - **Forever** plays the animation endlessly.
2. Press Return/Enter to apply the setting.

TIP The first time the animation plays is not counted in the Loop control. So, to play the animation four times, set the loop number to three.

To set looping in the Export Preview:

1. Choose **File** > **Export Preview**.
2. Click the Animation tab to display the Loop controls at the bottom of the Animation Frames list **49**.
3. Click the Play once icon to have the animation play one time and then stop.
4. Click the Loop icon.
5. Open the Numbers list and choose how many times the animation should play.

Looping Trick

Normally, GIF animations start on frame 1 and end on the last frame of the animation. If the first frame of your animation contains the most important information, here's how to have an animation stop on the first frame.

Duplicate the first frame and position it at the end of the animation. Set the timing for the duplicate first frame to a small amount.

When the animation runs, it appears to run full circle and stop on the first frame. It actually stops on the last frame—the duplicate of the first frame.

Fireworks also lets you control the *frame disposal.* This is a sophisticated way to control transition of the pixels on one frame to the next frame or the background. Frame disposal can help speed the download of a GIF animation.

To set the transition of the frames:

1. Select a frame in the animation options panel of the Export Preview.

2. Use the Disposal method list ⑤⓪ to control the blends between frames.

    *   **Unspecified** has Fireworks choose the most efficient disposal method.
    *   **None** leaves any pixels that are not covered by the next frame visible. This option is useful when objects are revealed in different areas of the frames.
    *   Select **Restore to Background** when transparency is turned on so that each frame changes from one to another.
    *   Select **Revert to Background** when objects appear over a frame created earlier. Revert to Background is not supported by all browsers.

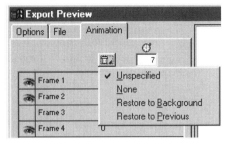

⑤⓪ *The* **Disposal method** *list.*

Fireworks is Disposal Smart

You don't have to worry about the disposal settings. As Macromedia says, Fireworks is disposal smart— that is, the Unspecified setting automatically chooses the most efficient disposal method.

For example, when the Unspecified setting is chosen and the background is transparent, Fireworks automatically uses the correct disposal method which is Restore to Background.

So, unless you have an overwhelming reason why you want to change the disposal setting, leave it set to Unspecified.

Frame Controls

51 Auto Crop *and* Auto Difference *are on by default to create the smallest possible files.*

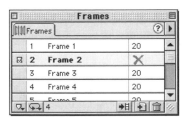

52 *The X marks the* **frame excluded from export** *in the Frames panel.*

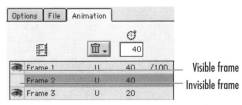

Visible frame
Invisible frame

53 *The* **visibility settings for frames.** *In this example, frames 1 and 3 are set to export but frame 2 is not set to export.*

The Export Preview has another way to control the final size of the animation: the Auto Crop and Auto Difference settings.

TIP These settings are on by default to give you the smallest possible files. If you export animations to other applications, such as Macromedia Director, you may need to turn off these settings.

To set the Auto Crop and Auto Difference:

1. Choose the Animation tab of the Export Preview dialog box. The Auto Crop and Auto Difference settings are at the bottom of the Animation panel **51**.

2. Check Auto Crop to have Fireworks automatically crop the image instead of sending the same information over and over.

3. Check Auto Difference to use a transparency to make the file size even smaller.

Even though you have created certain frames, you don't have to export them in the final animation.

To set the frames to export in the Frames panel:

1. Open the Frames Properties control for the frame you want to omit *(see page 274).*

2. Deselect Include When Exporting.

3. Close the control. A red X next to the frame **52** indicates that the frame will not export as part of the animation.

To set the frames to export in Export Preview:

1. Choose **File** > **Export Preview**.

2. Click the Animation tab to display the Frame list.

3. Click the Show/Hide icon in the Animation tab **53**. If the icon is visible, the frame exports. If the icon is not visible, the frame does not export.

Optimizing Animations

After you have finished the frames of the animation, you use the Optimize panel or Export Preview to fine tune the settings and export the file.

To set the animation export options:

1. Open the Optimize panel .

   or

   Choose **File** > **Export** to open the Export Preview window.

2. Choose Animated GIF from the Format list ⑤⑤.

3. Set the GIF color and transparency options as desired *(see Chapter 15, "Optimizing")*.

4. Use the Export commands to export the file *(see Chapter 20, "Exporting")*.

⑤④ *Choose* **Animated GIF** *from the Optimize panel before exporting an animated GIF.*

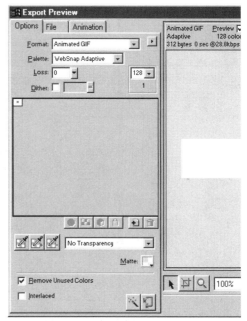

⑤⑤ *Choose* **Animated GIF** *from the Export Preview dialog box to export an animation.*

HOTSPOTS AND LINKS **17**

Imagine you are creating a magical machine that transports people all over the world. How would you design the controls? One way might be to start with a map of the world. Your users would simply touch a certain part of the map and they would be instantly transported to where they wanted to go.

That's the idea behind image maps for Web graphics. You embed different areas of an image with information that sends the viewer to different Web pages or performs a certain action. All the viewer needs to do is click inside each area of the image and they are transported to a new Web page.

The special areas on the image are created using the Fireworks hotspot tools. The information that sends you to a new Web page or performs the action is called a link.

Creating Hotspots

You can draw hotspots directly on your image using one of the three hotspot tools: the Rectangle, Circle, and Polygon hotspot tools.

To draw a rectangular or circular hotspot object:

1. Choose the Rectangle or Circle hotspot tool in the Tools panel ❶.
2. Drag to create a rectangle or circle that defines the hotspot area ❷.

TIP Hold the Shift key to constrain the Rectangle to a square.

TIP Hold the Opt/Alt key to drag from the center outward.

TIP Hotspots are automatically placed on the Web layer even if that layer is not the selected layer.

To draw a polygon hotspot object:

1. Choose the Polygon hotspot tool in the Tools panel ❶.
2. Click to set the first point of the polygon.
3. Click the next corner of the polygon to make the first line segment.
4. Continue clicking to set additional points.
5. Close the hotspot object by clicking again on the first point ❷.

Circle
hotspot tool

Rectangle
hotspot tool

Polygon
hotspot tool

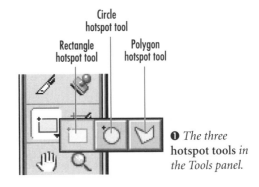

❶ *The three* **hotspot tools** *in the Tools panel.*

❷ **Hotspots** *can be rectangular, circular, or irregular polygons.*

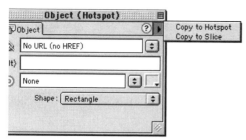

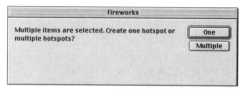

❸ *The Object panel menu lets you copy and convert regular paths into hotspot objects.*

❹ *You can choose if one hotspot or multiple hotspots are created from multiple selected paths.*

You can also copy and convert any Fireworks path into a hotspot object. This is much easier than trying to match the exact size of an object.

To convert a single object into a hotspot:

1. Select the path you wish to convert.

2. Choose **Insert** >**Hotspot**.

   or

   Choose Copy to Hotspot from the Object panel menu **❸**.

   or

   Drag the object square in the Layers panel from the object layer to the Web layer. *(For more information on working with the Layers panel, see page 104.)* This copies the shape of the selected object into a hotspot object.

TIP When curved objects are converted to hotspots they are converted to polygons with a series of small straight line segments.

You can also copy and convert multiple Fireworks paths into hotspots.

To convert multiple objects into hotspots:

1. Select the paths you wish to convert.

2. Choose one of the choices for step 2 in the previous exercise. A dialog box appears asking whether you want to convert the multiple objects into one hotspot or several **❹**.

3. Click One to create a single hotspot that covers all the selected paths.

   or

   Click Multiple to create individual hotspots that follow the shapes of the selected paths **❺**.

❺ *Selected vector paths can be converted into polygon hotspot objects.*

Creating Hotspots

Modifying Hotspots

Once you have created hotspot objects, you can still modify them.

To move and modify hotspot objects:

1. Choose either the Selection or the Subselection tools in the Tools panel.

2. Drag inside a hotspot object to move it to a new positon.

3. Drag one of the anchor points of the hotspot object to change its shape ❻.

You can also convert hotspot objects from one shape to another.

To change hotspot shapes:

1. Choose the hotspot object you want to convert.

2. Choose a shape from the Hotspot Object panel Shape list ❼.

The Web layer allows you to control the visibility of hotspots.

TIP You may want to hide hotspots in order to select or modify the paths below the hotspots.

To show and hide hotspot objects:

1. To hide the hotspot objects, click the Show/Hide icon for the Web layer ❽.

2. To show the hotspot objects, click the empty area in the Show/Hide icon column for the Web layer.

   or

   Use any of the hotspot tools on the image. The Web layer automatically becomes visible.

TIP You can show and hide hotspots using the Show/Hide controls at the bottom of the Tools panel.

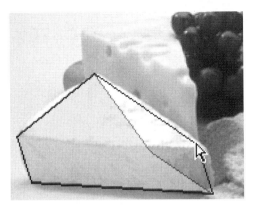

❻ *Use the Selection or Subselection tools to* **modify hotspot objects.**

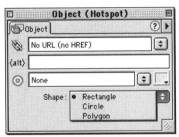

❼ *The* **Shape menu** *of the Hotspot Object panel.*

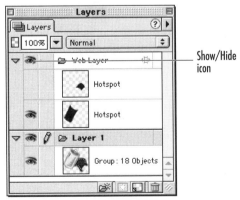

❽ *The* **Show/Hide icon** *for the Web layer.*

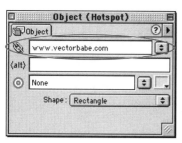

❾ The **Links** field *in the Hotspot Object panel.*

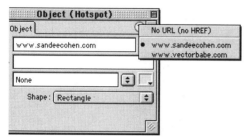

❿ The **Link list** *in the Hotspot Object panel.*

Understanding URLs

URL stands for *uniform resource locator*. It contains information for the browser to perform an action. The most common types of URLs are http, mailto, and ftp.

http stands for HyperText Transfer Protocol. These are the links that send visitors to new Web pages.

mailto is used to send e-mail.

ftp stands for File Transfer Protocol. It directs the browser to download a file located in a specific location.

Fireworks supports all these types of links. For more information on working with URLs, you can read *HTML 4.0: No Experience Required* by Stephen Mack and Janan Platt.

Assigning Hotspot Attributes

Once you have created hotspot objects, you can then apply URL links to them. If you need to apply only one or two links you can easily type them directly into the Object panel.

To link a hotspot to a URL:

1. Select the hotspot object.
2. Type the URL in the Links field in the Hotspot Object panel **❾**.

As you apply or create URL links a record of each link is retained as the Link list. You can use the list to reapply a URL link without having to type it.

To apply links from the Link list:

1. Select the hotspot object you want to apply a URL link to.
2. Press the pop-up Link list next to the Links field in the Hotspot Object panel **❿**.
3. Choose the link you want to apply to the hotspot.

TIP Only the links that have been applied to objects are kept in the Link list. Other links are discarded when you quit Fireworks. If you want a permanent record of all the URL links, you can add the list to a URL library *(see page 285).*

Hotspots don't have to have URL links. A hotspot can also be used as the trigger for a behavior. *(See Chapter 19, "Behaviors.")*

To detach a URL link from a hotspot:

1. Select the hotspot.
2. Choose No URL (no HREF) from the Link list.

TIP The No URL (no HREF) is the default entry for new hotspots.

(see page 285).

Assigning Hotspot Attributes

In addition to the URL links, there are other settings for hotspot objects. The (alt) tag contains the text that is displayed while the image is loading or if the image can't be found.

To set the (alt) tag:

◆ Type the text in the (alt) field **11**.

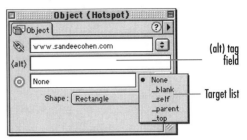

11 *The* **Hotspot panel commands.**

The Target field controls where the Web page requested by a link appears. Targets are usually used as part of framesets.

To set the target:

◆ Use the Target list or type in the field **12** the window or frame you want the link to open to.

 • **None** and **_self** open the destination page in the same location that the button was in.
 • **_blank** opens the destination page in a new browser window.
 • **_parent** opens the destination page in the parent frameset of the link.
 • **_top** replaces all the frames in the current browser window and opens the destination page in that window.

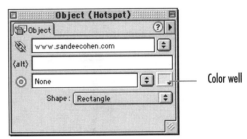

12 *The* **Hotspot color well** *allows you to change the color of the overlay.*

Hotspots are displayed with a see-through overlay. You can change the overlay color to help organize different links.

To change the hotspot color:

◆ Use the hotspot color well **12** to set the color for different hotpsots.

TIP Darker colors make it easier to see through the overlay.

Assigning Hotspot Attributes

⓭ *The* URL *panel allows you to manage multiple URLs.*

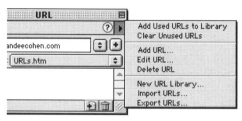

⓮ *The* URL panel menu.

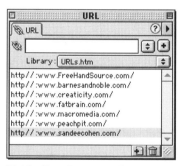

⓯ *The* list of URLs *in the URL panel.*

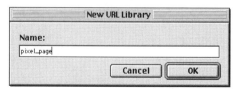

⓰ *The* New URL Library *dialog box.*

Managing Links

Typing URL links is fine if you only have a couple of links to add. However, complicated Web sites can have hundreds of links. Fireworks offers you many features for working with large numbers of links. Rather than type links one by one you can import URLs from any HTML file, Netscape Navigator bookmarks, or Internet Explorer favorites.

To import links:

1. If the URL panel **⓭** is not visible, choose **Window > URL Manager**.

2. Choose Import URLs from the panel menu **⓮**.

3. Navigate to select an HTML file, Navigator bookmarks file, or Internet Explorer favorites file. The URLs appear as a list in the panel **⓯**.

You can also create *libraries,* or groups of URLs. This allows you to group all the URLs for a certain Web site or client.

To create a URL library:

1. Choose New URL Library from the URL panel menu. This opens the New URL Library dialog box **⓰**.

2. Type the name of the library and click OK. This adds the library to the library list.

TIP Libraries can be used by multiple documents.

TIP To delete a library from the list, delete the library file located in the folder Fireworks:Configuration:URL Libraries.

You can add the current URL assigned to an object to a URL Library.

To add the current URL to a Library:

1. Create a new library or choose a library from the list.

2. Click the Add Current URL in the URL panel menu ⓱. The URL appears as part of the URL Library.

⓱ *The* **Add Current URL button** *(circled) allows you to add the URL of a selected object to the URL Library.*

The URL panel keeps a list of used URLs in all the documents for that session of Fireworks. This list is erased when you quit Fireworks. You can make the list permanent by adding the used URLs to a library.

To add used URLs to a Library:

1. Create a new library or choose a library from the list.

2. Choose Add Used URLs to Library from the URL panel menu.

Add URL Delete URL

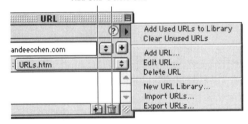

⓲ *Click the* **Add URL icon** *or choose Add URL from the menu to add URL links to a library.*

To add a new URL link to a Library:

1. Select the library that you want to add the URL link to.

2. Choose Add URL from the URL Manager menu or click the Add URL icon ⓲. This opens the New URL dialog box ⓳.

3. Type the URL in the field and then click OK. This adds the URL to the library.

⓳ *The* **New URL dialog box** *lets you type in new links for the selected library.*

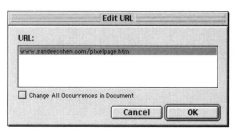

⑳ *The* **Edit URL dialog box** *lets you edit URLs and apply the changes to all occurrences of the URL in the document.*

To delete URL links:

1. Choose a link in the library.
2. Choose Delete URL from the URL panel menu or click the Delete URL icon.

URL links change continually. Fortunately, Fireworks provides a simple way to edit URL links in a document.

To edit URL links:

1. Click the URL you want to edit.
2. Choose Edit URL from the URL panel menu. This opens the Edit URL dialog box **⑳**.
3. Make whatever changes you want to the URL.
4. Check Change all Occurrences in Document to change all the objects that use that URL.

Managing Links

SLICES 18

Why would anyone spend hours creating an intricate Web graphic and then cut it up into different pieces? Well, the technique is called *slicing* and it allows you to define regions of an image that you can set to behave differently.

For instance, you might want to slice an image so that each slice has its own optimization settings depending on the type of artwork. You might want to slice an image into sections so that you can easily update new products or news stories. You can also slice an image so that it contains plain HTML text rather than an image.

Macromedia Fireworks makes it easy to control where to put the slices and to apply special attributes to each slice region.

Using Ruler Guides to Slice

If you're in a hurry, and don't need to set any different optimization settings, the easiest way to slice an image is to use ruler guides.

To slice using ruler guides:

1. Drag a guide from a ruler around the side of the area you want to slice *(see pages 38–39)*.

2. Drag additional guides until you have defined all the slices for the image ❶.

3. When you export the file, set the Slicing to Slice Along Guides *(see Chapter 20, "Exporting.")*

> **TIP** Fireworks opens Adobe Photoshop files with the Photoshop guides in place. They can then be used as ordinary slices in Fireworks.

> **TIP** Use hotspot objects *(see Chapter 17, "Hotspots and Links")* to add links to slices created by guides.

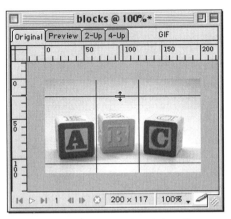

❶ *Ruler guides can be used to define slices.*

Why Slices? (Part One)

Slices make it easier to update the images on a Web site. For instance, you might have a portion of a graphic that changes periodically. Slicing that part of the image makes it easier to update.

Sliced images appear to download faster. Some Web servers can send out multiple images. So the individual slices of an image are downloaded together. This gives the impression that the image is downloading faster.

Also, the first time visitors view images those images are cached, or stored, on their computers. The next time visitors come to that image, even if it's on a different page, it appears faster because it is already downloaded.

Using Ruler Guides to Slice

❷ *When ruler guides are used to slice an image they may cut into other images that you don't want sliced such as the slices through the images of the statue and Mt. Rushmore.*

Slice object   Slice guide

❸ *Slice objects create slice guides that keep the slices to a minimum and avoid cutting through other slice objects.*

❹ *The* **Rectangular Slice tool** *in the Tools panel.*

❺ *Drag the* **Slice** *tool to create a* **Slice object.**

Creating Slice Objects

Ruler guides do not provide enough control to slice all the areas of the image accurately. For instance, a guide around one area may cut through an area that you don't want sliced ❷. Slice objects create slices around specific areas of your image. Other areas are sliced only if necessary.

TIP Slice objects create slice guides that create the minimum amount of slices necessary to slice the rest of the image ❸.

To use the Rectangular Slice tool:

1. Choose the Rectangular Slice tool from the Tools panel ❹. (Be careful, it's sharp.)

2. Drag a rectangle around the area that you want to slice ❺. This creates a rectangular slice object.

TIP If slice objects overlap, the top object will be used to control optimization, behaviors, and actions.

3. Use the Selection tools to move or modify slice objects.

TIP Slice objects can be copied, pasted and duplicated just like ordinary objects *(see Chapter 6, "Working with Objects.")*

Creating Slice Objects

291

To use the Polygon Slice tool:

1. Choose the Polygon Slice tool from the Tools panel ❻.
2. Click to create a point that defines each segment of the polygon that defines the slice ❼.
3. Use the Selection tools to move or modify slice objects.

To create slices from objects:

1. Select the object or objects you want to slice. This includes placed images.
2. Choose **Insert > Slice**. This creates a slice object around the selected object.

TIP If you select multiple objects, a dialog box will ask if you want to create multiple slices or a single slice.

❻ *The* **Polygon Slice tool** *in the Tools panel.*

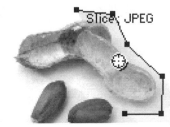

❼ *Click to create segments of a polygon slice.*

When should you use Polygon Slices?

Polygon slices are useful when you want to add behaviors or hotspots to intricate graphics or where rectangular slices would overlap.

However, the Polygon Slice tool doesn't really create polygon-shaped slices. You can't have anything except rectangular slices in your image.

The area under a Polygon Slice is actually a hotspot image with as many rectangular sub-slices as necessary to create the irregular shape.

Many slices means more images that need to be handled as your Web page loads. This can slow down the display of your page.

Bottom line: Use the Polygon Slice tool not because you *can,* but because you *must!*

Show/Hide icon

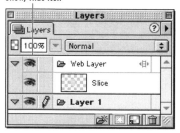

❽ *Use the* **Web Layer Show/Hide icon** *to control the display of slice objects.*

Hide Web   Show Web
Layer   Layer

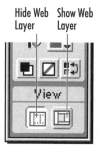

❾ *Use the* **Show/Hide Web Layer icons** *in the Tools panel to control the display of slice objects.*

Viewing Slice Objects and Guides

You may find it difficult to select or work with objects that have slices over them. You can control whether or not the slices or the slices guides are displayed.

To show and hide slice objects:

◆ Click the Show/Hide icon for the Web Layer in the Layers panel ❽.

or

Click the Show or Hide Web Layer icons at the bottom of the Tools panel ❾.

To show and hide slice guides:

◆ Choose **View** > **Slice Guides.** This hides and displays the slice guides.

Why Slices? (Part Two)

Slicing also comes in handy when you need to use more than one export format for an image.

For instance, artwork that contains primarily flat colors should be exported as GIF files. Artwork with photographic images is usually exported in the JPEG format.

You can also use slices so that GIF images contain their own unique color tables.

Viewing Slice Objects and Guides

Setting the Slice Options

You set the options for slice objects using the Slice Object panel. Its controls are similar to the Hotspot options. *(For more information working with the URL settings, see Chapter 17, "Hotspots and Links.")*

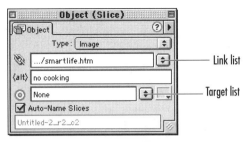

⑩ *The Slice Object panel allows you to set the links and other attributes for slice objects.*

To set the slice options:

1. If the Object panel is not visible, choose **Window>Object**.

2. Select a slice object to display the slice object options **⑩**.

To set the link for a slice object:

1. Use the link list to choose a link from either the current Link list or the Library selected in the URL Manager.

2. To enter a link not in the list, type the link directly into the Link field.

TIP The no URL (no HREF) setting lets you slice an image without a URL link.

Like hotspot objects, slice objects let you enter the (alt) text and target information. *(For a description of the (alt) text and target fields, see page 284.)*

To set the (alt) text and target:

1. Type the text for the (alt) field.

2. Use the Target field or list to set a specific frame or window for the link.

You can also control the color of the slice object. This doesn't affect the slicing itself but can be useful to help organize slices or see them over different backgrounds.

To set the slice object display color:

◆ Use the Color Well to set the display color for the Slice object.

Why Slices? (Part Three)

You also need to slice images to assign JavaScript behaviors such as rollovers and Swap Images. Fortunately, Fireworks makes it easy to create the slices and tables necessary for JavaScript actions. *(For more information on working with behaviors, see Chapter 19, "Behaviors.")*

Putting Slices Back Together

Once you set the slices for an image, you need some way to reassemble the slices on your Web page. That is the function of an HTML table.

Putting slices in your document creates a HTML table.

When you export the images, Fireworks creates the HTML table necessary to reassemble the slices. *(See Chapter 20, "Exporting" for more information on exporting slices and HTML code.)*

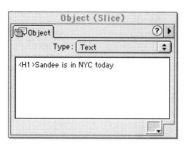

⑪ *The slice object* **Text Settings**.

⑫ *The* **information in a text slice** *is shown inside the selected slice object.*

Sandee is in NYC today

⑬ *Use the* **Preview in Browser** *command to see an actual preview of a text slice.*

You can set a slice so that it displays ordinary HTML text in the sliced area. This makes it easy to update the information without creating new graphics.

To create a text slice:

1. Select the slice object and set the Object panel's Type list to Text (No Image). The text settings appear **⑪**.

2. Type whatever text you want in the image. The text is displayed inside the slice **⑫**.

TIP Use HTML codes to set the style, color, size, and other attributes of the text.

TIP The area inside a text cell is transparent and uses the canvas color as its background.

To preview the text slice in a browser:

◆ Choose **File > Preview in Browser** and then choose either the primary or secondary browser listing in the menu.

TIP You need to preview in a browser in order to see the effects of any HTML formatting you insert into the text slice field **⑬**.

Optimizing Slices

One of the most important reasons to slice images is so you can set separate optimizations for the areas under each slice object. This allows you to set different optimization settings within an image.

To optimize slices:

1. Select one or more slice objects .

2. Use the Optimize panel to set the optimization for the area under the slice object **⑮**. *(For more information on working with the Optimize panel, see Chapter 15, "Optimizing.")*

TIP Hold the Shift key to select multiple slice objects. You can then set the optimization for all the selected slice objects.

TIP Each slice object is labeled with its optimization setting.

⑭ *Select individual slice objects to create* **different optimization settings**.

⑮ *The* **Optimize** *panel for a slice object lets you set the optimization for that object.*

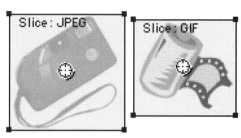

⑯ *Slices let you mix JPEG and GIF images in the same file.*

Empty areas—areas not covered by slices—can be optimized separately from the slices.

To optimize the empty areas:

1. Make sure no slice objects are selected.

2. Use the Optimize panel to set the optimization. This setting will be applied to all empty areas in the document.

Optimizing Strategies

Setting different optimization settings for the slices can help you lower the file size.

For instance, you can set a photograph to be a JPEG and flat art to be a GIF image **⑯**.

You can set the critical areas of an image to a higher JPEG quality and the background to a lower quality to create smaller images.

You can use different GIF palettes for separate areas. This lets you set a limited number of colors individually for different images.

Watch out, though! Slices have to be reassembled using HTML tables and the table code can take up its own space and add to the download time.

Optimizing Slices

BEHAVIORS 19

People expect Web pages to do more than just display information. They want to click onscreen buttons that whisk them away to new pages. And they expect those buttons to light up or do something when the mouse passes over them or look like they're in the up or down position.

With Macromedia Fireworks you can easily create interactive elements using behavior commands. For instance, a simple rollover behavior changes the appearance of a button as the mouse passes over it. A more complex behavior gives users four different looks as the user moves over the area and clicks the button. Behaviors also let visitors move the cursor over one area to display pictures or animations elsewhere on the page. Behaviors also let you create pop-up menus with a list of choices.

Interface designers know that adding behaviors to Web pages is a great way to give visual feedback to the navigational elements. (They're also lots of fun to play with!)

Understanding the Rollover States

How do you let people know where to click on your Web page? An image map *(see Chapter 18, "Hotspots and Links")* is too primitive. It hardly gives any feedback that there is something to click ❶.

Rollovers are more sophisticated. You can create a rollover so that it changes dramatically when the viewer passes the cursor over the button area ❷.

Fireworks gives you four different choices for the appearance of a rollover ❸:

- **Up** is the appearance of the rollover when there is no cursor inside the image area. This is also called the normal state of the rollover.

- **Over** is the appearance of the rollover when the cursor is moved inside the area of the rollover. The Over state alternates with the Up state when the cursor moves in and out of the rollover.

- **Down** is the appearance of the rollover after the mouse clicks inside the area. The Down state is "sticky" in that it stays down after you click it.

- **Over While Down** is the appearance of the rollover when the cursor passes over a rollover that is in the Down state. This Over While Down state alternates with the Down state when the cursor moves in and out of the rollover.

TIP The Down and Over While Down states are best used with framesets so that the rollover is seen in one frame while the new page appears in another.

❶ *When the mouse* **passes over an image map,** *it changes from an arrow to a simple hand cursor.*

❷ *When the mouse* **passes over a rollover,** *it not only shows the hand cursor but the image also changes to the Over state. In this case the image changed its size and color and added a beveled edge and a drop shadow.*

❸ *The* **four rollover states** *can be set for whatever looks you want. Each state can display a distinct image in response to the action of the mouse.*

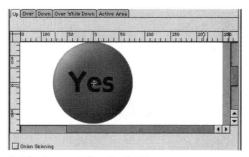

❹ *The Button Editor in the* **Up** *state.*

❺ *The Button Editor in the* **Over** *state.*

❻ *The Button Editor in the* **Down** *state.*

❼ *The Button Editor in the* **Over While Down** *state.*

Creating a Button Symbol

The easiest way to create a rollover is to create a Button symbol. *(For information on graphic and animation symbols, see Chapter 16, "Animations.")*

To create a button symbol:

1. Choose **Insert** > **New Button**. This opens the Button Editor.

2. Click the tabs to create the artwork for each of the states *(see the following exercise)*.

3. Set the active area for the rollover *(see the following page)*.

4. Use the Link Wizard to set the following attributes for the button *(see page 303)*.

To create the button symbol artwork:

1. With the Up tab selected create the artwork for the Up state **❹**.

2. Click the Over tab **❺** to switch to the work area that controls the appearance of the Over state of the button.

3. Click the Copy Up Graphic to bring the artwork from the Up window into the Over window. You can then make any adjustments as desired.

   or

   Use any of the Fireworks tools and commands to create a new graphic for the Over state of the button.

4. Repeat steps 2 and 3 for the Down **❻** and Over While Down states **❼**.

TIP You can create a simple button with just the Up and Over states.

Creating a Button Symbol

The active area is the "hot" area that responds to the presence of the cursor.

To set the active area for a button:

1. Select the Active Area tab ❽.

2. Use either of the selection tools to increase or decrease the size of the green rectangle that covers the button.

TIP Don't make the active area smaller than the artwork for any of the states. If the artwork for any of the states lies outside the active area rectangle, that artwork will not be seen during the rollover.

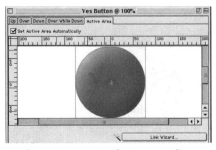

❽ *The* **Active Area** *in the Button Editor.*

As you work on a button symbol, you may want to see how one state relates to another. You turn on Onion Skinning to see the states for a button ❾.

To view multiple states of a button:

1. Select Onion Skinning in any of the button states.

2. Use the Onion Skinning controls in the Frames panel to change which states are visible. *(See pages 271 for working with the Onion Skinning controls.)*

TIP The Up, Over, Down, and Over While Down states corresponds to frames 1, 2, 3, and 4 of the Frames panel.

Ordinarily a button is first displayed with the Up state visible. However, you can set the button so the Down state is first displayed when the page is opened.

To control the opening display of a button:

1. Select the Down state tab.

2. Choose Show Down State Upon Load.

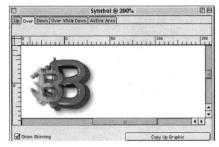

❾ **Onion skinning** *lets you see a combination of the different button states.*

Save Outside the Button Editor

The Save command does not work when you are working inside the Button Editor. You must close the Editor and then choose the Save command to save your work. Other commands such as Revert also don't work while in the Editor.

Don't despair, though. The commands you need to work with objects—such as Align, Arrange, Group, and so on—are all available while you're in the Button Editor.

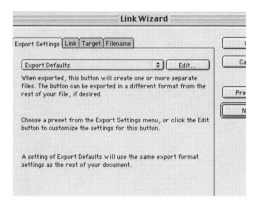

⑩ *The* **Link Wizard Export Settings** *let you set the optimization for a Button Symbol.*

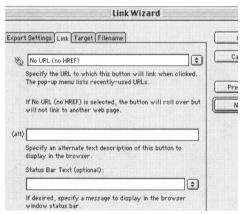

⑪ *The* **Link Wizard Link settings** *control the URL, (alt) tag, and Status Bar Text for a Button Symbol.*

Using the Link Wizard

Despite its name, the Link Wizard does more than just set the link for a button. It also controls the export settings, link, target, and file name.

To set the Export settings in the Link Wizard:

1. Click the Active Area tab for a button.
2. Click the Link Wizard. This opens the Link Wizard dialog box.
3. Click the Export Settings tab **⑩**.
4. Choose one of the Export Presets listed in the pop-up menu.

   or

   Click the Edit button. This opens the Export Preview dialog box.
5. Make whatever changes you want to the Export Preview and click OK. The settings are applied to the button.

TIP The Previous and Next buttons let you move between the Link Wizard tabs.

To set the Link settings in the Link Wizard:

1. Click the Link tab in the Link Wizard **⑪**.
2. Use the Link field to set the URL link for a button. *(See Chapter 17, "Hotspots and Links for more information on URL links.)*

TIP Leave the field set for No URL (no HREF) if you do not want to create a link for the button.

3. Type the alt tag in the (alt) field.

TIP The (alt) tag is the information displayed when images are turned off.

4. In the Status Bar Text field type the message to be displayed in the browser's Status Bar when the cursor passes over the button.

TIP The Status Bar text is optional but is considered a helpful addition to your Web site.

To set the Target in the Link Wizard:

1. Click the Target tab in the Link Wizard **⓬**.

2. Set the Target control as follows:
   - **None** or **_self** opens the destination page in the same location that the button was in.
   - **_blank** opens the destination page in a new browser window.
   - **_parent** opens the destination page in the parent framset of the link.
   - **_top** replaces all the frames in the current browser window and opens the destination page in that window.

   TIP If you have your own name for a frame you can type the custom frame name in the target field.

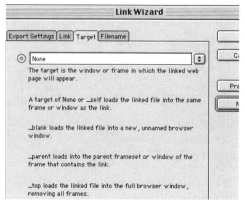

⓬ *The* **Link Wizard Target settings** *let you set where the destination page opens.*

You can give your button a custom name. This makes it easier to identify the images exported for the button.

To set the Filename in the Link Wizard:

1. Click the Filename tab in the Link Wizard **⓭**.

2. Deselect Auto-Name to open the Filename field.

3. Type the custom name to be used when the file is exported.

   TIP You can also open the Link Wizard by selecting a button symbol on the page and clicking Link Wizard in the Object panel **⓮**. This lets you go directly to the Link Wizard without opening the Symbol Editor.

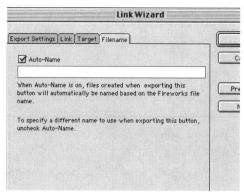

⓭ *The* **Link Wizard Filename settings** *let you customize the name when the button is exported.*

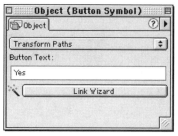

⓮ *The Object panel lets you open the* **Link Wizard** *for individual instances of a button symbol.*

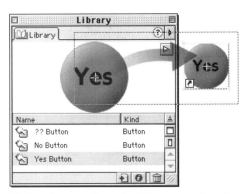

⓰ Drag buttons from the Library panel *to the canvas to create the buttons for a Nav Bar.*

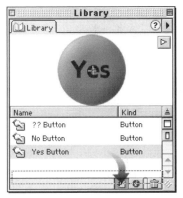

⓰ Duplicate a button *by dragging it onto the New Symbol icon.*

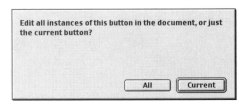

⓱ *You can edit all the buttons in a document or just the selected instance.*

Working with Button Symbols

It's a rare Web site that only has one button on a page. So you're going to want to duplicate and modify instances of buttons.

To add a button from the Library:

◆ Drag the button symbol from the Library panel onto the canvas **⓰**.

TIP Instances of button symbols automatically create slice areas. This is so they can display the different rollover states.

To duplicate an instance on the canvas:

1. Select the button on the canvas.

2. Use any duplication commands or Opt/Alt-drag to create a second instance of the button.

To duplicate a symbol in the Library:

◆ Drag the symbol onto the New Symbol icon in the Library panel **⓰**.

or

◆ Choose Duplicate from the Library panel menu.

You can easily convert an instance of one button into a new button.

To modify an instance on the canvas:

1. Double-click the instance on the canvas. A dialog box appears asking you if you want to edit just this instance of the button or all instances of it **⓱**.

2. Select All to open the Button Editor for the button.

or

Select Current to open a new Button Editor for a new button.

3. Edit the button in the Button Editor.

TIP The new symbol will have the same name as the original button plus a numerical suffix. Use the Symbol Properties dialog box to change the name.

Working with Button Symbols

The Fireworks team recognizes that text is one of the most common elements of a button that need to be modified. So they made it especially easy to change it.

To edit the text for a button symbol:

1. Select the instance of the button symbol on the canvas.

2. In the Object panel change the text listed in the Button Text field 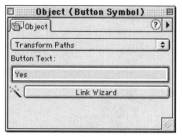.

TIP If there is more than one instance of the button symbol a dialog box appears. You can change the text for all instances of the button or just the instance that is currently selected.

TIP If you edit the text for one instance of a button symbol that is used elsewhere on the canvas, you actually create a new button symbol in the Library panel ⓳.

TIP Use the Symbol Properties dialog box to change the name of the new button symbol.

You may also want to change the link properties of a button. The Object panel gives you easy access to the Link Wizard.

To change the links for a button:

1. Select the instance of the button symbol on the canvas.

2. In the Object panel, click Link Wizard.

TIP If there is more than one instance of the button a dialog box appears that asks if you want to change all instances of the current button or the instance that is currently selected.

3. Choose All to change all instances or choose Current to change just the selected instance.

4. Select the Link tab of the Link Wizard and set the link (see page 303).

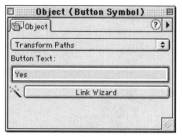

� ⓲ *Use the **Button Text field** in the Object panel to change the text for all the states of a button.*

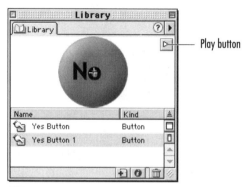

⓳ *If you make changes to the text or links of a current instance of a button, you create a new button in the Library panel.*

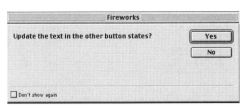

⓴ *You can change the text for all the button states while working in the Button Editor.*

Designing Buttons

As you create the artwork for buttons, keep in mind you're actually designing an application that visitors use to navigate to the different pages on your Web site.

Try to design your Web page interface so that it's clear to your visitors where the buttons are, what will happen if they click a particular button, and whether or not they have in fact clicked that button. Probably the most obvious way to indicate the presence of a button is to have color changes in the different rollover states.

By the way, you don't need to use the words "Click here!" to indicate that you can click a certain element.

Fireworks also makes it easy to update the text on all the states of a button while working in the Button Editor.

To update the text on the button states:

1. Double-click the preview of the button symbol in the Library panel.

   or

   Select the listing of the button and choose Edit Symbol from the Library panel menu. The Button Editor opens.

2. Double-click the text block to change the text on any of the button states.

3. Click OK to apply the text change. A dialog box appears ⓴.

4. Click Yes to apply the text change to all the other button states.

   or

   Click No to apply the change to just the current button state.

You can preview the different states of a button symbol in the Library panel.

To preview button states:

1. Choose the button symbol in the Library panel.

2. Click the Play button in the Library panel ⓳. The button cycles through all four states.

Working with Button Symbols

Creating a Nav Bar

A Nav Bar (from the term *navigation bar*) is a set of button symbols that work together to move to different Web pages. You first create the button symbols and then assemble them into a graphic symbol that acts as the Nav Bar.

To create a Nav Bar:

1. Create the button symbols you want to use for the Nav Bar.

2. Choose **Insert** > **New Symbol**. This opens the Symbol Properties dialog box.

3. Set the Symbol type as Graphic ㉑. Name the Symbol and click OK. This opens the Symbol Editor.

TIP Although a Nav Bar contains button symbols, it is actually a graphic symbol with nested button symbols.

4. Use any of the tools to create the background artwork for the Nav Bar.

5. Drag the button symbols from the Library panel into the Symbol Editor for the Nav Bar symbol ㉒.

6. Choose Share This Layer from the Layers panel menu to set the layer to be seen across all frames ㉓.

TIP The Share Layer setting ensures that the buttons change their states without white areas around them.

7. Use the Add Frames command in the Frames panel menu to add as many frames as there are states in the symbol buttons.

TIP Two-state buttons need a total of two frames. Four-state buttons need four.

8. Close the Symbol Editor. An instance of the Nav Bar appears in the Library panel ㉔.

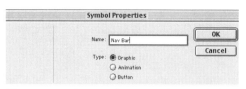

㉑ *A Nav Bar is created as a* **Graphic symbol.**

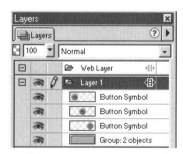

㉒ **Drag buttons** *from the Library panel onto the artwork for the Nav Bar graphic symbol.*

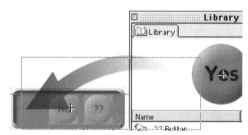

㉓ *The* **artwork for a Nav Bar** *must be on a shared layer.*

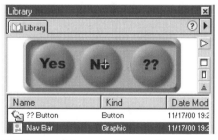

㉔ *The* **Graphic symbol** *for the Nav Bar appears in the Library panel.*

(side margin) **Creating a Nav Bar**

㉕ *If you make changes to the text or links of a current instance of a button, you create a new button in the Library panel.*

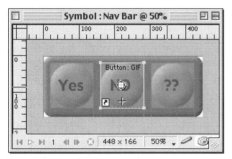

㉖ *The Symbol Editor for a Nav Bar contains the button symbols for the Nav Bar buttons.*

Plan, plan, plan!

The biggest mistake designers make has nothing to do with file sizes or HTML—it's not planning ahead.

Before you create your buttons and Nav Bars make sure you know what your page names are going to be.

You can't believe what a pain in the neck it is to re-do your Nav Bar just because you didn't make you buttons big enough to accommodate the word or phrase with the most characters!

To use a Nav Bar:

1. Drag the graphic symbol for the Nav Bar from the Library panel onto the canvas.

2. The Nav Bar appears on the canvas as a single instance containing both the background and the buttons **㉕**.

To edit a Nav Bar:

1. Double-click the instance of the Nav Bar on the page.

   or

   Double-click the preview of the Nav Bar in the Library panel. This opens the Symbol Editor.

2. Make whatever changes you want in the background artwork for the Nav Bar.

3. Close the Symbol Editor to apply the changes to the Nav Bar in the document.

   TIP Double-click the instances of the button symbols of a Nav Bar to launch the Button Editor for those buttons symbols **㉖**.

   TIP The Nav Bars you create for one document can be imported and used in other documents. *(See page 310 for importing symbols from one document into another.)*

Ordinarily a button is first displayed with the Up state visible. Many designers want Nav Bars to look like a radio button— when the page that the button is linked to appears, the button for that page is displayed in its down state.

To control the opening display of a button:

1. Select the Down state tab in the Button Editor.

2. Select Show Down State Upon Load.

Creating a Nav Bar

Sharing Symbols

You can re-use button symbols created for one document in other documents as well. In fact, these techniques for sharing and editing symbols apply equally well to the graphic symbols and animation symbols covered in Chapter 19.

To place a symbol in a document:

1. Open the document that contains the button symbol you want to use.

2. Open the document in which you want to use the button.

3. Drag the button symbol from either the document window or the Library panel into the new document.

You can also import many symbols from one document to another.

To import symbols into a document:

1. Choose Import Symbols from the Library panel menu **29**.

2. Navigate to find the file from which you want to import the symbols.

3. Click OK. This opens the Import Symbols dialog box **27**.

4. Select the symbols you want to import.

TIP Hold the Shift key to select contiguous symbols in the Import dialog box. Hold the Cmd/Ctrl key to select non-contiguous symbols in the dialog box.

5. Click Import to add the selected symbols to the document. The word *imported* appears after the name of an imported symbol in the Library **28**.

TIP The Symbol Properties dialog box shows a path to the original source file of an imported symbol.

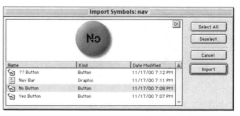

27 *The* **Import Symbols dialog box** *lets you select symbols used in other documents and import them into the current document.*

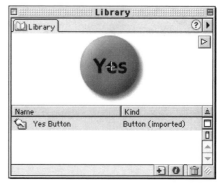

28 *An* **imported symbol** *is identified in the Library panel.*

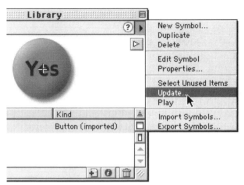

㉙ *Use the* **Update command in the Library panel** *to change an imported symbol so that it reflects changes made to the original symbol.*

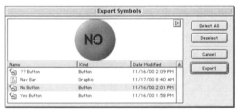

㉚ **Exported symbols** *retain their link to the original file.*

Symbols imported from other documents retain a link to the original symbol. If you edit the symbol in the original document, you can then update the imported instance.

To update an imported symbol:

1. Edit the symbol in the original document.

2. Save that file.

3. Select the imported symbol in the second document.

4. Choose Update from the Library panel menu **㉙**. A dialog box appears indicating that the object was updated.

TIP Imported instances of an edited symbol do not update unless you specifically apply the Update command. This allows you to edit the symbol in one document without affecting other documents.

You can also export symbols from one document into a new one.

To export symbols to a new document:

1. Choose Export Symbols from the Library panel menu. The Export Symbols dialog box appears **㉚**.

2. Select the symbols you want to export.

3. Click Export. This opens a standard dialog box that lets you name and save the file with the selected symbols.

TIP Exported symbols are still linked to their original file so you can update them to reflect changes in the originals, if you choose.

Sharing Symbols

Sometimes you want to sever the relationship between the original symbol and copies that you imported into other documents. You can break the link by editing the symbol.

To edit an imported symbol:

1. Double-click the symbol in the document window or Library. A document box appears asking if you want to break the link ③.

2. Click OK. This releases the symbol from the link to the original file.

3. Make any changes to the symbol.

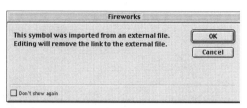

③ Editing an imported instance *breaks the link between the instance and the original symbol.*

Fireworks ships with four libraries of animations, buttons, bullets, and themes you can use in your own documents.

To import the Fireworks library elements:

1. Choose one of the following:
   - **Insert > Libraries > Animations** to open the animation symbols.
   - **Insert > Libraries > Buttons** to open the set of button symbols.
   - **Insert > Libraries > Bullets** to open the set of graphic symbols.
   - **Insert > Libraries > Themes** to open button and graphic symbols that can be used as a coordinated theme.

2. Use the Import dialog box to import any of the items from the libraries.

TIP The four libraries are located at Fireworks 4:Configurations:Libraries.

You can have your own files appear in the Libraries menu.

To add symbols to the Libraries menu:

1. Create a file that contains the symbols you want to use.

2. Save the file in Fireworks4:Configurations:Libraries. The file appears under the **Insert > Libraries** menu.

Different from Flash

If you are familiar with Macromedia Flash you know how the symbols work in that program. Fireworks symbols are slightly different.

Symbols in Fireworks do not reduce the final file size. There is no difference in final file size if a symbol is used when creating a GIF or JPEG.

However, just like Flash, the symbols in Fireworks make it easy to make changes within a document or among many documents.

Sharing Symbols

Trigger object   Target image

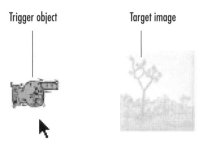

③② *When the cursor is outside the trigger object, the target image displays its normal state.*

③③ *When the cursor is inside the trigger object, the target image displays a second state.*

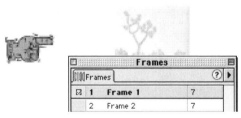

③④ Frame 1 *displays the trigger object and the* **normal state of the target image.**

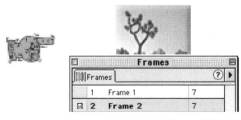

③⑤ Frame 2 *displays the trigger object and the* **second state of the target image.**

Creating a Disjointed Rollover

You can also use a *swap image* behavior to create a *disjointed rollover*. In a disjointed rollover moving the cursor over one area of the image shows something elsewhere in the image **③②**–**③③**.

You need to create certain elements to create a disjointed rollover. The order that you create these elements is important.

To create the elements of a disjointed rollover:

1. Create the frames with different images under the area to be changed.

2. Create a slice object (not a hotspot) to define the *target image*—the area to be changed by the behavior *(see the next page)*.

3. Create either a hotspot or slice object to define the *trigger object*—the area that triggers the behavior *(see the next page)*.

4. Assign a swap image behavior to the trigger object hotspot or slice object *(see page 248)*.

To create the frames for a disjointed rollover:

1. Create a frame that displays the normal state of the target image **③④**.

2. Create a second frame that displays the second state of the target image **③⑤**.

TIP The same area can be used for other target images. Simply put the artwork on other frames.

After you create the frames, you then need to add a slice object that defines the target image for the disjointed rollover.

To define the target image:

1. Create a slice object that completely covers the area to be changed **36**.

2. In the Object panel, leave the Link as No URL (no HREF).

3. Deselect Auto-Name Slices. This opens the text field for a custom name.

4. Give this slice a distinctive name.

TIP Although a distinctive name is not necessary, it can help as you assign the area for the disjointed rollover.

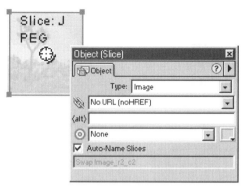

36 *The target image of a swap image behavior must be covered with a slice object.*

You can use either a hotspot or slice object to define the trigger object of the disjointed rollover.

To define the trigger object:

1. Select the path or object that triggers the change.

2. To create a hotspot area the same shape as the path, choose **Insert > Hotspot** **37**.

   or

   Use any of the hotspot tools to define the area for the rollover.

   or

   To create a slice object that can trigger the change, choose **Insert > Slice**.

TIP Using a hotspot object allows you to make a non-rectangular area for the trigger object.

TIP Using a slice object to trigger the change allows you to have that area also change its appearance.

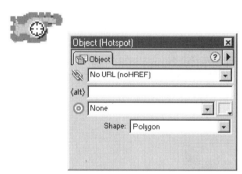

37 *The trigger object can be defined with either a hotspot or a slice object.*

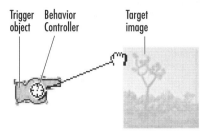

Trigger object   Behavior Controller   Target image

38 *Drag from the* **Behavior Controller** *of the trigger object to the target image of the disjointed rollover.*

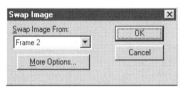

39 *Use the* **Swap Image From** *control to choose the frame or external file that displays in the target image area.*

40 *The* **curved line** *shows there is a Swap Image behavior between the hotspot and the slice.*

With all the elements in place, you are now ready to actually assign the swap image behavior to create the disjointed rollover.

To assign the swap image behavior:

1. Select the hotspot or slice object that triggers the change. A Behavior Controller appears.

2. Press and drag out from the Behavior Controller. A line appears.

3. Drag the line onto the slice area for the swap image **38**.

4. Release the mouse. The small Swap Image dialog box appears **39**.

5. Use the Swap Image From list to choose which frame should appear for the swap image behavior.

6. Click OK to apply the swap image behavior. A curved line connects the trigger object to the swap area. This indicates that the swap image behavior is in place **40**.

   or

   Click More Options to modify the swap image behavior. This opens the large Swap Image dialog box. *(See the first exercise on the next page for details.)*

If you want to refine the swap image behavior, you can use the options in the large Swap Image dialog box **⓵**.

To modify the swap image behavior:

1. Select Image File to swap an external file instead of a frame within the document.

TIP The external file should be the same size as the slice area or the image will be distorted when it is swapped. You must also specify the correct path to that file and the path must be in the site folder.

TIP You can use an animated GIF as the file for the swap image behavior.

2. Choose Preload Images to download the hidden images along with the rest of the artwork. This slows down the initial download but makes the swap occur faster. (This setting is on by default.)

3. Deselect Restore Image onMouseOut to keep the swapped image displayed after the cursor leaves the trigger area. (This setting is on by default.)

TIP See the next exercise for how to modify what actions trigger the swap image behavior.

4. Click OK to return to the document. The swap image appears in the Behaviors panel **⓶**.

TIP To see if the swap image behavior is working correctly, click the Preview tab. Note that to see any external files used, you need to chose **File > Preview in Browser**.

The More Options button in the small Swap Image dialog box opens the large Swap Image dialog box. If you want to go directly to the large Swap Image dialog box you can use the Behaviors panel.

To re-open the second Swap Image dialog box:

♦ Double-click the Swap Image listing in the Behaviors panel. This opens the large Swap Image dialog box.

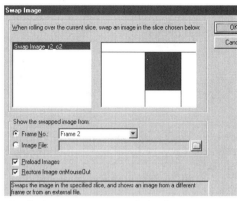

⓵ *The larger Swap Image dialog box gives you more controls over the settings for the Swap Image Behavior.*

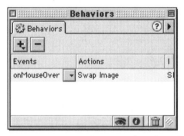

⓶ *A swap image action is listed in the* **Behaviors** *panel.*

43 *The* Events list *allows you to choose which mouse action will trigger the behavior.*

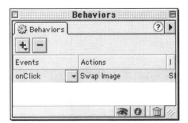

44 *You can set your own custom event for a Swap Image Behavior.*

Working with the Behaviors Panel

The Behaviors panel gives you still more control over behaviors. For instance, you may want a Swap Image behavior to be activated by a mouse click rather than moving the mouse over the image.

To modify the swap image events:

1. Select the hotspot or slice object that triggers the change.

2. Select the behavior in the Behaviors panel. A small triangle control appears in the Events column.

3. Click the Events triangle control. This opens the Events list **43**.

4. Choose the type of Mouse action that should trigger the behavior from the following:

   - **onMouseOver** triggers the action as the mouse moves inside the hotspot area.
   - **onMouseOut** triggers the action as the mouse leaves the hotspot area.
   - **onClick** triggers the action when the mouse button is clicked inside the hotspot area.
   - **onLoad** automatically triggers the action as the images are loaded.

   TIP The custom event appears in the Behaviors panel **44**.

To delete a behavior:

   ◆ Click the Minus (–) sign in the Behaviors panel to delete a selected behavior.

   or

   Click the Delete icon in the Behaviors panel.

You can also add a setting to control how the swap image behavior is restored when the mouse leaves the trigger object. For instance, you can add a behavior so that the image is restored when the mouse moves inside the trigger area.

To change the restore behavior:

1. Select the hotspot or slice object that triggers the change.

2. Click the Plus (+) sign in the Behaviors panel. This opens the Behaviors list **45**.

3. Choose Swap Image Restore. This adds a listing for the Swap Image Restore behavior **46**.

4. Use the Events control to change the mouse action for how the image is restored.

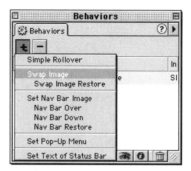

45 *The* **Behaviors** list *allows you to add behaviors to hotspots or slices.*

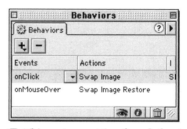

46 *This* **custom setting for a behavior** *displays the image on a mouse click and restores the image when the mouse passes over it.*

My Favorite Swap Image Settings

I like to create two or more trigger areas that swap images on different frames under the same slice.

Then I use onClick to swap the image rather than onMouseOver. I also use onMouseOver to apply the Swap Image Restore **46**.

When the mouse clicks inside the first trigger area, the image is swapped. However, when the mouse leaves the first trigger area the image is not restored.

When the mouse enters the second trigger area that's when the onMouseOver event restores the image. A click swaps the new image.

This setup allows the trigger for one area to change the image swapped by a different trigger area.

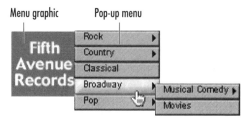

Menu graphic   Pop-up menu

47 Pop-up menus *let you create navigational elements of various categories.*

48 *Use the contextual menu to choose* **Add Pop-up Menu** *from the Behavior Controller.*

Creating Pop-up Menus

Another type of behavior is the Pop-up Menu behavior. This allows you to create sophisticated pop-up menus that give visitors menus and submenus of destinations to choose **47**.

To create a Pop-up menu:

1. Create the menu graphic. This is the area that is clicked to open the pop-up menu.

2. Create a hotspot or slice object to define the trigger area for the pop-up menu *(see the next exercise)*.

3. Add the Pop-up Menu behavior to either the hotspot or slice *(see the next exercise)*. This opens the Set Pop-up Menu dialog box.

4. Use the first part of the Set Pop-Up Menu dialog box to enter the menu and submenus listings *(see the next page)*.

5. Use the second part of the Set Pop-Up Menu dialog box to format the appearance of the pop-up menu *(see page 321)*.

6. Adjust the position of the pop-up menu *(see page 322)*.

To add the Pop-up Menu behavior:

1. Create the hotspot or slice to be used as the trigger for the Pop-up Menu.

2. Press the Behavior Controller and choose Add Pop-up Menu from the menu **48**.

    or

    Choose **Insert** > **Pop-up Menu**. This opens the Set Pop-Up Menu dialog box.

To add the menu items for the Pop-up menu:

1. With the first part of the Set Pop-Up Menu dialog box open , enter a menu listing in the Text field.

2. Enter the target frame for the listing in the Target field.

3. Enter the URL in the Link field.

TIP You can rearrange the order of the listings by dragging items up or down in the dialog box.

4. Click the Create Menu button to move a listing to a new column on the right ⑤⓿. This creates a submenu.

5. Click the Promote Menu button to move a listing back to a column on the left ⑤⓿. This elevates a submenu item to the next level up.

6. Press the Plus (+) button or the Return/Enter key to apply the listing and clear the Text field for a new listing.

7. Repeat steps 1 through 6 as many times as necessary to create all the listings and sub-listings for the menu.

8. Click the Next button to format the appearance of the menus.

To correct errors in the listings:

1. Select the listing that has the error.

2. Make a change in the Text, Link, or Target fields.

3. Click Change to update the listing.

To delete a listing:

1. Select the listing that you want to delete.

2. Press the Minus (-) button.

⑭⑨ *The first part of the* Set Pop-Up Menu *dialog box lets you enter the listings and sub-listings for the pop-up menu.*

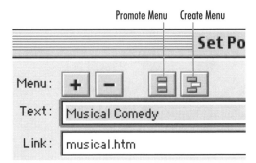

⑤⓿ *The* Menu controls *of the Set Pop-Up Menu dialog box.*

Creating Pop-up Menus

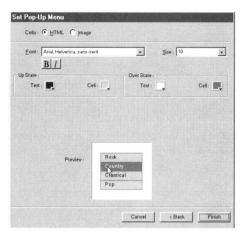

51 *The* **HTML controls** *of the Set Pop-Up Menu dialog box control the appearance of menus that are formatted using HTML code.*

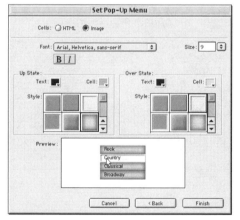

52 *The* **Image controls** *of the Set Pop-Up Menu dialog box control the appearance of menus that are formatted using graphic styles.*

The cells of the pop-up menus can be formatted as HTML code or as graphic images. HTML code menus tend to download faster. Graphic image menus create more sophisticated effects.

To set the HTML formatting:

1. Select HTML from the Cells choices. The HTML formatting appears **51**.

2. Choose the font from the Font list.

3. Set the point size from the Size list.

4. If desired, set the text style for bold or italic.

5. Use the color wells to set the text and cell colors for the Up state or Normal state of the Pop-up Menu.

6. Use the color wells to set the text and cell colors for the Over State of the pop-up menu.

7. Click Finish to apply the formatting and return to the document window.

TIP Use the Back button to go back to the listings for the Pop-up Menu.

TIP Use the Events list of the Behaviors panel so that the pop-up menu is revealed by a click or onMouseout.

To set the Image formatting:

1. Choose Image from the Cells choices. The Image formatting appears **52**.

2. Use the steps in the previous exercise to set the font, point size, style, and colors.

3. Use the Style lists to choose one of the graphic styles for the Up state and the Over state.

4. Click Finish to apply the formatting and return to the document window.

TIP The style graphics are grayscale images that are colored using the choices in the color wells.

Creating Pop-up Menus

The pop-up menu can be repositioned so it is closer to, or further away from, the trigger area.

To reposition the pop-up menu:

1. Select the hotspot or slice that acts as the trigger area for the Pop-up Menu. An outline of the pop-up menu appears.

2. Press and drag the outline of the pop-up menu to a new position 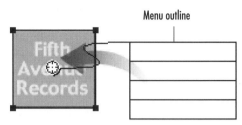.

Menu outline

53 *Drag the* **pop-up menu outline** *to reposition the pop-up menu.*

You can create your own styles for the Image settings of the Pop-up Menu. This gives you more creative choices than the default styles that ship with Fireworks.

To customize the Image formatting:

1. Create the styles you want to have available for the Image Styles.

2. Select the styles and choose Export Styles from the Style panel menu.

3. Save the exported styles file in Fireworks4:Configurations:Nav Menu.

Changing the Menu Alignment

You can reposition the pop-up menu relative to the trigger area so that the menu is closer to or further away from the trigger area. However, Fireworks does not have a way to change the alignment of the sub-menus. Fireworks automatically overlaps the sub-menus and positions them slightly down from the previous menu.

You may not like this default position. Unfortunately, the only way to change the position of sub-menus, is to open and edit the JavaScript code that Fireworks creates when you export the menu.

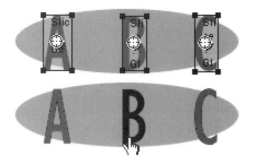

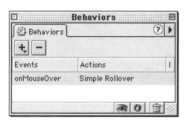

54 *The* **Simple Rollover** *assigned to the slice objects allows you to rollover the objects on Frame 2 without matching the background oval.*

55 *Use the Behaviors panel to assign a* **Simple Rollover** *to slice objects.*

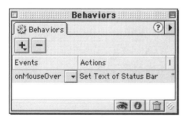

56 *The Set Text of Status Bar dialog box lets you type the message that appears in the browser's Status Bar.*

Setting Other Behaviors

The Behaviors panel also lets you create Simple Rollovers using elements on the page rather than with button symbols. This lets you use artwork for rollovers without worrying about matching the background area in the frames **54**.

To create a Simple Rollover:

1. Create the first frame with the image for the Up state.

2. Create the second frame with the images for the Over state.

TIP Simple Rollovers contain only two states.

3. Create the slices over the areas that you want to change.

4. Select the slices.

5. Click the Plus (+) sign in the Behaviors to assign a Simple Rollover **55**.

The Behaviors panel also lets you add text that appears in the browser's Status Bar **56**. This gives your visitors additional information about the page they are viewing.

To add a Status Bar message:

1. Select the hotspot or slice that you want to trigger the message.

2. Click the Plus (+) sign in the Behaviors panel to add the Set Text of Status Bar behavior. This opens the Set Text of Status Bar dialog box.

4. Type the text in the message field.

5. Click OK. The behavior is listed in the Behaviors panel **57**.

TIP Use the Events triangle to change the action that triggers the display of the message.

57 *Use the Behaviors panel to set a Status Bar message for hotspots or slices.*

You can also use the Behaviors panel to create Nav Bars from elements on the page.

To create a Nav Bar on the page:

1. Create the frames for the four Nav Bar states as follows:
   - Frame 1 displays the Up state.
   - Frame 2 displays the Over state.
   - Frame 3 displays the Down state.
   - Frame 4 displays the Over While Down state.

2. Create the slices over the areas that you want to act as the Nav Bar triggers.

4. Select the slices.

5. Use the Behaviors panel to assign a Nav Bar to the slices **58**. This opens the Set Nav Bar Image dialog box **59**.

6. Select Include Over While Down State if desired.

7. Select Show Down Image Upon Load if desired.

8. Click OK to apply the Nav Bar.

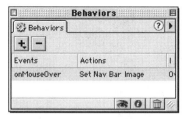

58 *Use the Behaviors panel to set a* **Nav Bar Image.**

59 *The* **Set Nav Bar Image** *dialog box.*

EXPORTING 20

U nlike print images, graphics created for the Web require special handling when it comes to exporting. Not only do you have to optimize to the proper file format but you also have to make sure you create the HTML code necessary to create the image maps or reassemble sliced graphics. That's where exporting comes in. Fortunately, Macromedia Fireworks makes it easy to export your graphics together with the HTML code. It even provides special export settings that make it easy to use your Web graphics with Macromedia Dreamweaver and Macromedia Director.

Finally, Fireworks lets you export files in formats that can be used by other applications such as Macromedia Flash, Adobe Illustrator, and Adobe Photoshop.

Understanding Exporting

There are several steps to exporting files. Each of the steps controls different aspects of the final output.

To export files:

1. Set the optimization settings as desired. *(See Chapter 15, "Optimizing.")*

2. Choose **File** > **Export**. This opens the Export dialog box.

3. If the file does not contain slices or image maps, export the file as a basic export.

4. If the file contains slices, set the slicing controls *(see the next page)*.

5. If the file contains slices or image maps, set the HTML properties *(see page 328)*.

6. Navigate to set the location of the images created by slicing.

7. Name the file.

8. Click Save to export the files.

Creating a Basic Export

If the file does not contain slices or image maps, it can be exported in one step. This is a basic export ❶.

To export without slices or image maps:

1. Choose **File** > **Export**. The Export dialog box appears.

2. Set Save As pop-up menu to Images only ❷.

TIP If you do not have slices or image maps in the file Fireworks automatically sets the Slices and HTML options to None.

❶ *A graphic, such as this photo, that does not contain slices or buttons can be handled as a basic export.*

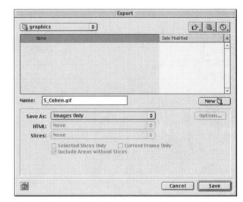

❷ *A plain graphic does not need any options for slices or HTML.*

❸ Sliced images *need special handling during exporting.*

❹ *The* Slices list *controls how the image is sliced.*

❺ *Choose* Selected Slices Only *to export only the areas under the selected slices.*

❻ *The* Contextual Menu *for a slice lets you export a single slice.*

❼ *The Export dialog box when* Export Selected Slice *is chosen from the contextual menu.*

Setting the Slices Controls

If you have slices, button symbols, or pop-up menus ❸, you need to set how the slices are exported.

To set the slice options:

1. In the Export dialog box use the Slices list ❹ to choose how to slice the file:
   - **None** turns off any slicing applied to the image.
   - **Export Slices** uses the slice objects to define the slices.
   - **Slice Along Guides** slices along the ruler guides.

2. Check Include Areas without Slices to also export those areas that are not covered by slice objects.

TIP If you deselect Include Areas without Slices, you create empty cells. *(See page 330 to control the appearance of these empty cells.)*

You can also export only selected slices. This makes it easy to update only certain parts of an image.

To export only the selected slices:

1. Select the slices you want to export.

2. In the Export dialog box, choose Selected Slices only ❺.

3. Choose Current Frame Only to limit the slices to the image in the currently selected frame.

You can also export a single selected slice.

To export one slices:

1. Select the slices you want to export.

2. Control-click (Mac) or right-mouse-click (Win) and choose Export Selected Slice from the contextual menu ❻.

3. Set the Slices options ❼.

TIP The HTML options are not available when you export a single slice.

Setting the HTML Properties

As soon as you create slices, button symbols, pop-up menus, or image maps you need to create HTML code that reassembles the slices or controls the behaviors.

You can create an actual HTML file or copy the HTML file to the computer clipboard.

To set the HTML destination:

◆ In the Export dialog box use the HTML list to choose the destination for the HTML code **❽**:

- **Export HTML File** creates an actual file containing the HTML information.
- **Copy to Clipboard** copies the HTML information to the computer clipboard.

TIP Copy to Clipboard allows you to switch to a program such as Dreamweaver and paste the code directly onto a page.

You can also set many options for exporting files in the HTML Setup.

To open the HTML Setup:

◆ In the Export dialog box click Options **❾**. This opens the HTML Setup dialog box **❿**:

or

With the document window open, choose **File > HTML Setup**.

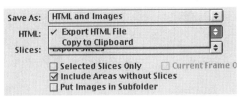

❽ *The* **HTML list** *lets you create an actual HTML file or copy the HTML to the clipboard.*

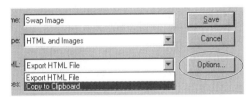

❾ *The* **Options button** *in the Export dialog box opens the HTML Setup controls.*

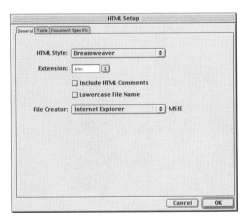

❿ *The* **General** *controls of the HTML Setup.*

Setting the HTML Properties

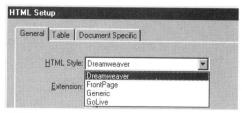

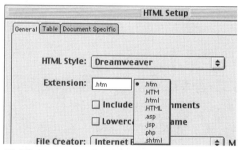

⓫ The **HTML Style list** *lets you match the HTML code to the application you use to create the Web page.*

⓬ The **Extension** list *lets you change the extension that is added to the file.*

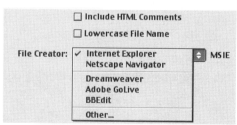

⓭ The **File Creator list (Mac)** *lets you assign a specific creator code to the HTML file.*

Setting HTML General Properties

The General tab of the HTML Setup contains several options for different aspects of the exported files.

To set the HTML General options:

1. Click the General tab in the HTML Setup dialog box:

2. Use the HTML Style list to choose the program that you want the HTML code to be inserted into **⓫**:
   - Choose among the programs Macromedia **Dreamweaver**, Microsoft **FrontPage**, or Adobe **GoLive**.
   - Choose **Generic** if you don't know the Web page layout program you will be using or if you will be hand coding the page.

3. Use the Extension list **⓬** to set the file extension applied to the HTML file.

4. Check Include HTML Comments to add the extra comments that explain the functions of the different codes and show how to copy and paste the code into your page layout.

5. Check Lowercase File Name to insure that no capital letters are used in naming the files.

TIP The Lowercase File Name option forces Fireworks to save your files with only lowercase letters—even if you have uppercase letters in the file names. This is helpful if your Web server does not display files that contain uppercase letters.

6. (Mac) Use the File Creator list to choose which application can be used to open the HTML code **⓭**.

Setting the HTML Table Properties

Fireworks lets you control the spacing options for the HTML tables.

To set the table spacing options:

1. Click the Table tab in the HTML Setup dialog box ⓮.

2. Use the Space with list to control the type of table ⓯:

   • **1-Pixel Transparent Spacer** creates a single table that uses a 1-pixel transparent GIF image to ensure the table cells display properly.

   TIP The transparent GIF image is called a spacer.gif and is created along with the other images for the file.

   • **Nested Tables - No Spacers** uses tables within tables to lay out the image. No spacer.gif images are used.

   • **Single Table - No Spacers** creates a single table without any spacer.gif images.

   TIP Single Table - No Spacers creates a simpler table but the result does not always display correctly in browsers.

You can also control the appearance of text slices *(see page 295)* as well as the empty cells created if you deselect Include Areas without Slices *(see page 327)*.

To control the empty cells:

1. Select Use Canvas Color to use the Fireworks background color.

2. If you deselect Use Canvas Color, use the Cell Color color well to choose a specific cell color.

3. Use the Contents list ⓰ to choose what should be included in the empty cells:

   • **None** adds nothing to the empty cell so that the cell remains blank. This creates the smallest possible file.

   • **Spacer Image** inserts a spacer.gif in empty cells.

   • **Non-breaking Space** inserts the HTML code for a space tag.

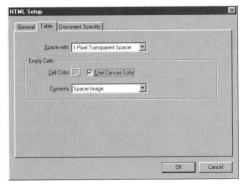

⓮ *The* **HTML Setup** *dialog box set to the* **Table** *controls.*

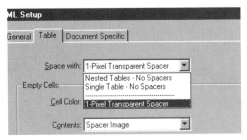

⓯ *The* **Space with list** *lets you control how the tables are created.*

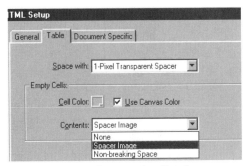

⓰ *The* **Empty Cells controls** *affect the appearance of non-image slices.*

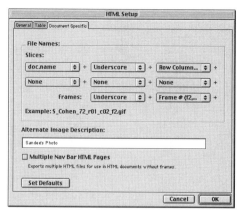

⑰ *The* HTML Setup *dialog box set to the* Document Specific *controls.*

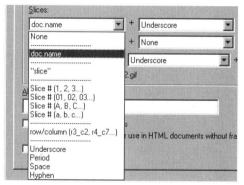

⑱ *The* Slices pop-up menus *let you assign the naming conventions for the files created from slicing.*

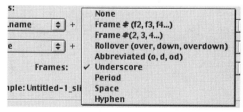

⑲ *The* Frames pop-up menu *lets you assign the naming conventions for the files created from frames.*

Setting HTML Document Properties

Use the Document Specific tab to set how Fireworks names the sliced images.

To set the File Names:

1. Click the Document Specific tab in the HTML Setup dialog box **⑰**.

2. Use the Slices pop-up menus under File Names to set the file naming as follows **⑱**:
   - **doc.name** sets where the name of the document should appear.
   - **"slice"** inserts the word slice into the file name.
   - **Slice#** options inserts a number for each slice.

   TIP The "slice" and Slice# options can be used together to number the slices in the table without using rows and columns.

   - **row/column** names the slice using the row and column where the slice appears in the table.
   - **Underscore, Period, Space**, or **Hyphen** adds those elements as dividers between the slice labels.
   - **None** adds no element in that space for the file name.

3. Use the Frames pop-up menu under File Names to set the file naming as follows **⑲**:
   - **Frame # (f2, f3, f4)** inserts the label f and the frame number.
   - **Frame # (2, 3, 4)** inserts just the frame number.
   - **Rollover (over, down, overdown)** adds the name of the rollover state of the frame.
   - **Abbreviated (o, d, od)** adds letter labels for the rollover state.

4. Choose Underscore, Period, Space, or Hyphen to add those elements as dividers between the slice labels.

5. Choose None to add no element in that space for the file name.

You can also set the Alternate Image Description. This alt text appears on the image place holder while the image is downloading from the Web or in place of an image if it fails to download. It may also appear as a tool tip when the mouse passes over the image.

To enter the Alternate Image Description:

- ◆ Enter the text in the Alternate Image Description field.

- **TIP** This Alternative Image Description applies to non-defined "virtual" slices and documents that don't use slices.

You can export the Multiple Nav Bar HTML as separate pages. This lets you use the Nav Bars on layouts that don't use framesets.

To export Multiple Nav Bar pages:

- ◆ Choose Multiple Nav Bar HTML Pages ➋⓿.

- **TIP** If you import the code created by the Multiple Nav Bar HTML Pages into existing pages that have different file names, you'll need to fix the URLs in the Behaviors that point to those files.

Finally, you can set the defaults for all the document specific settings.

To set the defaults:

- ◆ Click the Set Defaults button ➋⓿. This makes the current Document Specific settings the defaults for new documents.

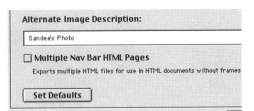

➋⓿ *The* **HTML list** *lets you create an actual HTML file or copy the HTML to the clipboard.*

Setting the Alternate Image Description

The Alternate Image Description is also called the alt tag. The alt tag is the text that is displayed while an image is downloading. If the viewer has turned off viewing images the alt tag is the only indication of what the image is supposed to be.

That's why you should give the alt tag a descriptive name that explains the image instead of something generic such as "image" or "graphic."

Many screen readers, which are used by those who are blind or have vision impairments, use the alt tag as the information read aloud for their listeners. Once again you will provide more information for the visitors to your site if you use descriptive alt tags.

㉑ *The* **Export Wizard** *takes you through the steps necessary to export files.*

㉒ *The* **Export Wizard button** *(circled) in the Export Preview dialog box.*

㉓ *The Export Wizard looks at the* **destination** *of the file to determine the best export options.*

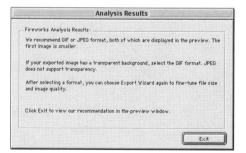

㉔ *The Export Wizard displays an* **analysis** *of its results.*

Using the Export Wizard

If you would like some help exporting files, Fireworks has an Export Wizard that can take you through the export steps.

To use the Export Wizard:

1. Choose **File** > **Export Wizard**. This opens the Export Wizard dialog box **㉑**.

   TIP You can also click the Export Wizard icon in the Export Preview dialog box **㉒**.

2. Click Select an export format to have the Export Wizard choose the format that is most appropriate for your image.

   TIP If you have opened the Export Wizard from the Export Preview dialog box you can choose Analyze current format settings to have Fireworks determine whether or not the current format is appropriate for the image.

3. Check Target export file size to limit the size of the final exported file.

4. Click Continue to choose the destination for the image **㉓**.

5. Choose one of the destinations listed.

6. Click Continue to have the Export Wizard analyze the export options **㉔**.

7. Click the Exit button to open the Export Preview set with the options chosen by the Export Wizard.

8. Click Export in the Export Preview.

   or

   Click OK to return to the document window. The Optimize panel will be set with the options chosen by the Export Wizard.

Cropping or Scaling Exported Images

Once you have created an image you can scale the image or crop it to export just a certain area.

To scale an image in Export Preview:

1. Choose **File** > **Export Preview** to open the Export Preview dialog box.

2. Click the File tab. This opens the File Scale and Export Area options **㉕**.

3. Use the percentage (%) slider or type in the field to scale the image to a percentage of its original size.

   or

   Enter an amount in the *W* (width) or *H* (height) fields to scale the image to an absolute measurement (in pixels).

   TIP With Constrain selected, the width and height of the image keep the proportions of the original image.

You can also crop an image while you are working inside the Export Preview area. This crops the exported image but does not crop any part of the original image.

To use the Export Area tool in the Export Preview:

1. Choose **File** > **Export Preview**.

2. Click the Export Area tool **㉖** at the bottom of the preview area.

3. Adjust the handles **㉗** so the rectangle surrounds the area you want to export.

4. Use the Export Preview dialog box to export the image.

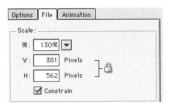

㉕ *The* **Scale controls** *of the File tab of the Export Preview dialog box.*

㉖ *The* **Export Area tool** *in the Export Preview dialog box.*

㉗ *Adjust the* **Export Area handles** *to set the area to be exported.*

㉘ *The* **Export Area tool** *in the Tools panel.*

You can also use the Export Area tool to select and export a portion of the image while working in the Document window.

To use the Export Area tool:

1. Choose the Export Area tool from the Tools panel **㉘**.

2. Drag a rectangle around the area you want to export **㉙**.

3. Adjust the handles so they are around the area you want to export.

4. Double-click inside the rectangle.

   or

   Click the Export button in the Tool Options panel. Only the selected area appears in the Export Preview window.

5. Use the Export Preview dialog box to export the image *(see page 333)*.

㉙ *Use the* **Export Area tool** *to* **drag a rectangle around the area you want to export.**

You can control the size of the export area numerically using the Export Area controls of the File tab.

To crop numerically in the Export Preview:

1. Choose **File** > **Export Preview**.

2. Choose the File tab **㉚**.

3. Use the *X* and *Y* fields to set the upper left corner of the area to be exported.

4. Use the *W* and *H* fields to set the width and height of the exported area.

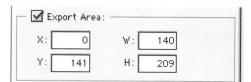

㉚ *Use the* **Export Area controls** *to numerically adjust the size of the exported image.*

TIP When you set the export area numerically, you see the same handles as when you use the Export Area tool. You can drag the handles in the box that surrounds the selected portion to adjust the selection.

Cropping or Scaling Exported Images

Exporting a Dreamweaver Library

In addition to exporting graphics and HTML code, Fireworks lets you export files in formats for use in other applications. For instance, you can export the HTML file with the special code that can be used as a Macromedia Dreamweaver Library.

TIP Dreamweaver Library items are HTML files with added code that identifies them as Dreamweaver Library items. Library items can be used in various places for a Web site. When the Library item is updated in Dreamweaver, the instances that use the Library item automatically update.

To export as a Dreamweaver Library:

1. In Fireworks, choose **File** > **Export**.

2. Choose Dreamweaver Library from the Save As list **❸❶**.

3. Navigate to place the Library (.lbi) in the Dreamweaver Library folder.

4. Set the Slice options as described on page 327.

TIP The HTML options are not available since the Dreamweaver Library format is already a type of code.

5. Select Put Images in Subfolder to navigate to locate the subfolder where images should be stored.

6. Click Save to export the artwork.

To use a Library item in Dreamweaver:

1. In Dreamweaver, choose **Window** > **Library** to open the Assets panel in the Library mode.

2. Drag the item from the panel onto the Dreamweaver page **❸❷**.

❸❶ *The export choices for saving files in the* **Dreamweaver Library** *format.*

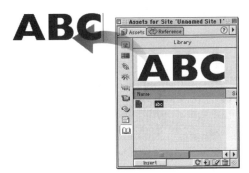

❸❷ *Drag a Dreamweaver Library element from the Library panel onto the page.*

Before You Export as a Dreamweaver Library

You need to do some preparation ahead of time before you export as a Dreamweaver Library (.lbi) item.

First, you should use Dreamweaver to define the local site root folder.

Then create a folder named Library (with a capital L) that is inside the local site root folder.

You can now use that Library folder for exporting Fireworks objects as Dreamweaver Library elements.

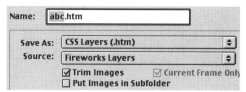

③ *The export choices for saving files in the CSS Layers (.htm) format.*

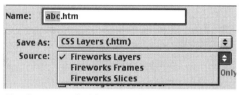

③ *The Source list lets you choose what elements should be used to create the CSS elements.*

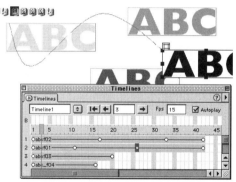

③ *CSS Layers can be animated using the Timelines in Dreamweaver.*

Exporting CSS Layers

You can also export Fireworks objects as Cascading Style Sheets (CSS) Layers. This allows you to export the individual layers or frames of a Fireworks document together with the HTML code necessary to create a CSS Layer.

To export as CSS Layers:

1. Create your Fireworks objects using layers, frames, or slices.

   TIP Artwork on a single frame should be separated by placing the different elements on separate layers. The elements for a button automatically appear on frames. An image that is sliced appears as a part of slices.

2. In Fireworks, choose **File > Export**.

3. Choose CSS Layers (.htm) from the Save As list **③**.

4. Use the Source list to choose how to separate the elements **③**.

5. Select Trim Images to discard any excess canvas area around the images.

6. Select Put Images in Subfolder to navigate to locate the subfolder where images should be stored.

7. Click Save to export the artwork.

To use the CSS Layers items in Dreamweaver:

1. In Dreamweaver, choose **File > Open** to open the HTML file created when you exported the artwork. The CSS elements appear inside the Dreamweaver document window.

2. Use the Timelines or other CSS options to animate the graphics **③**.

Exporting to Director

You can also export artwork from Fireworks together with the code necessary to reassemble it in Macromedia Director. This makes Fireworks the perfect tool for creating bitmap images for Director. It also allows you to add Fireworks effects such as shadows or bevels to Director movies.

To export as Director objects:

1. Create your Fireworks objects using any combination of layers, frames, or slices.

TIP Artwork on a single frame should be separated by placing the different elements on separate layers. Or you can use slices to divide the artwork into separate elements.

2. In Fireworks, choose **File** > **Export**. This opens the Export dialog box.

3. Choose Director (.htm) from the Save As list **36**.

4. Use the Source list to choose Fireworks Layers or Fireworks Slices **37**.

5. Choose Trim Images to discard any excess canvas area around the images.

6. Choose Put Images in Subfolder to navigate to locate the subfolder where images should be stored.

7. Click Save to export the artwork.

To use the object in Director:

1. In Director, choose **Insert** > **Fireworks** > **Images from Fireworks HTML** to open the HTML file created when you exported the artwork. The artwork appears as part of Director's Internal Cast.

2. Use any of the Director techniques to animate the imported elements **38**.

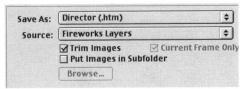

36 *Fireworks's export choices for saving files in the* **Director** *format.*

37 *Fireworks's* **Source** *list lets you choose what elements should be used to create the Director images.*

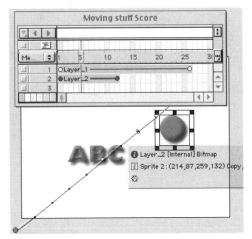

38 *The elements exported into Director can be animated using Timelines.*

39 *The* **Layers to Files** *option separates Fireworks layers into individual files.*

40 *The* **Frames to Files** *option separates Fireworks frames into individual files.*

Naming Multiple Files

Fireworks automatically names the multiple files created when you break up layers or frames into individual files.

Layers converted to files are named with the layer name replacing the original file name.

Frames converted to files are named by adding the label _f01, _f02, and so on to the original file name.

Breaking Up Files

As sad as it sounds, sometimes you need to break up files. Perhaps you need to separate the frames of a rollover into individual artwork for a print ad. You may need to separate the layers of a file to use in a presentation or for video. Fireworks lets you separate layers or frames into their own files.

To convert layers to files:

1. Create your Fireworks objects using layers.
2. Set the Optimize panel to the final format.
3. Choose **File** > **Export**.
4. Choose Layers to Files from the Save as list **39**.
5. Choose Trim Images to discard any excess canvas area around the images.
6. Click OK to export the artwork.

To convert frames to files:

1. Create your Fireworks objects using frames.
2. Set the Optimize panel to the final format.
3. Choose **File** > **Export**.
4. Choose Frames to Files from the Save as list **40**.
5. Choose Trim Images to discard any excess canvas area around the images.
6. Click Save to export the artwork.

You can also break up files into the format used by Lotus Domino Designer. This allows you to use Fireworks rollovers and other artwork as part of pages for the groupware database program Lotus Notes.

To export to Lotus Domino Designer:

1. Create your Fireworks objects using frames.

2. Set the Optimize panel to the final format.

3. Choose **File** > **Export**.

4. Choose Lotus Domino Designer from the Save as list ⓭.

5. Use the Source list to choose one of the following ways to break up the file:
   - **Fireworks Layers** uses the Layers panel.
   - **Fireworks Frames** uses the Frames panel.
   - **Fireworks Slices** uses the slice objects.

   TIP The Trim Images setting does not affect the final file created by the Lotus Domino Designer export. To trim the image use **Modify** > **Trim Canvas**.

6. Click Save to export the file ⓮.

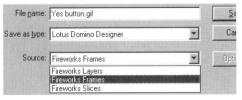

⓭ *The export choices for saving files in the* **Lotus Domino Designer** *format.*

⓮ *The Lotus Domino Designer format places all the images on one file with a line between them.*

Keep Your Originals!

No matter what format you export your files as, don't lose the original PNG file. All the export formats rasterize the artwork into non-editable pixels. This means you will lose your text, paths, effect settings, and other parts of the artwork.

If you have to make changes to the exported artwork, it is easier to go back to the original Fireworks PNG file and then re-export.

Personally, I find it easier to keep track of the Fireworks PNG file when it's in the same folder with the exported files.

43 *Most of the Fireworks formatting is lost when you* **export as vectors**.

44 *Choose* **Illustrator 7** *to export files in the vector format.*

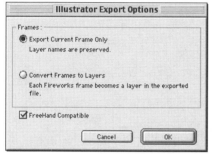

45 *The* **Illustrator Export Options** *controls how objects are converted into vector files.*

Don't Be Disappointed

You may be surprised how different your artwork looks when you export it into vectors.

Anti-aliasing, feathering, effects, opacity, blending modes, textures, patterns, Web dither fills, slices, hotspots, many text formatting, guides, grids, and canvas color will be discarded.

Gradient fills and bitmap images will also be discarded if FreeHand Compatible is chosen.

Exporting as Vector Artwork

Fireworks lets you export its vector artwork into vectors that can be opened by programs such as Adobe Illustrator or Macromedia FreeHand.

TIP Much of the formatting is lost when you export as vectors. If you need to use the artwork in Illustrator, you may want to use the TIFF format which maintains the formatting. However, if you want only the path shapes, you can export as vectors **43**.

To export as vector artwork:

1. Choose **File** > **Export**.

2. Choose Illustrator 7 from the Save As list **44**.

TIP Fireworks saves the vectors in the Illustrator 7 format. However, the current version of Illustrator and FreeHand can open these files.

3. Click Options to open the Illustrator Export Options dialog box **45**.

4. Select Export Current Frame Only to keep the artwork on individual layers.

   or

   Select Convert Frames to Layers. This converts each Fireworks frame into a layer.

5. Select FreeHand Compatible to discard those objects that FreeHand is unable to open. *(See the sidebar on this page to find out which elements are discarded when converting to vectors.)*

6. Click OK to return to the Export dialog box.

7. Click Save to export the artwork.

Exporting as Flash SWF

You can export Fireworks images in the Macromedia Flash SWF format. This lets you convert animations created in Fireworks into SWF animations. The benefit of exporting as Flash SWF is that the SWF file can be uploaded to the Web or inserted into a Web page without opening Macromedia Flash. However, the exported files lose their link to the original Fireworks artwork.

As mentioned in Chapter 15, you can also import the native Fireworks PNG file into Flash. Importing PNG files into Flash keeps a link to the PNG file. This may be a better way to use Fireworks artwork in Flash animations.

To export Flash SWF files:

1. Choose File > **Export**.

2. Choose Macromedia Flash SWF from the Save As list **46**.

3. Click the Options button to open the Flash SWF Options dialog box.

4. Set the SWF options as explained on the following page.

5. Click Save to export the file.

TIP The SWF files created by Fireworks can be played by any application that supports the SWF format. This includes the Flash Player and Apple QuickTime. You can also play SWF animations by opening them in a browser such as Internet Explorer or Netscape Navigator that has the Flash plug-in.

TIP For very simple animations you may find it better to export a single frame and then create the animation in Flash itself. This allows you to create symbols that keep the file size down.

46 *Choose* **Macromedia Flash SWF** *to export files as Flash animations.*

Flash Replaces GIF?

Not too long ago, many companies would not use SWF animations in their Web pages. Too many people had to first download a plug-in to see the SWF animation.

However, a survey conducted in September of 2000 reports that 96.4% of all Web users can view SWF content without having to download and install a player.

Today, more and more Web sites are integrating SWF—either by inserting Flash buttons and animations or by creating entire sites using Flash.

My own feeling is that within a very short period of time, Flash animations will completely replace GIF animations—with good reason. A small size, five-frame GIF animation can take up 5K of file space. The same animation saved in the SWF format is less than 1K.

Exporting as Flash SWF

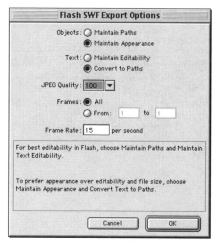

🐝 *The* **Flash SWF Export Options** *control how objects are converted into Flash SWF.*

Fireworks image

Flash image

🐝 Maintain Paths *and* Maintain Editability *create Flash objects that can be edited but the Fireworks effects and transformations are discarded.*

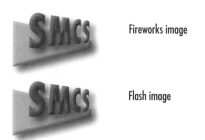

Fireworks image

Flash image

🐝 Maintain Appearance *and* Convert to Paths *create Flash objects that look the same as their original Fireworks artwork.*

To export Flash SWF files:

1. Use the Objects controls to choose how Fireworks objects are exported to Flash SWF **🐝**:
   - **Maintain Paths** converts Fireworks paths into editable Flash paths **🐝**.
   - **Maintain Appearance** converts paths into bitmapped images **🐝**.

2. Use the Text controls to choose how text is exported:
   - **Maintain Editability** converts Fireworks text into Flash text which can be edited **🐝**.
   - **Convert to Path** converts Fireworks text into artwork **🐝**.

3. Set the JPEG quality for bitmapped images.

TIP The lower the quality, the smaller the file size.

4. Use the Frames controls to choose which frames should be exported.

5. Choose a Frame Rate to control the speed of the animation.

6. Click OK to return to the Export dialog box.

Exporting as Flash SWF

Exporting as Photoshop Files

It must be an indication of how popular Fireworks has become because not only can you import files from Adobe Photoshop you can also export Fireworks files back into Photoshop. This makes it easy for you to do all your work in Fireworks and then send the files back to those who have to work in Photoshop.

50 *The export choices for saving files in the* **Photoshop** *format.*

TIP Exporting to Photoshop always converts Fireworks paths into bitmap images.

To export as Photoshop files:

1. Choose File > **Export**.

2. Choose Photoshop PSD from the Save As list **50**.

3. Choose the controls from the Settings list **50** as follows:

   • **Maintain Editability over Appearance** converts objects to layers, keeps effects editable, and converts text into editable text.

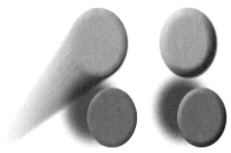

51 *Effects such as the Motion Blur are discarded when the file is exported in the Photoshop format.*

TIP Only those Fireworks effects that have Photoshop equivalents will be kept. Effects such as the Eye Candy Motion Blur don't remain editable **51**.

   • **Maintain Fireworks Appearance** converts objects into layers, renders the effects as part of the layer, and turns text into images.

   • **Smaller Photoshop File** flattens each Fireworks layer into a fully rendered image.

   • **Custom** allows you to control the individual settings for objects, effects, and text. *(See the following exercise.)*

4. Click Save to export the file.

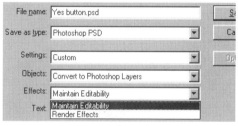

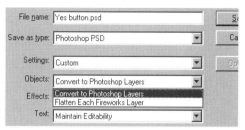

52 *The* **Objects list** *controls how objects are converted into the Photoshop format.*

53 *The* **Effects list** *controls how Live Effects are converted into the Photoshop format.*

54 *The* **Text list** *controls how text is converted into the Photoshop format.*

To set the custom Photoshop export settings:

1. Choose Custom from the Settings list.

2. Choose the controls from the Objects list **52** as follows:
   - **Convert to Photoshop Layers** creates a new Photoshop layer for each Fireworks object.
   - **Flatten Each Fireworks Layer** merges all the objects on each Fireworks layer into one Photoshop layer.

   TIP If you choose Flatten Each Fireworks Layer, you will not have any choices for Effects and Text.

3. Choose the controls from the Effects list **53** as follows:
   - **Maintain Editability** converts the Fireworks effects into the equivalent Photoshop effect. Effects that have no equivalent are discarded.
   - **Render Effects** rasterizes the Fireworks effects as part of the image.

3. Choose the controls from the Text list **54** as follows:
   - **Maintain Editability** converts the text into the equivalent Photoshop text.
   - **Render Text** rasterizes the text into a Photoshop layer.

   TIP Fireworks text on a path has no equivalent in Photoshop and will be converted into linear text.

Updating HTML

You may find that you want to change the HTML code and images that have already been imported into a Web page along with other HTML text and graphics. If so, Fireworks gives you a powerful command that searches for specific HTML inside a Web page and updates it.

To update HTML inside an existing page:

1. Choose File > Update HTML. This opens a dialog box where you can navigate to find the HTML page you want to change.

2. Select the file.

3. A dialog box asks you where to put the graphics for the updated HTML.

TIP If Fireworks cannot find the proper HTML code to update, it adds the code for the selected image to the end of the document.

COMPARED TO PHOTOSHOP 21

Without question, Adobe Photoshop is one of the most successful computer graphics applications. It's hard to find anyone working with computer graphics who doesn't have a copy of Photoshop installed.

When Macromedia Fireworks was first introduced people wondered just how Macromedia intended to go up against the Photoshop juggernaut. Yet with each version of Fireworks more and more people are using the product—switching over from the combination of Photoshop and Adobe ImageReady.

One reason is the excellent integration between Fireworks and Macromedia Dreamweaver. Another reason is the vector drawing tools in Fireworks and object-oriented graphics make it easy to edit artwork.

This chapter is especially for those who have moved from Photoshop to Fireworks. It gives you side-by-side comparisons of the features in the two programs. You can look through this chapter for Photoshop features and learn what are their equivalent Fireworks features. Then you can skip back to previous chapters for more details.

TIP Each of the figures displays the Fireworks items on the left and the Photoshop items on the right.

Working with Tools

Many of the tools in Photoshop are found in Fireworks. There are some vector tools in Fireworks that Photoshop does not have. Similarly, there are some imaging tools that Fireworks does not have.

Bitmap Selection Tools

- The marquee selection tools in Fireworks are similar to the marquee selection tools in Photoshop ❶. There are no equivalents to the Single Row or Single Column tools. *(See page 205.)*

  TIP Many older Photoshop tutorials use these marquee tools to create shapes. The equivalent in Fireworks is to use the object shapes, not marquee selections.

- Fireworks's two lasso tools are directly comparable to the Lasso and Polygon Lasso in Photoshop ❷. Fireworks does not have a Magnetic Lasso tool. *(See page 206.)*

- The Magic Wand in Fireworks works similarly to the Magic Wand in Photoshop ❸. *(See page 207.)*

  TIP As soon as you use any of the bitmap selection tools Fireworks switches into the Bitmap Mode.

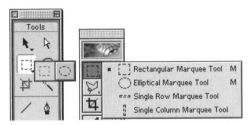

❶ *The two marquee selection tools in Fireworks are the equivalent to the two marquee tools in Photoshop.*

❷ *The two lasso tools in Fireworks are the equivalent to the Lasso and Polygon Lasso tools in Photoshop. Fireworks does not have a Magnetic Lasso.*

❸ *The Magic Wand in Photoshop is similar to the Magic Wand in Fireworks.*

Stop Using the Marquee Tools

One of the most common errors students make when switching from Photoshop to Fireworks is that they use the marquee tools to create selections and then try fill the selections with colors.

Use Fireworks's object tools to create actual objects that can be filled rather than the marquee tools which only create selections.

Working with Tools

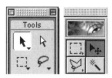

❹ *Photoshop's Move tool is used to move bitmap images. Fireworks uses the Selection tool to move bitmap images.*

❺ *Photoshop's object selection tools are equivalent to the two selection tools in Fireworks.*

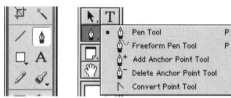

❻ *Photoshop displays several different pen tools. Fireworks uses keyboard modifiers to change the functions of the Pen tool.*

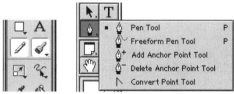

❼ *Fireworks's Pencil and Brush tools provide much of the function of Photoshop's Freeform Pen tool.*

Object Selection Tools

- Photoshop's Move tool is used to move bitmap images ❹. Fireworks uses the regular Selection tool to move bitmap images. *(See pages 76 and 211.)*

- Photoshop's two object selection tools are used to manipulate paths and the objects used in clipping paths ❺. Fireworks's two selection tools are used to move objects and manipulate points in the same manner. *(See pages 76 and 211.)*

Pen Tools

- Photoshop displays each of its Pen tools in the Toolbox ❻. Fireworks displays only the Pen tool. The Add Anchor Point, Delete Anchor Point, and Convert Point tools are obtained in Fireworks using keyboard modifiers. *(See page 64.)*

- Photoshop's Freeform Pen tool is similar to the Fireworks Pencil and Brush tools ❼. *(See pages 69 and 70.)*

TIP Fireworks allows you to add strokes to open paths. Photoshop's stroke command will automatically close paths when applied to clipping path layers.

Working with Tools

Object Drawing Tools

- The Rectangle, Rounded Rectangle, Ellipse, and Polygon tools all have direct equivalents in both programs **❽**. *(See page 60–63.)*

- Fireworks has no equivalent to Photoshop's Custom Shape tool. However, any vector image can be imported into Fireworks and then transformed or modified as desired. *(See page 225.)*

- The Line tools in both programs are almost identical **❾**. *(See page 62.)*

Text Tool

- The Text tool in Fireworks is the equivalent to Photoshop's Text tool **❿**. *(See page 154.)*

Crop Tool

- The Crop tool in Fireworks works the same as the Crop tool in Photoshop **⓫**. *(See page 35.)*

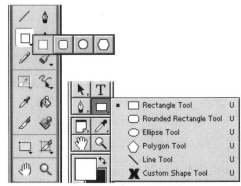

❽ *Fireworks's object tools correspond to the first four Photoshop object tools. However, Fireworks does not have a Custom Shape tool.*

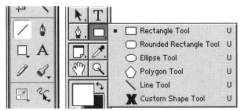

❾ *Fireworks's Line tool is the equivalent of the Line tool in Photoshop.*

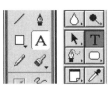

❿ *Fireworks's Text tool is the equivalent of the Text tool in Photoshop.*

⓫ *Fireworks's Crop tool is the equivalent of the Crop tool in Photoshop.*

⑫ *Fireworks's Rubber Stamp tool is the equivalent of the Clone Stamp tool in Photoshop.*

⑬ *Use the Airbrush settings in the Stroke panel to have Fireworks's Brush tool duplicate the Airbrush tool in Photoshop.*

⑭ *There are no equivalents to Photoshop's History Brush or Art History Brush tools.*

⑮ *There are no equivalents to the Blur, Sharpen, or Smudge tools in Photoshop.*

⑯ *There are no equivalents to Photoshop's Dodge, Burn, or Sponge tools.*

⑰ *Fireworks does not have a Gradient tool. Instead, gradients are applied from the Fill panel.*

Bitmap Drawing Tools

- The Rubber Stamp tool in Fireworks works the same as the Clone Stamp tool in Photoshop **⑫**. *(See page 215.)*

TIP You must switch to the Bitmap Mode in order to use the Rubber Stamp tool.

- The Airbrush in Photoshop can be duplicated in Fireworks by using the Brush tool and then changing the Stroke panel settings **⑬**. *(See pages 69 and 123.)*

- The Brush in Fireworks is the equivalent of the Paintbrush in Photoshop. *(See page 69.)*

TIP You must switch to the Bitmap Mode in order to use the Brush tool on images. Otherwise, the Brush tool creates stroked paths.

- Fireworks has no equivalents to Photoshop's History Brush or Art History Brush tools **⑭**.

- Fireworks has no equivalents to Photoshop's Blur, Sharpen, or Smudge tools **⑮**.

- Fireworks has no equivalents to Photoshop's Dodge, Burn, or Sponge tools **⑯**.

- Fireworks does not have a Gradient tool **⑰**. Instead, gradients are added using the Fill panel.

Working with Tools

Eraser Tool

- In the Bitmap Mode, the Fireworks Eraser tool works like the Photoshop Eraser **18**. *(See page 217.)*

- In the Object Mode, the tool changes into the Knife tool **19**. *(See page 98.)*

Image Map Tools

- Photoshop's Rectangle, Circle, and Polygon Image Map tools are the equivalent of the same Hotspot tools in Fireworks **20**. *(See page 280.)*

- Fireworks does not have an Image Map Select tool. All hotspot objects in Fireworks can be selected using any of the object selection tools. *(See page 76.)*

Slice Tools

- Photoshop's Slice tool is the same as the Slice tool in Fireworks **21**. *(See page 291.)*

- Fireworks does not have a Slice Select tool. All slice objects in Fireworks can be selected using any of the object selection tools. *(See page 76.)*

18 *The Fireworks's Eraser tool can be used in the Bitmap Mode like the Photoshop Eraser tool.*

19 *If you are working in the Object Mode, Fireworks's Eraser is replaced by the Knife tool.*

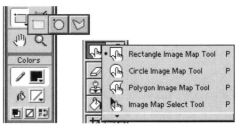

20 *Fireworks's Hotspot tools are the equivalent of Photoshop's Image Map tools.*

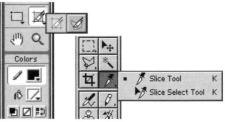

21 *The Slice tool in Photoshop is equivalent to Fireworks's Rectangular Slice tool.*

㉒ *The Eyedropper tool in Photoshop is similar to the Eyedropper tool in Fireworks.*

㉓ *The Paint Bucket tool in Photoshop is similar to the Paint Bucket tool in Fireworks.*

㉔ *The Hand tool in Photoshop is similar to the Hand tool in Fireworks.*

㉕ *The Zoom tool in Photoshop is similar to the Zoom tool in Fireworks.*

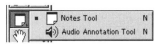

㉖ *There is no equivalent to Photoshop's Notes and Audio Annotation tools.*

Eyedropper Tool

- Photoshop's Eyedropper tool is the same as the Eyedropper tool in Fireworks **㉒**. *(See page 217.)*

TIP You can also get the Eyedropper in Fireworks by using any of the Color Wells.

- Fireworks does not have a Color Sampler tool or a Measure tool.

Paint Bucket Tool

- Photoshop's Paint Bucket tool works the same as the Paint Bucket tool in Fireworks **㉓**. *(See page 217.)*

Hand Tool

- Photoshop's Hand tool works the same as the Hand tool in Fireworks **㉔**. Both tools also have the same keyboard shortcuts. *(See page 44.)*

Zoom Tool

- Photoshop's Zoom tool works the same as the Zoom tool in Fireworks **㉕**. Both tools also have the same keyboard shortcuts. *(See page 42.)*

Notes and Audio Annotation Tools

- Fireworks does not have any equivalents to the Notes or Audio Annotation tools **㉖**.

Working with Tools

Working with Palettes

Photoshop calls its onscreen elements *palettes*. Fireworks calls its elements *panels*. Many Photoshop palettes have equivalent panels in Fireworks.

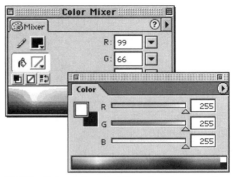

Color palette

- The Color palette in Photoshop is similar to the Color Mixer panel in Fireworks **㉗**. *(See page 48.)* The foreground and background colors in Photoshop are replaced by the Fill and Stroke colors in Fireworks. *(See page 26.)*

㉗ *The Color palette in Photoshop is equivalent to the Color Mixer in Fireworks.*

- **TIP** Because Photoshop is used for print production, it lets you mix colors using CMYK values. Because Fireworks is designed exclusively for Web graphics, it uses CMY values to mix colors.

Swatches palette

- The Swatches palette in Photoshop is similar to the Swatches panel in Fireworks **㉘**. *(See page 52.)*

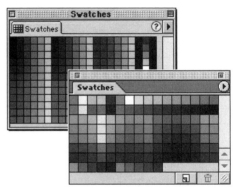

Channels palette

- There is no equivalent to Photoshop's Channels palette **㉙**. Fireworks does not display channels of an image. You can, however, save a single selection along with the image. *(See page 213.)*

㉘ *The Swatches palette in Photoshop is equivalent to the Swatches panel in Fireworks.*

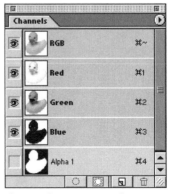

㉙ *Fireworks does not have an equivalent to Photoshop's Channels palette.*

Working with Palettes

30 *Fireworks does not have an equivalent to Photoshop's Paths palette.*

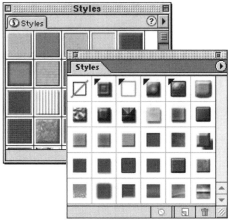

31 *The Styles palette in Photoshop is equivalent to the Styles panel in Fireworks.*

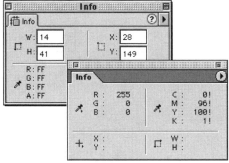

32 *The Info palette in Photoshop is equivalent to the Info panel in Fireworks.*

Paths palette

- There is no equivalent to Photoshop's Paths palette **30**. Fireworks displays paths as part of the artwork for the image. *(See page 106.)*

Styles palette

- The Styles palette in Photoshop is the equivalent of the Styles panel in Fireworks **31**. *(See page 183.)*

TIP Fireworks does not save the button states as styles as ImageReady does. However, Fireworks does have text styles.

Info palette

- The Info panel in Photoshop is the equivalent of the Info palette in Fireworks **32**. *(See page 86.)*

TIP The Info palette in Fireworks can be used to re-size and reposition objects.

Working with Palettes

Navigator palette

- There is no equivalent to Photoshop's Navigator palette **33**.

33 *Fireworks does not have an equivalent to Photoshop's Navigator palette.*

History palette

- The History palette in Photoshop is similar to the History panel in Fireworks **34**. *(See page 194.)*

Actions palette

- Fireworks does not have a direct equivalent to Photoshop's Actions palette **35**. However, you can use Fireworks's History panel to replay a set of steps. Fireworks's History panel can also save a selected set of steps as an action in the Commands menu. *(See page 195.)*

34 *Photoshop's History palette is equivalent to the History panel in Fireworks.*

35 *Many of the features in Photoshop's Actions palette can be duplicated by Fireworks's History panel.*

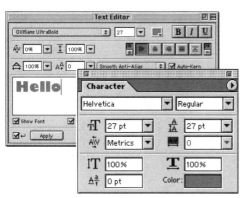

❸❻ *Fireworks's Text Editor serves the function of Photoshop's Character palette.*

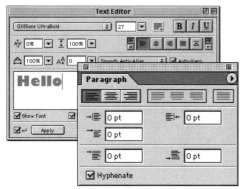

❸❼ *Fireworks's Text Editor serves the function of Photoshop's Paragraph palette.*

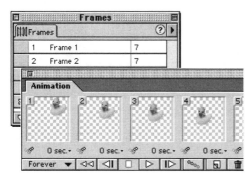

❸❽ *ImageReady's Animation palette is equivalent to the Frames panel in Fireworks.*

Character palette

- Fireworks formats character styling using the Text Editor. Photoshop uses a Character palette **❸❻**. *(See page 155.)*

Paragraph palette

- Fireworks formats paragraph attributes using the Text Editor. Photoshop uses a Paragraph panels **❸❼**. *(See page 155.)*

When you work with Photoshop, you have to switch to ImageReady for many Web features. Fireworks contains all the Web features in one program.

Animation palette (ImageReady)

- The Animation palette in ImageReady is similar to the Frames panel in Fireworks **❸❽**. *(See page 258.)*

Working with Palettes

Rollover palette (ImageReady)

- The Rollover palette in ImageReady is used to create buttons. This is similar to the Button window in Fireworks **39**. *(See page 301.)*

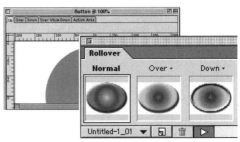

39 *Fireworks's Button Editor serves the functions of ImageReady's Rollover palette.*

Slice palette (ImageReady)

- The Slice palette in ImageReady is used to control the features of slices **40**. This is similar to using the Object panel when a slice is selected in Fireworks. *(See page 294.)*

Image Map palette (ImageReady)

- The Image Map palette in ImageReady is used to control the features of image map objects **41**. This is similar to using the Object panel when a hotspot object is selected in Fireworks. *(See page 283.)*

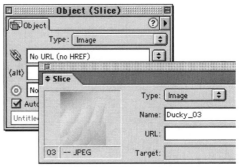

40 *ImageReady's Slice palette is the equivalent of Fireworks's Object panel for a selected slice.*

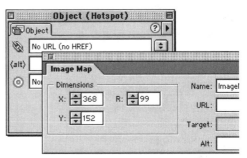

41 *ImageReady's Image Map palette is the equivalent of Fireworks's Object panel for a selected hotspot.*

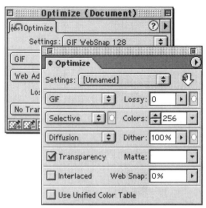

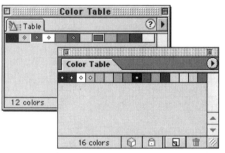

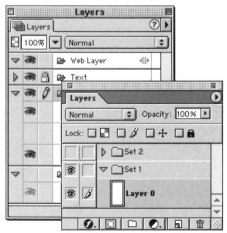

42 *Fireworks's Optimize panel serves the functions of ImageReady's Optimize palette.*

43 *Fireworks's Color Table panel serves the functions of ImageReady's Color Table palette.*

44 *Fireworks's Layers panel serves the functions of Photoshop's Layers palette.*

Optimize palette (ImageReady)

- The Optimize palette in ImageReady is similar to the Optimize panel in Fireworks **42**. *(See page 235.)*

Color Table (ImageReady)

- The Color Table palette in ImageReady is similar to the Color Table panel in Fireworks **43**. *(See page 237.)*

Layers palette

- The Layers palette in Photoshop is the equivalent of the Layers panel in Fireworks **44**. *(See page 104.)*

TIP The next section covers the Fireworks equivalents to Photoshop's Layers palette features.

Working with Palettes

Working with Layers

Fireworks Layers owe more of its heritage to vector drawing programs such as Macromedia FreeHand and Adobe Illustrator. For instance, you can place as many objects as you want on a single layer. You can even have two bitmap images on the same layer without merging their pixels.

Layer Effects

- Many of the features of Photoshop's Layer Effects are duplicated in Fireworks's Effects panel ⑮. (*See page 132.*)

Adjustment Layers

- The effects found under Fireworks's Adjust Color submenu provide many of the same features as Photoshop's Adjustment layers ⑯. (*See page 142.*)

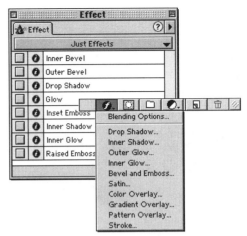

⑮ *Some of Photoshop's Layer Effects are duplicated by Fireworks's Effects panel.*

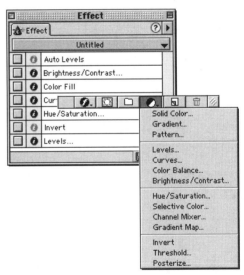

⑯ *Some of Photoshop's Adjustment Layers are duplicated by the Fireworks's Adjust Colors effects.*

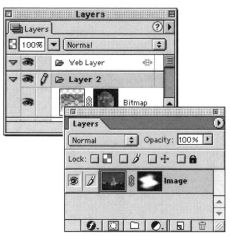

④⑦ *Photoshop's Layer Masks are duplicated by using a bitmap image as a mask in Fireworks.*

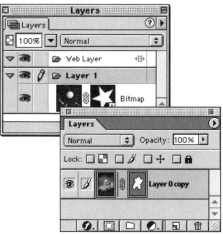

④⑧ *Photoshop's Layer Clipping Paths are duplicated by using a vector object as a mask in Fireworks.*

Layer Masks

- The Layer Masks in Photoshop are similar to using bitmap images as masks in Fireworks **④⑦**. *(See page 214.)*

Layer Clipping Paths

- The Layer Clipping Paths in Photoshop are similar to using vector objects as masks in Fireworks **④⑧**. *(See page 167.)*

Use Masks Instead of Deleting Pixels

If you haven't used Photoshop's Layer Masks, you most likely have resorted to deleting pixels to create silhouettes or vignettes.

Take the opportunity to learn how to use Fireworks's masking features. It is much better to mask out areas than permanently deleting pixels.

Working with Layers

Miscellaneous Features

Photoshop Filters

- Fireworks also lets you use many Photoshop filters **49**. However, they are not like Photoshop filters that can only be applied once and not modified. Instead Fireworks uses the filters as live effects that can be modified or discarded at any time. *(See page 152.)*

TIP You can also point Fireworks to the folder that holds Photoshop 5.5 filters. Your Photoshop filters will appear under the Fireworks Effect panel. Unfortunately, at the time of this writing Fireworks 4 can't use the filters that ship with Photoshop 6.

Canvas Color

- Photoshop creates a background layer when you first create a document. That background layer becomes the background color for the file **50**. The layer itself must be modified to change the background color. Fireworks uses a Background Color command to set the background color. This color can be changed or modified at any time.

49 *Many Photoshop filters appear in Fireworks's Effect panel.*

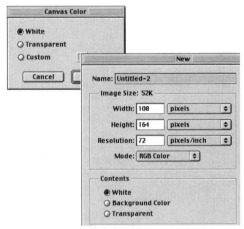

50 *Photoshop creates a separate layer that displays the background color. The background color of a Fireworks document is controlled electronically.*

KEYBOARD SHORTCUTS

A s you become more familiar with the various Fireworks features, you should begin to use the keyboard shortcuts for the commands you use most often. For instance, rather than use the mouse to choose **File**>**Export**, it is much faster and easier to use the keyboard shortcut.

This appendix lists the shortcuts for Macromedia Standard set of Fireworks menu commands. These are the commands that ship as the default setting with Fireworks. As shown on pages 27–29, you can change these keyboard commands.

Most of these shortcuts are also displayed along with the command on the menus. So you do not have to use this list to find the shortcut for the commands you use the most.

Windows Keyboard Shortcuts

The following are the keyboard shortcuts for the Windows platform. These are the abbreviations used for the keys.

Ctrl . . . . Control key
Alt . . . . Alt key
Up . . . . Up arrow key
Down . . . . Down arrow key
Left . . . . Left arrow key
Right . . . . Right arrow key
Space . . . . Spacebar

File Menu

New . . . . Ctrl+N
Open . . . . Ctrl+O
Close . . . . Ctrl+W
Save . . . . Ctrl+S
Save As . . . . Ctrl+Shift+S
Import . . . . Ctrl+R
Export . . . . Ctrl+Shift+R
Export Preview . . . . Ctrl+Shift+X
Preview in Browser F12
Preview in Secondary Browser . . . . . Shift+F12
Print . . . . Ctrl+P
Exit . . . . Ctrl+Q

Edit Menu

Undo . . . . Ctrl+Z
Redo . . . . Ctrl+Y, Ctrl+Shift+Z
Cut . . . . Ctrl+X
Copy . . . . Ctrl+C
Copy HTML Code . . . . Ctrl+Alt+C
Paste . . . . Ctrl+V
Clear . . . . Backspace, Del
Paste Inside . . . . Ctrl+Shift+V
Paste Attributes . . . . Ctrl+Alt+Shift+V
Select All . . . . Ctrl+A
Deselect . . . . Ctrl+D
Duplicate . . . . Ctrl+Alt+D
Clone . . . . Ctrl+Shift+D
Find and Replace . . . . Ctrl+F
Preferences . . . . Ctrl+U

View Menu

Zoom In . . . . Ctrl+=,
Zoom In . . . . Ctrl+Num +,
Zoom In . . . . Ctrl+Shift+=
Zoom Out . . . . Ctrl+-,
Zoom Out . . . . Ctrl+Num -
Fit Selection . . . . Ctrl+Alt+0
Fit All . . . . Ctrl+0
Full Display . . . . Ctrl+K
Hide Selection . . . . Ctrl+L
Show All . . . . Ctrl+Shift+L
Rulers . . . . Ctrl+Alt+R
Show Grid . . . . Ctrl+Alt+G
Snap to Grid . . . . Ctrl+Alt+Shift+G
Show Guides . . . . Ctrl+;
Lock Guides . . . . Ctrl+Alt+;
Snap to Guides . . . . Ctrl+Shift+;
Slice Guides . . . . Ctrl+Alt+Shift+;
Hide Edges F9
Hide Panels . . . . F4, Tab

Magnification

50% . . . . Ctrl+5
100% . . . . Ctrl+1
200% . . . . Ctrl+2
400% . . . . Ctrl+4
800% . . . . Ctrl+8
3200% . . . . Ctrl+3
6400% . . . . Ctrl+6

Insert Menu

New Symbol . . . . Ctrl+F8
Convert to Symbol F8
Hotspot . . . . Ctrl+Shift+U
Slice . . . . Alt+Shift+U

Modify Menu

Trim Canvas. . . . . Ctrl+Alt+T
Fit Canvas . . . . Ctrl+Alt+F
Animate Selection . . . . Alt+Shift+F8
Tween Instances. . . . . Ctrl+Alt+Shift+T
Edit Bitmap. . . . . Ctrl+E
Exit Bitmap Mode . . . . Ctrl+Shift+E
Select Inverse . . . . Ctrl+Shift+I
Convert to Bitmap . . . . . . Ctrl+Alt+Shift+Z
Numeric Transform . . . . Ctrl+Shift+T
Rotate 90° CW . . . . Ctrl+9
Rotate 90° CCW . . . . Ctrl+7
Bring to Front. . . . . Ctrl+Shift+Up
Bring Forward . . . . Ctrl+Up
Send Backward . . . . Ctrl+Down
Send to Back. . . . . Ctrl+Shift+Down
Align Left. . . . . . Ctrl+Alt+1, Ctrl+Alt+Num 1
Align Center Vertical . . . . Ctrl+Alt+2
Align Center Vertical . . . . . Ctrl+Alt+Num 2
Align Right . . . . Ctrl+Alt+3
Align Right . . . . Ctrl+Alt+Num 3
Align Top . . . . Ctrl+Alt+4
Align Top . . . . Ctrl+Alt+Num 4
Align Center Horizontal . . . . Ctrl+Alt+5
Align Center Horizontal . . . . Ctrl+Alt+Num 5
Align Bottom . . . . Ctrl+Alt+6
Align Bottom. . . . . Ctrl+Alt+Num 6
Distribute Widths. . . . . Ctrl+Alt+7
Distribute Widths . . . . Ctrl+Alt+Num 7
Distribute Heights . . . . Ctrl+Alt+9
Distribute Heights . . . . Ctrl+Alt+Num 9
Join. Ctrl+J
Split. . . . . Ctrl+Shift+J
Group. . . . . Ctrl+G
Ungroup. . . . . Ctrl+Shift+G
Bold . . . . Ctrl+B
Italic . . . . Ctrl+I
Text Align Left . . . . Ctrl+Alt+Shift+L
Text Align Center . . . . Ctrl+Alt+Shift+C
Text Align Right . . . . Ctrl+Alt+Shift+R
Text Align Justified. . . . . . . Ctrl+Alt+Shift+J
Text Align Stretched. . . . . . Ctrl+Alt+Shift+S
Attach to Path. . . . . Ctrl+Shift+Y
Convert to Paths . . . . Ctrl+Shift+P

Xtras

Repeat Xtra . . . . Ctrl+Alt+Shift+X
Invert . . . . Ctrl+Alt+Shift+I

Window Menu

New Window . . . . Ctrl+Alt+N

Toolbars

Stroke. . . . . Ctrl+Alt+F4
Fill . . . . Shift+F7
Effect . . . . Alt+F7
Info . . . . Alt+Shift+F12
Object. . . . . Alt+F2
Behaviors . . . . Shift+F3
Color Mixer . . . . Shift+F9
Swatches . . . . Ctrl+F9
Tool Options . . . . Ctrl+Alt+O
Layers. F2
Frames . . . . Shift+F2
History. . . . . Shift+F10
Styles. . . . . Shift+F11
Library F11
URL. . . . . Alt+Shift+F10
Find and Replace. . . . . Ctrl+F

Help

Using Fireworks F1

Miscellaneous

Clone and Nudge Down . . . . Alt+Down
Clone and Nudge Down Large. . Alt+Shift+Down
Clone and Nudge Left . . . . Alt+Left
Clone and Nudge Left Large. . . . Alt+Shift+Left
Clone and Nudge Right . . . . Alt+Right
Clone and Nudge Right Large. . Alt+Shift+Right
Clone and Nudge Up . . . . Alt+Up
Clone and Nudge Up Large. . . . . Alt+Shift+Up
Nudge Down . . . . Down
Nudge Down Large . . . . Shift+Down
Nudge Left . . . . Left
Nudge Left Large. . . . . Shift+Left
Nudge Right . . . . Right
Nudge Right Large . . . . Shift+Right
Nudge Up . . . . Up
Nudge Up Large. . . . . Shift+Up
Paste Inside . . . . Ctrl+Shift+V
Play Animation . . . . Ctrl+Alt+P
Previous Frame. . . . . Page Up
Previous Frame . . . . Ctrl+Page Up
Fill Pixel Selection . . . . Alt+Backspace
Next Frame . . . . Page Down
Next Frame . . . . Ctrl+Page Down

Windows Keyboard Shortcuts

Macintosh Keyboard Shortcuts

The following are the keyboard shortcuts for the Macintosh platform. These are the abbreviations used for the keys.

Cmd	Command key
Opt	Option key
Up	Up arrow key
Down	Down arrow key
Left	Left arrow key
Right	Right arrow key
Space	Spacebar

File

New	Cmd+N
Open	Cmd+O
Close	Cmd+W
Save	Cmd+S
Save As	Cmd+Shift+S
Import	Cmd+R
Export	Cmd+Shift+R
Export Preview	Cmd+Shift+X
Preview in Browser	F12
Preview in Secondary Browser	Shift+F12
Print	Cmd+P
Quit	Cmd+Q

Edit Menu

Undo	Cmd+Z
Redo	Cmd+Y, Cmd+Shift+Z
Cut	Cmd+X
Copy	Cmd+C
Copy HTML Code	Cmd+Opt+C
Paste	Cmd+V
Clear	Delete, Delete
Paste Inside	Cmd+Shift+V
Paste Attributes	Cmd+Opt+Shift+V
Select All	Cmd+A
Deselect	Cmd+D
Duplicate	Cmd+Opt+D
Clone	Cmd+Shift+D
Find and Replace	Cmd+F
Preferences	Cmd+U

View Menu

Zoom In	Cmd+=
Zoom In	Cmd++
Zoom In	Cmd+Shift+=
Zoom Out	Cmd+-
Hide Selection	Cmd+L
Show All	Cmd+Shift+L
Rulers	Cmd+Opt+R
Show Grid	Cmd+Opt+G
Snap to Grid	Cmd+Opt+Shift+G
Show Guides	Cmd+;
Lock Guides	Cmd+Opt+;
Snap to Guides	Cmd+Shift+;
Slice Guides	Cmd+Opt+Shift+;
Hide Edges	F9
Hide Panels	F4, Tab

Magnification

50%	Cmd+5
100%	Cmd+1
200%	Cmd+2
400%	Cmd+4
800%	Cmd+8
3200%	Cmd+3
6400%	Cmd+6
Fit Selection	Cmd+Opt+0
Fit All	Cmd+0
Full Display	Cmd+K

Insert Menu

New Symbol	Cmd+F8
Convert to Symbol	F8
Hotspot	Cmd+Shift+U
Slice	Opt+Shift+U

Modify Menu

Trim Canvas . . . . Cmd+Opt+T
Fit Canvas . . . . Cmd+Opt+F
Animate Selection . . . . Opt+Shift+F8
Tween Instances . . . . Cmd+Opt+Shift+T
Edit Bitmap . . . . Cmd+E
Exit Bitmap Mode . . . . Cmd+Shift+E
Select Inverse . . . . Cmd+Shift+I
Convert to Bitmap . . . . . Cmd+Opt+Shift+Z
Numeric Transform . . . . Cmd+Shift+T
Rotate 90° CW . . . . Cmd+9
Rotate 90° CCW . . . . Cmd+7
Bring to Front . . . . . . Cmd+Shift+Up Arrow
Bring Forward . . . . Cmd+Up Arrow
Send Backward . . . . Cmd+Down Arrow
Send to Back . . . . . Cmd+Shift+Down Arrow
Align Left . . . . Cmd+Opt+1
Align Center Vertical . . . . Cmd+Opt+2
Align Right . . . . Cmd+Opt+3
Align Top . . . . Cmd+Opt+4
Align Center Horizontal . . . . . . Cmd+Opt+5
Align Bottom . . . . Cmd+Opt+6
Distribute Widths . . . . Cmd+Opt+7
Distribute Heights . . . . Cmd+Opt+9
Join . . . . Cmd+J
Split . . . . Cmd+Shift+J
Group . . . . Cmd+G
Ungroup . . . . Cmd+Shift+G
Bold . . . . Cmd+B
Italic . . . . Cmd+I
Align Text Left . . . . Cmd+Opt+Shift+L
Align Text Center . . . . . . Cmd+Opt+Shift+C
Align Text Right . . . . . . Cmd+Opt+Shift+R
Align Text Justified . . . . . Cmd+Opt+Shift+J
Align Text Stretched . . . . Cmd+Opt+Shift+S
Attach to Path . . . . Cmd+Shift+Y
Convert to Paths . . . . Cmd+Shift+P

Commands Menu

Repeat Xtra . . . . Cmd+Opt+Shift+X
Invert . . . . Cmd+Opt+Shift+I

Window Menu

New Window . . . . Cmd+Opt+N
Stroke . . . . Cmd+Opt+F4
Fill . . . . Shift+F7
Effect . . . . Opt+F7
Info . . . . Opt+Shift+F12
Object . . . . Opt+F2
Behaviors . . . . Shift+F3
Color Mixer . . . . Shift+F9
Swatches . . . . Cmd+F9
Tool Options . . . . Cmd+Opt+O
Layers F2
Frames . . . . Shift+F2
History . . . . Shift+F10
Styles . . . . Shift+F11
Library F11
URL . . . . Opt+Shift+F10
Find and Replace . . . . Cmd+F

Help Menu

Help . . . . F1, Cmd+Shift+/, Cmd+/

Miscellaneous

Clone and Nudge Down . . . Opt+Down Arrow
Clone and Nudge Down Large . Opt+Shift+Down
Clone and Nudge Left . . . . . Opt+Left Arrow
Clone and Nudge Left Large . . . Opt+Shift+Left
Clone and Nudge Right . . . . Opt+Right
Clone and Nudge Right Large . Opt+Shift+Right
Clone and Nudge Up . . . . Opt+Up
Clone and Nudge Up Large . . . . Opt+Shift+Up
Fill Selected Pixels . . . . Opt+Delete
Page Down . . . . Cmd+Page Down
Nudge Down . . . . Down Arrow
Nudge Down Large . . . . Shift+Down
Nudge Left . . . . Left
Nudge Left Large . . . . Shift+Left
Nudge Right . . . . Right
Nudge Right Large . . . . Shift+Right
Nudge Up . . . . Up
Nudge Up Large . . . . Shift+Up
Paste Inside . . . . Cmd+Shift+V
Play Animation . . . . Ctrl+Opt+P
Previous Frame . . . . Page Up
Previous Frame . . . . Cmd+Page Up

Macintosh Keyboard Shortcuts

INDEX

E

M

Index

P